SOCIAL THEORY
AFTER POSTMODERNISM

SOCIAL THEORY
AFTER POSTMODERNISM
Rethinking Production, Law and Class

Anthony Woodiwiss

PLUTO **PRESS**
London • Winchester, Mass

First published 1990 by Pluto Press
345 Archway Road, London N6 5AA
and 8 Winchester Place, Winchester
MA 01890, USA

British Library Cataloguing in Publication Data
Woodiwiss, Anthony
  Social theory after postmodernism : rethinking production, law
  and class.
  I. Title
  301

  ISBN 0-7453-0387-0 hb

Library of Congress Cataloging-in-Publication Data
Woodiwiss, Anthony.
  Social theory after postmodernism.

  Includes bibliographical references.
  1. Sociology–Methodology. 2. Marxian school of
sociology. 3. Postmodernism. I. Title.
HM24.W66 1990   301'.01   89-25553
ISBN 0-7453-0387-0
ISBN 0-7453-0472-9 (pbk.)

Typeset in Stone by Stanford Desktop Publishing Services
Printed in Great Britain by Billing and Sons Ltd, Worcester

Contents

Acknowledgements   vii
Introduction: After the Crisis   1

Part I: Metatheoretical Starting Points
1. Realism, Non-humanism and Deconstruction   25

Part II: Rethinking Production
2. Against Metaphors   39
3. The Discourses of Production   57

Part III: Rethinking Law
4. The Egalitarian Premiss   81
5. A New Theory of Law   101
6. Law and the Development of Capitalism   124

Part IV: Rethinking Class
7. Law and Production   145
8. Deconstructing 'Class'   151
9. Reconstructing 'Class'   170

Conclusion: Towards a Sociology without Metaphors   185

Bibliography   190
Index   202

Acknowledgements

My deepest intellectual debt is to Frank Pearce, my very *alter* ego, without whose conversation I doubt very much that the current text could have been produced. My deepest personal debt is to Kathyanne Hingwan, upon whose love I have grown to depend. Many other people have contributed significantly to the realisation of this project personally, intellectually and usually in both ways, often without realising it. Those I can remember are: Harold Wolpe, Bob Jessop, Ted Benton, Ian Craib, George Kolankiewicz, Mary McIntosh, Sheldon Leader, Elaine Stavro, Anne Beech, Ken Plummer, Chris Bartram, Ernesto Laclau, Mick Mann, Dennis Marsden, David Rose, Orly Sullivan, Roy Todd, Peter Fitzpatrick, Frankie Todd, Colin Prescod, Mike Gonzalez, Pete Utting, Amalia Chamorro, Mike Woodiwiss, Lennox Sylvester, Min Woodiwiss, Roger Woodiwiss, Angela Woodiwiss, Lady Audrey Lawrence, Terry Wordingham and all the students to whom I have ever taught theory. Since this is my first work of theory, I would like also to thank two very different but equally inspirational theory teachers: Alan Dawe and Paul Hirst. In the present climate, which is extremely hostile to work such as this, I also feel it important to express my immense admiration for all my colleagues at the University of Essex for the way in which they have sustained the values and indeed the mutual respect that are so essential to free enquiry. Amongst these colleagues are Carole Allington, Brenda Corti, Mary Girling, Geraldine Shanks, and Barbara Winstanly without whose 'input' the present text could never have been read by anyone. Because of all this help, the sad truth is that I can blame no one but myself for the inadequacies I hope my readers will take the trouble to discover.

To Kathyanne

There are more things in heaven and earth, Horatio,
Than are dreamt of in your philosophy.
(*Hamlet, act 1, scene 5*)

Let us speak of the peacock, a bird twice monstrous, which wears so many feathers, and such long ones, that it cannot fly. As though evolution had made a mistake, by excess, it shows us a hundred eyes we dream can see, but know cannot. When it struts, it shows an ocellated tail on which it exposes only feather eyes ... The immobile fowl ... will show us, should it proudly strut, our dead theory. Sight looks blankly upon a world from which information has already fled. A disappearing species, only ornamental, the peacock asks us to admire, in the public parks and gardens where gawkers gather, the old theory of representation. (*Serres, 1989, pp. 25, 47*)

Don't panic.
(*lapel button, c. 1979*)

Introduction: After the Crisis

The crisis has passed. For ten years or more, the practitioners of the social theory born of the latter part of the nineteenth century have been close to a state of panic. Their position has been threatened by the rise of an explicitly anti-sociological, neoliberal discourse of political rule born of the latter part of the eighteenth century. Their resilience has been reduced by the belated discovery of the long-repressed sins of their 'fathers', as symptomised by their difficulties in coming to terms with 'the new social movements'. And, as if all this were not enough, their very words have been questioned by a fiercely iconoclastic 'postmodernism', which has consistently refused their reassurances concerning their 'fathers', as well as their own good intentions. Not surprisingly, social theorists, not to mention their colleagues, have sometimes appeared to have lost confidence in the scientific worth of their vocation. Nevertheless, encouragingly, no social theorist of any stature has yet apostatised and sought the comforts to be found beneath the warm skirts of neoliberal authority.

Although the anxiety is only slowly receding, there have been signs of renewed confidence, and several major attempts to revitalise theory have been published (for example, Alexander, 1982; Giddens, 1985; Unger, 1986).

Significantly, however, the response to these efforts has been very low key. There has been little, if any, of the excitement that greeted the appearance of new books or articles by an earlier generation of theorists, most notably by Parsons, Habermas and Althusser. And this despite the recent texts' possession of the very ingredients that made those of their predecessors so exciting, and so reassuring – new pictures of society inspired by new conceptualisations.

Postmodernism and the Mortality of Social Theory

In my view the source of this resistance lies in a widely shared if barely conscious perception that the more recent theorists have

1

failed, despite their staggering but somewhat anxious productivity, to come to terms with the ultimate cause of their discomfort. For good or ill, in an age of simulacra, painting pictures no longer has the significance, therapeutic or otherwise, it once had. Besides, today, as in the past, the problems thus posed are better investigated by artists, whatever their media, than by social theorists. Despite the many differences between them and their shared distance from Parsons, the recent authors nevertheless all repeat the latter's representationalism. Thus the prime cause of their anxiety is not fear of neoliberalism, although there are signs of this in the resort of some to such notions as 'rational choice'. Nor is it guilt consequent upon the discovery of the sins of their fathers, although there are signs of this too, in this instance welcome. Rather, the cause is a still largely unconscious shame associated with a thought which it is only just becoming possible to confront, namely the possibility that these sins were committed by mistake. The same mistake, moreover, that renders the goals they share with their fathers still impossible to achieve.

Most social theorists today continue to assume that the aim of social theory is to provide verifiably accurate, if supposedly abstract, representations of social reality. What they appear not to realise is that, in maintaining this assumption, they impose serious constraints upon their sociological imaginations – they can only hope to picture whatever the received wisdom tells them is present, which even today is typically only ever human beings. In the meantime, as a result of the 'deconstructive' methodological effects of the arrival of the concept of 'discourse', Althusser's ostensibly rather different approach has been turned against itself, with the result that representationalism and some of its problematic consequences have been found to characterise it too (see below, pp. 48–50). This is largely the result of a few former 'structuralist Marxists' questioning the validity of representationalism as such, whether practised by functionalists, Weberians, Marxists or the always more numerous empiricists. And this on the basis, utterly shocking to some, of an assumption as to the pan-discursive validity of the results produced by that very 'postmodernism' that is both a cause and, as I will suggest below, a symptom of the current anxiety. These are results which expose the very claim to representation as the product of a mistaken understanding of the nature of language and of a simultaneous and equally mistaken 'humanism', whereby the individual human subject is deemed to be the fundamental social atom, that is, the origin and the sole active substance of sociality.[1]

Representation, Signification and Sociality

According to the traditional, representational theory best exemplified in Wittgenstein's *Tractatus*, language consists of humanly created symbols which name and so may be understood, more or less complicatedly, to stand for the things that humans wish to talk about. By contrast, according to the significatory theory first enunciated by Saussure, words (including theoretical terms) do not represent extra-linguistic things. Rather, they are arbitrary combinations of systematically differentiated aural and/or graphic images (signifiers) with similarly differentiated mental ones (signifieds), which owe their existence as elements of language, not to human beings but to such additional non-human but equally active and substantive systems of difference and opposition as syntaxes and lexicons, which in turn are better conceptualised as the properties of social formations than as the products of individual or collective subjects.

All sociologists, if not all social theorists, have sought to advance beyond the truism that humanity and sociality are consubstantial with one another. Unfortunately, however, thanks to the pervasiveness of that mythic representation which Parsons (1949, p. 90) famously termed 'the Hobbesian problem of order', they have too often continued to assume that human consent, whether free or forced, is critical to social order and hence that social structures are ultimately reducible to the relations between individual and/or collective subjects. Most of the thoughts prompted by the presence of this subversive trace of political discourse may be put to one side in the present context. The only one that will be followed up here is the thought that there is in fact no necessity to believe that because social relations are always mediated through human beings, then the latter are always (falsely) conscious of being implicated in and hence always critical to the existence of those relations. Sometimes they may be but at least as often either so-called 'non-human' institutional subjects or even, as I intend to suggest, still more abstract entities turn out to be the prime movers in social relations.

Thus in what follows the problem of (false) consciousness will not hold centre stage and the focus of theoretical concern will thus be on inter-structural relations rather than on those between individuals. Put another way, what follows will be coloured throughout by a desire to see all questions as to the social and sociological significance of human agency temporarily removed to the margins of sociological texts. The purpose is to demonstrate that, freed from the necessity of assuring what Weber termed the 'meaningful adequacy' of sociological constructs, one is able to imagine non-human entities whose existence makes a better sense of the patterning, if that is not too strong a term, of the positionings of subjects than has proved possible thus far on the basis of the traditional, ideal-typical representations of what are commonly supposed to be the same entities.

Because of their representationalism and for all the acknowledged artificiality of ideal-type constructs, their proponents nevertheless have to assume that the boundaries of groups and institutions are marked by lines that include some individuals and exclude others. Hence their obsession with classifying and counting individuals. (Here again is another trace of political discourse, although this time one related more to the needs of the state rather than to arguments over the form it should take; see Kay, Mott, 1982.) The assumption that produces this result loses its plausibility once one rejects representationalism and is prepared instead to imagine that society is structured by non-human entities. This is because the existence of such entities in no way depends upon the extent to which they position whole individuals – in extreme cases, a wave of the hand, a day's work, a vote or even a statement may exhaust the sociological significance of a particular individual. Thus the effort to draw boundary lines around segments of the population is here regarded as an impossible and anyway pointless task.

That said, rejection of the traditional mode of empirically supporting conceptions of what are imagined to be structural entities immediately prompts the question as to what mode of empirical support is appropriate in the case of non-human entities? To my mind this question has been best answered by Foucault (1974, Chapter 3) in response to the cognate question, 'What is a discourse?' Paraphrasing his answer and applying it to non-human entities in general, evidence for their existence may be gained by investigating (a) whether or not any particular conditions are required for their possibility; (b) whether or not particular types of subjects were or are positioned by them; (c) whether or not there were or are any specific effects ascribable to such positionings; and, finally (d) whether or not such effects could have been produced by any other entity or in any other way.

In short, the materiality or otherwise of any imagined non-human entity may be established by investigating the differences it depends upon and makes to social relations.

Inspired by such adepts of significatory theory as Foucault and

Derrida, Althusser's more positive critics have written texts which attempt to draw out the consequences for social theory of a rejection both of representationalism and of the humanism that underpins it. Amongst the most important of these consequences is the aforementioned view, which regrettably has seldom been taken far enough, that the objects of social scientific inquiry should no longer be human beings or aggregates of them but rather non-human entities and the relations between them. These are entities and relations which may only be 'seen' thanks to the beneficence of theory and which may well turn out never to have existed in the forms in which they are first observed, much as has been the case with many of the particles that have been known to physics. The texts where such ideas appear have been described variously as 'post-structuralist', 'post-Marxist' or 'postmodernist': in the first case, because they refuse the stability of meaning often assumed by structuralists, despite the latter's foundational rejection of representationalism; in the second, because they refuse the economic reductionism of Marxism as well as its claims to provide the basis for a comprehensive knowledge; and in the third, because, inspired by Nietzsche, they refuse the belief in, or even the belief in the desirability of (it has too often been asssociated with 'totalitarianism'), intellectual and social progress that underpins the aforementioned beliefs and claims, whether made by Marxists, structuralists or others.[2]

The choice of label varies with the concerns of the labellers, but since each implies the other, what is signified thereby remains more or less the same. Thus the choice of any of them to describe a social-scientific text suggests that it rejects and distrusts any social theory that claims, no matter how, to have transcended its own linguistic nature and so to have produced knowledge of the world beyond itself. Many observers, including the postmodernists proper, have taken the appearance of texts so labelled as portending the death of theory and especially of so-called 'grand theory'. Indeed Laclau has gone a step further and spoken (like the neoliberals?) of 'the impossibility of society'.

Realism, Postmodernism and the Revitalisation of Social Theory

This will not be the position taken here, where the metaphysical, or as I prefer to call it 'metatheoretical', stance will be that of a variant of what has become known as 'scientific realism'. Although, unbeknownst to most postmodernists, such realists agree with the proposition that knowledge claims can never be verified or falsified, even probabilistically, they nevertheless insist that knowledge of the extra-discursive is possible. It may be gained by undertaking reflexive, theoretically informed observation (Bhaskar, 1978; Benton, 1977; Keat, Urry, 1975), whose results must be stoically accepted as necessarily never anything other than utterly fallible. What distinguishes the stance taken here from that to be found in most realist texts and therefore insulates it from the criticisms that postmodernist writers otherwise correctly level at them, is the fact that it shares and indeed, because of the positive nature of its scepticism, takes further postmodernism's rejection of representationalism and humanism.

Very much against the grain of the current, self-destructively dogmatic, postmodernist orthodoxy, according to which realism and representationalism imply one another (see Lawson and Appignanesi, 1989, intro., for example), the adoption of a realist stance will be taken here to require the rejection of representationalism. In the absence of one, the promise implicit in the other cannot be fulfilled.

Representationalism and humanism thrive on the assumption that there can be certainty, whilst the assumption that there can be certainty depends for *its* plausibility on the thought that, in the end, the objects of social scientific concern are the visible bodies of human beings, whose activities are observed every day and which one day we may hope to picture accurately. It is my view that only the positive scepticism fundamental to realism and the imaginative space it opens up can finally free social science from the limitations inherent in representationalism/humanism and thereby save its critical practitioners from sitting on their theoretical hands like the postmodernist epigoni, alternately laughing and railing at past mistakes. The writing of ironic 'theoretical' narratives cannot substitute for the revivification of social theory, not least because, nicely, such narratives have yet to free themselves from tacitly depending upon the same representationalism/humanism (see below pp.170-1).

Unempowered by realism's positive scepticism, the postmodernists have restricted themselves to providing critiques of particular concepts (for example, 'class', see Cutler et al, 1977; and 'society', see Laclau and Mouffe, 1985) on the grounds of their claimed incoherence, and, by aggregating or generalising from these, they have suggested the delusory nature of much of what we take to be 'theory'. By contrast, the present text will begin by drawing out the consequences of the rejection of representationalism and humanism for the activity of theorising as such and only afterwards will it move on to consider the fate of particular concepts. The net result will be that, although the problems uncovered are profound, they will not be treated as insuperable, since they are understood to originate in an approach to theory rather than to be intrinsic to it.

According to the present metatheoretical stance, knowledge as a set of discourses is as much a social fact and thus as much a material 'thing' as any of the objects to which we may suppose it to refer. For realists this should mean that one can never be sure as to whether or not knowledge as such exists, let alone any particular instance of it. Thus the pursuit of certainty so enthusiastically taken up by the various epistemological protagonists is based upon a fundamental misrecognition as to the status of knowledge. I include amongst the victims of this misrecognition the Pragmatists and the many scientific realists who, despite their shared scepticism, unfortunately also share a commitment to the dangerously question-begging notion of worldly usefulness or 'practical adequacy' as a surrogate for a guarantee that at least some part of the truth has been grasped. ('Question-begging' because we can never be at all certain as to why or how any knowledge we think we have possesses whatever practical adequacy it has. 'Dangerous' because the judgement as to practical adequacy has to be a human one, which thereby puts at risk the fundamental realist postulate that the world, including the social world, exists independently of whether or not we are in any way aware of it – cp Trigg, 1981, intro.). The misrecognition of concern here is that which results from the Cartesian assumption that because the realm of knowledge is the habitat of our conscious minds at their sharpest, the scepticism that is otherwise *de rigueur* as regards all other truth claims may be suspended with respect to knowledge's own existence. In other words, the privileging of knowledge is yet another of the problems bequeathed to us by the long-established hegemony of humanist discourses in the social sciences. 'Certainty' and for that matter 'practical adequacy' are humanly fabricated objects of desire, which only make sense to human beings. The remainder of the world, whether natural or social, is utterly indifferent to them, as also should be those who seek knowledge of that world.

Fundamental to the present position is the rigorous observance of a radically transformed version of a distinction whose importance has often been noted before but seldom respected – that between 'the analytic' or the conceptual and 'the concrete' or the empirical.

Here, prompted by Saussure, this distinction will be recast as one between mutually irreducible social scientific things composed of signifiers and their signifieds, the latter including empirical data as well as concepts, and the extra-social scientific things to which they are made to refer. In other words, the view taken here is that the role of theory and the empirical research with which it should always be conjoined is to provide the means whereby what can never be more than a flickering and unreliable light may be thrown upon other things. However, the denial of the mutual irreducibility of social scientific things and their referents is precisely what occurs when those who adopt a representationalist/humanist stance argue that, in the end, social institutions are only ever the temporary crystallisations of human interactions. The result is that, misdirected by the hope of 'certainty', they repeatedly violate their own protocols and confuse 'the analytic' with 'the concrete'; for example, the question 'Is "class" a concept or a real group of people?' has seldom, if ever, been answered unambiguously even within a single text.[3]

In my view, the confusion of social scientific things with the things to which they refer is the proximate cause of the incoherences detected by the postmodernists. Unfortunately, the latter do not agree. On the contrary, for them, the ultimate cause of these incoherences lies in the assumption that the two may be separated, and more specifically in the assumption that the extra-discursive may ever be thought of as in any way separable from the discursive. (For the unintended idealism that is the metatheoretical consequence of this view see below, p. 68, and p. 70.)

A Non-Representationalist Approach to Theory

The proper conception of theory is, then, not one that considers concepts to be stable representations of the extra-theoretical world and its 'inner workings'. Rather, it is one that considers concepts to be inherited but inherently changeable and irredeemably abstract signs, which to a degree and because of their semiological character, are manipulable without any necessary reference to the extra-theoretical world. Nevertheless, as social scientific signs they are and/or should be *made* to illuminate or refer to that world in an explicit and visible way by the operation of a number of processes: that is, by the historical and social specifics of their constitution as discourses (see below, pp. 30–2); by the research process; and by the myriad other social processes (for example, those relating to education) that account for their being read as referring to the extra-theoretical world. In sum, the achievement of ordinary but consciously controlled reference rather than of any specially verified or falsifiable 'truth' is all that can or need be sought.

By insisting upon the scepticism that is intrinsic to realism and upon the semiological character of theoretical terms, I have already indicated why 'reference' is all that can be sought. A few additional words are required to explain why it is all that need be sought. This is because reference, once established, is extremely resilient even in the face of the strongest counter–indications and arguments. Thus the question that should be addressed is not, 'How does one achieve certainty?' – despite its impossibility, it all too often automatically follows the achievement of reference – but, 'How does one consciously achieve reference and maintain its corrigibility?' The answer proposed here is that corrigible reference may only be achieved if one makes reference as explicit and transparent as possible. Thus it may be agreed with Pearce (1989, intro.) that one very important indicator of 'quality' as regards social theory is the degree to which it is 're-readable' and reusable in different historical and cultural contexts.

In sum, social theorists *qua* theorists should aim to provide not pictures of social reality but rigorously interrelated ensembles of signs that have been made to refer to extra-theoretical reality. This is a more difficult task than it might at first appear, and not just because of the metatheoretical and methodological protocols that must be respected if such reference is to be rigorously and corrigibly established. However, abstinence from the major stimulant of humanism, and from related but on their own less potent stimulants such as empiricism and, especially in the case of Marxism, economic reductionism and theoreticism, should help towards a more ascetic approach. An approach, moreover, which because of its inherent distrust of not just the received wisdom but also of its primary supports, should help to exclude historically anachronistic, as well as male-centred, homophobic and ethnocentric preconceptions from sociological research – if only because it is that much harder to import the prejudices of everyday life when the objects of such research are non-human rather than human entities.

By refusing what might be termed 'the rush to representation', such abstinence should also enhance the likelihood of a deferred and potentially more fruitful union between theory and observation: one that is systematically counter-intuitive and unafraid of abstraction; one in which the role of observation is to control abstraction rather than initiate, verify or falsify it; and one, finally, that is capable of bringing to light non-human social entities of whose possible existence we have hitherto heard only rumours. Such rumours have seldom hardened into referentially supported 'facts' because they have been too often and too quickly denied. Instead, we accept far too readily: (a) that the objects of social scientific inquiry should only be human beings (humanism); (b) that we should only trust the evidence of our senses (empiricism); (c) that every lasting structure must have a set of foundations (economic reductionism); and, finally (d) that theory is a self-validating instance of 'second-sight' (theoreticism).

Thanks to such supports, the hold of representationalism is so tenacious that even those who have sought most diligently to free themselves from its thrall have failed: humanism, in no matter how vestigial a form, makes it all too easy to think that social scientific categories refer directly to some thing, namely human behaviour; empiricism has a reinforcing effect in that what we can most readily observe is human behaviour; economic reductionism has a similar effect, both because foundations are ultimately supposed to be uncoverable and hence visible, and also because in the face of its often demonstrated implausibility, the antidote typically recommended is an admonition to observe 'actual human behaviour'; and, finally, theoreticism too has a reinforcing effect in that unfortunately thus far the work of those who have sought to advance a non-representationalist approach to social theory has seldom been rooted in, or even been followed up by, empirical research – thus, the all-too-human pendulum of fashion rather than an abstractly derived research agenda has tended to determine the nature of their topics of concern. In sum, humanism is the key support, not only because it privileges human beings as the representers, but also because, narcissistically, it privileges them as the things to be represented.

On the basis, then, of a non-representationalist and non-humanist variant of 'scientific realism', what will be presented hereafter are the further results of an imagined, reciprocally critical dialogue between postmodernism and Marxism, a dialogue that was conducted with a view to aiding the recuperation of social theory rather than speeding its death. As the intellectual anxiety subsides, the sometimes liberatory, sometimes reactionary nihilism implicit in postmodernist thought may be seen for what it is – an hallucinatory anticipation ('figuration') of the calm that follows a crisis. The quotidian remains as complex and opaque as ever and certainly not susceptible to being wished away as if it too were only the product of imaginations, fevered or otherwise. Society is not so much an impossible concept as a difficult reality to understand.

Despite some claims to the contrary, postmodernism is no more a self-guiding and self-subsistent body of discourse than any other. If it has a referent beyond itself which makes it more than just an assemblage of abstractions, it is because of a wider set of social changes of which it is a part (for preliminary efforts to specify what these might be see Jameson, 1984; Kellner, 1989; Harvey, 1989). It is this which also makes it, alongside its competitor for peer group leadership, neoliberalism, symptomatic of a social condition, a *malaise* even, where the quest for the new and/or the better often seems an impossible and even foolish waste of time. This condition must be acknowledged and reflected upon. And not simply negatively, since there is a lot to learn from it, some of which is 'good news', not least for the environment and the peoples of 'Eastern Europe' (for examples of non-humanist interventions in the debate on the environment that are compatible with the present position see Benton, 1984, 1988). However, no more than any other is it a condition that may be understood, let alone surpassed, exclusively in the terms that are part of the symptoms it presents. *Munchhausen* effects are as implausible in the social sciences as anywhere else, or ought to be.

Postmodernism after Realism

In what follows the reader will encounter none of the spaciousness and *grandeur* traditionally found in 'the house of theory'. A jobbing professional draughtsman with a sneaking regard for Escher rather than a great artist like Piranesi is my model. Instead of the equivalent of a fantastically detailed front elevation, what will be found below are the equivalents of a series of rather spare but, on occasion, perceptually surprising sections through some of the principal rooms behind the façade. What the reader will encounter is a somewhat austere but, I hope, provocative effort at conceptual reasoning of a fundamentally modernistic and specifically Marxist kind, written in the course of a receptive but critical dialogue with the postmodernist *avant garde*. The influence of the latter is apparent both in the present text's refusal of humanism and representationalism and also in its acceptance of what might be called 'a postmodernist intellectual ethic', which values modesty, pragmatism and cooperation: 'modesty' because hitherto theorists have tended to make excessive claims; 'pragmatism' because, in the absence of miraculous solutions to conceptual and social problems, the latter require elucidation and their pursuit provides the most promising context within which to attempt theoretical advance; and 'cooperation' because its necessity is implied by the others.

Given 'scientific realism' and the re-reading of the pertinent post-modernist texts that it provokes, such a combination of modernism and postmodernism as is proposed here is possible, contrary to polemical and popular opinion, because as a result of their shared verificational scepticism the opposition between them need no longer be sustained. Thus one may value modesty without giving up hope on the possibility of 'grand theory'; one may work on a pragmatic basis without thinking that because something appears to 'work' it is necessarily true; and finally, provided one pays attention to the issue of metatheoretical consistency, one may accept help from other thinkers and other traditions without losing coherence. In sum, it should now be possible to theorise in a new key, allowing a wider range of voices to harmonise with one another.

The discovery of the possibility, necessity even, of a non-representationalist approach to theorising is not the only benefit that may be derived for social theory from acknowledging the significatory nature of language. In addition, such an acknowledgement provides a means of more directly uncovering aspects of social reality that have otherwise remained invisible. Thus, more substantively, this effort at theorising will proceed by using the concept of discourse and a variant of the deconstructive method, successively and cumulatively, to rethink not just the language-borne phenomena of ideology but also and as a consequence three of the concepts central to classical social thought: 'production', 'law' and 'class'. In general terms the argument to be advanced here is that the discursive/ideological realm is one that Marxism in particular has ignored, that this is no longer a supportable position, and that the entire corpus of Marxist theory has now to be rethought. By implication, the more reactive varieties of non-Marxist theory such as Weberianism also stand in need of equally radical rethinking.

The present text arises out of an ongoing programme of research on the sociology of labour law in Britain, Japan and the United States (Woodiwiss, 1987b; 1988c; 1990a). It is because I have attempted to theorise within this context, whose more specific pertinence will become apparent as the text proceeds, that I hope that I may be judged to have actually played and not merely bluffed the best hand in the Pragmatists' game, namely that based upon the strategy that knowledge should be pursued rather than worried about (Rorty 1979, 1982). Bluffing, one suspects, is all too often the case when the practical goal invoked to justify theoretical activity is merely a vaguely defined political one (for example, 'the struggle for socialism').[4]

The Centrality of Law

More will be said in Chapter 1 about the theoretical and methodological underpinnings of this text and how they will affect the deconstruction to be attempted herein as compared to that practised in those of the postmodernists proper. However, first, something should be said about why so much of the argument that follows proceeds by way of a discussion of the law. The reasons for this are twofold. The first is the present author's belief that new ways of thinking about the law in general, and about labour law in particular, will open the way to new ways of thinking in many other theoretical and substantive areas. For too long the law has been understood by sociologists, for example, as an institutional 'black box' whose social role may be understood without knowing much about its internal life. Since the death of sociology's founding fathers, but with the exception of Unger among recent general theorists, it has been deemed sufficient to know that the civil law guaranteed the right to private property. All kinds of conclusions have been drawn from this far from uncontestable statement. Those conclusions have affected the way in which aspects of the world are seen in areas that are far removed from the purview of the law.

The case in point will be the theory of class as developed by Marxists. Here the assumption that the law guarantees private property in the means of production has long served as a conceptual guy-rope, whose peg only needs to be banged in for virtually any structure to remain upright. Thus, once the sociologically critical rethinking of the nature of production has been completed, the substantive theoretical question, whose posing will most directly structure this narrative, is: 'What happens to the Marxist theory of class after the theory of law, upon which it has hitherto rested, has been rejected?' The second reason for the attention paid to law is that, both as a topic of intellectual interest and as a sphere of social activity, it is in the throes of a great but slow-motion upheaval that is central to the politics of the present. The immediate symptoms of this upheaval cannot be addressed directly in this text. All that can be said is that these may well turn out to be connected with the industrial upheaval consequent on the transformations in the nature of production that have recently been taken further by the rise of what is becoming known as 'post-Fordism' (Jessop, 1987; Lipietz, 1985).[5]

What can and will be directly addressed here, however, are the problems associated with the theoretical prerequisites for understanding the causes of both upheavals, particularly their class-structural aspects, since these relate to at least part of the context within which the significance of the transition to post-Fordism has to be understood. Thus, as well as being long overdue for analytical reasons, an interest in the law appears to be a sign of the times (*vide* the recent emergence in Britain of the movement for constitutional reform known as 'Charter 88').

Reconstructing the Law: Two Debates

This is also a period of some legal and juristic unease in the countries of the advanced capitalist world. Legal systems and the academic approaches to their study, which, like social theory, still owe much to the nineteenth century, have recently begun to experience challenges of a radicalness unparalleled since those which they themselves represented in relation to their own ramshackle inheritance. Strong, executive-led antinomian forces have arisen as part of what has often been seen as an emergent corporatism but which has gained force with the rise of a neoliberalism which, contradictorily, shares corporatism's preference for vaguely phrased, enabling legislation. They have so challenged 'the rule of law' and indeed the constitutional primacy of legislatures that the resistances represented by the belated creation of a body of administrative law in the common law countries, by the rise or revival of judicial review, by the occasional strengthening of individual and civil rights, and/or by the promulgation of the various human rights conventions, all seem very puny. And not least because they are themselves the objects of often bitter disputes amongst those who have most to lose from the law's derogation. This, then, is one context within which a debate about legal reconstruction has arisen: the legal system itself.

The other context for such a debate has been the academy, wherein, since the realist revolt of the 1920s in the United States and, belatedly, since Hart's use of the phrase 'descriptive sociology' to describe his work in the Britain of the 1960s, jurisprudence, at least, has become an ever more fully interactive part of the social sciences – a process recently confirmed by Dworkin's (1986) apparently *a posteriori* claim to dependence on the hermeneutics of Habermas and Gadamer. Admission of such kinship and of an associated need for self-reconstruction has been widely acknowledged as necessary if jurisprudence is both to understand what is happening to the law and to participate in its reconstruction. As will be indicated shortly, all schools of jurisprudence have participated in this effort at self-reconstruction. However, one such effort is of particular interest in this text and will be actively pursued here, namely that undertaken within the ambit of the Marxist theory of law.

Reconstructing Legal Theory in the United States and Britain

Since at least 1971 and the publication of Rawls' *A Theory of Justice*, a debate has been joined in the United States around the theme of *Reconstructing American Law* (Ackerman, 1983). Many individuals and schools have contributed to this debate, ranging from conservatives, through several types of liberal to the Critical Legal Theorists. Many of the latter have taken up postmodernist themes, most implicitly (for example, Kennedy, 1979; Stone, 1981) and some explicitly (for example, Balkin, 1987; Dalton, 1985). At stake is the nature of the jurisprudence and associated legal practice that should replace the hitherto dominant Legal Realism.[6] In one way or another all these proposals for reconstruction argue for the legal pertinence of phenomena that have been regarded previously as impertinent, whether they are Dworkin's 'principles' (1977), Posner's 'market' (1981), the 'alienation' of concern to some of the Critical Legal Theorists (Kairys, 1982) or 'the justice of multiplicity' of concern to the postmodernists among them (Lyotard, 1985, p. 100). Their practical aim has been to move beyond the 'particularism' of realism, whereby what is idiosyncratic in a case is overemphasised to the detriment of any serious consideration of 'the systematic structural tensions of social life' (Ackerman, 1983, p. 20). What are being recommended, therefore, are various strategies for broadening the allowable 'facts of the case', so that new questions may be brought to law, new clients represented and new legal outcomes made possible. What the questions should be, who the clients should be and what outcomes are considered desirable of course varies across the political spectrum according to the political commitments of the reconstructionists.

In Britain the arguments for the legal pertinence of many of the phenomena pointed to by US jurists have been repeated and elaborated upon, as is evidenced by the recent collection of essays entitled *Legal Theory and the Common Law* (Twining, 1986). Interestingly, a reading of these essays fails to reveal either the same sense of crisis that seems to permeate the American literature or the same degree of mutual hostility between the proponents of the competing positions. These differences may reflect a greater equability amongst British jurists or, more likely, a certain fatalism that is the product of the more embattled position of all legal theorists in Britain.

Sugarman's contribution to the British collection, in which he discusses the history of British legal education, suggests why such a stance should be both advised and accompanied by a certain fatalism. Briefly put, Sugarman's suggestion is that the 'classical law dons' of the nineteenth century so emphasised their positivism (to gain acceptance in the universities) and their expository role (to gain acceptance from the profession) that when their approach was vulgarised after their passing, there was little in their legacy to support the critical spirit that informed their own work. Sugarman considers that critical spirit to be essential if interest in theory is to thrive and, by extension, if jurisprudence is to pull its social scientific weight. Plausible though this suggestion is within the compass of Sugarman's essay, it does not on its own explain the differences between British and US jurisprudence that are of concern here. The reason for this insufficiency is that, of course, US law teaching was initially at least as positivistic and expository as that in Britain, and for the same reasons (see below pp. 137–8).

To obtain a more adequate explanation of the differences between the literatures and between the contemporary politics of law in the two societies, one has to acknowledge at least two points of dissimilarity between their legal and social contexts. Legally, the rationalisation that the 'classical law dons' achieved in Britain was not premissed upon the primacy of property in the same almost exclusive way that it was in the United States (Woodiwiss, 1989, Ch. 4). As Sugarman pointed out in an earlier paper (1984, pp. 32–6), the rights of property holders in Britain never attained the autonomy from and priority relative to the rights and powers of the state that they did in the United States. This fact, coupled with the judicially unqualified constitutional supremacy of Parliament and the comparatively early development of an economically and politically powerful as well as ideologically influential labour movement, has meant that the law has never presented the obstacle to the labour movement's encroachment on state power that it did in the latter part of the nineteenth century in the United States. Then the doctrine of 'judicial supremacy' held sway and led to the Supreme Court's recurrent declarations that 'pro-labour' statutes were unconstitutional (Boudin, 1968). Thus, in Britain apart from when the courts consider industrial relations issues upon which the statutes are silent, the phrase 'due process of law' carries few, if any, of the negative connotations that it carries for progressive jurists in the United States even today.

Law and the Politics of Production in Contemporary Britain

The underlying issue of which conditions allow and which threaten legal autonomy will be discussed further at the end of Chapter 5. The politics of law and their relation to the economy have been mentioned at this point simply to suggest why the debate over 'the reconstruction of law' has not been joined so fiercely in Britain, thus far. The qualification is necessary because the Employment Acts passed by the present British government signify the possible casting aside of the very device (the 'immunities') that since the 1870s has preserved the coherence of what is still a property-centred legal system, notwithstanding Parliamentary supremacy and the occasional access to state power of the labour movement. The 'immunities' enjoyed by the trades unions may have been an affront to the dignity of the law and may indeed have undermined the very idea of 'the rule of law', because they may also be construed as 'privileges' (Dicey, 1914). Nevertheless, they also constrained that same challenge to 'individualism' by 'collectivism' that so concerned Dicey. This was a challenge which, given Labour governments, otherwise might just have had to have been met within the discourse of property itself, as indeed has been the case in Sweden (see below, p. 100), rather than outside it. Such an eventuality would have undermined still further the coherence although not necessarily the autonomy of the law, as well as had unpredictable but most probably negative consequences for capital. In short, it might have involved a significant qualification to the powers that otherwise inhere in ownership and allow it its privileged position in law and society.

Contemporarily, it remains possible that the passage of the recent Employment Acts may turn out inadvertently to have provided an opening for the labour movement. This ambiguity in what the Acts might eventually come to signify is suggested by the movement's recent, partial and grudging acceptance of them, and by its ever more enthusiastic participation in the debate on ownership that has commenced between the Labour Party ('social ownership', 'industrial democracy' etc.) and the Conservatives ('profit related pay', 'wider share ownership' etc.). The debate has been joined most directly on the issue of the wider social significance of Employee Share Ownership Plans (ESOPs) – do they presage socialisation or worker-capitalism? It is, thus, just possible that the equability of the British legal profession is about to be tested by a far more radical effort to 'reconstruct the law' than is at present conceivable in the United States (but see Woodiwiss, 1990a, conclusion). If this proves to be the case, any fatalism on the part of British theorists, whether of law or sociality, will lose whatever justification it may have had. In the meantime they are being propelled, willy nilly, into the centre of juristic and indeed political debate by Thatcherism's attempt to eradicate socialism from our national life.

Law and Economics

Returning to the academic debate about the reconstruction of the law, apart from its qualified affiliation with postmodernism, what immediately differentiates this text from those written by other participants, except some by Critical Legal Theorists, is its refusal of the validity of what is otherwise considered to be the most pertinent non-legal premiss of the efforts at reconstruction. This assumption is the notion that equal exchange in the market is all that is required for social justice to be assured. The specific site of this refusal is the market of central concern here, the market where production, law and class are inextricably intertwined, namely the labour market.

As it relates to capitalist societies and given the 'labour theory of value', Marxist social scientific discourse is premissed, correctly in my view (see Chapter 2), upon an assumption as to the intrinsic inequality of the wage-bargain. According to Marx's argument in *Capital*, the origin of this inequality was the process of 'so-called primitive accumulation', whereby property in the means of production was monopolised by a class of owners, under a sign of private property and to the inescapable detriment of those who consequently had only their labour-power to sell. Thenceforth and because of the peculiarity of labour-power as a commodity – that is, its 'use-value possesses the peculiar property of being a source of value, whose actual consumption ... is itself an embodiment of labour, and consequently, a creation of value' (Marx, 1965, p. 167) – there has been a specifically capitalist element of compulsion, exploitation and therefore inequality intrinsic to the labour market which qualitatively distinguishes it from other markets and which has to be acknowledged even in abstract theorising.

Marxism and Postmodernism

This said, it must be admitted immediately that so powerful was the discovery of the peculiarity of the labour market, and the derived one of 'class', that it has had some very unfortunate effects on Marxist theory, particularly when the latter has been deployed to explain non-economic social phenomena. Specifically, the determinative power of the economy and/or class with respect to other aspects of social relations has been exaggerated, with the result that political and ideological determinations, for example, have been neglected or assigned only a secondary significance. For this reason Marxist discussions of law and class have been criticised often and correctly for an oversimplified reductionism. It is in order to try to prevent the repetition of this criticism that the present text has been written, using the metatheoretical, conceptual and methodological advances made possible by the belated arrival of the concept of 'discourse'.

Interestingly, postmodernism has had, thus far, its greatest social scientific impact in British Marxist circles. Although the concept of 'discourse' arrived more than ten years ago (Hindess and Hirst, 1977), its significance is still unclear and subject to a great deal of often vociferous debate. On the one hand there are those, like Laclau and Mouffe (1985), for whom it has provided a means for moving on to a 'post-Marxist' position. On the other there are those, like Anderson (1983, p. 40), for whom its current prominence illustrates a more general structuralist 'exorbitation of language' (for a similar critique, but from a non-Marxist position see Rose, 1984). The latter group often appear to prefer to fasten their hopes for the renewal of Marxist theory upon either Critical Theory (Dews, 1988) or the self-described 'no bullshit Marxism' associated with Cohen (1978) and Elster (1985).

There is, however, a third way through these debates, one which has had a considerable influence among what might be called, to echo C.W. Mills (1963), 'ordinary Marxists'. It is apparent amongst social historians (for example, Stedman-Jones, 1983), literary theorists (for example, Easthope, 1983; 1988) and between the covers of

Marxism Today and *Economy and Society*. According to this approach, and irrespective of the many differences between its protagonists, the concept of discourse promises the enrichment of the tradition that Marx founded rather than either its corruption or transcendence. This text is offered as a contribution to this third way.

Notes

1. I will use the term 'non-humanism' rather than the more common 'anti-humanism' to refer to the opposite of humanism, since the latter has too often been used to denote simply the denial of the originary power of the human subject.

2. Since this is determinedly a work *of* rather than *about* theory, no attempt will be made here to outline postmodernist or any other pre-existing set of ideas in any systematic way. Fragments of such discourses will be outlined in what follows but only in so far as knowledge of them is necessary to advance the argument. Those readers requiring more systematic treatments of the principal sets of ideas upon which this text draws are recommended to consult the following: Benton (1984); Dews (1988); Dreyfus and Rabinow (1982); Jessop (1986); Norris (1982); Sturrock, (1986).

3. An ambiguous response to such questions has proved particularly hard to resist when those to whom they have been addressed have opted to couch all or some of their causal arguments in terms of the language of surveys and statistics. There are two main reasons for this. The first is that the latter almost always partakes of one or other variant of the probabilistic empiricist rhetoric of 'certainty'. The second is that representationalism is implicit in the very term 'survey', and it becomes explicit both in the language of the relevant textbooks (for example, de Vaux, 1986; Marsh, 1988) and every time the opinion pollsters utter their standard caveat to the effect that their polls are merely 'snapshots' of the electorate at particular points in time. Moreover, even such advanced concepts and techniques as 'Lorenz curves,' '*gini*-coefficients,' 'odds ratios,' 'log-linear analysis' and 'smoothing' simply provide means whereby the representations produced by surveys and polls may be mechanically enhanced so that their snapshots are that much clearer. (For additional, compatible and more specifically realist criticisms of the privileging of what is normally somewhat misleadingly called 'observation', as well as of over-reliance on statistics more generally, see Sayer, 1984,

Ch. 6.) Fortunately, the provision of an answer to the question as to whether or not statistical concepts and techniques may be recast so that they may be made compatible with non-empiricist conceptions of causality is beyond the scope of the present study.

4. Given the realism of this text, a subsidiary aim is to suggest, if implicitly, to those still mesmerised by the concept of discourse, and who would join Rorty in his view of 'science as [but] one genre of literature' (1982, p. xiii), that the opposition that he sees between pragmatism and realism is false and is a consequence of him being committed to a view of language, a conflation of moral and natural phenomena and a reading of Foucault, which are in no way necessarily the only ones with which pragmatism's ontological confidence may co-exist.

5. As the use of the term 'post-Fordism' suggests, this text shares with its originators in the 'regulation school' their insistence on the continued centrality of production to the structures of advanced capitalist societies. It also shares with them their desire to understand production in a way that is not economically reductionist. Indeed it is as a clarification of how a non-reductionist account of production and of the social formation more generally might be produced that I hope the present text might be of interest to the regulationists and those whom they have inspired, such as the authors of the British Communist Party's *Manifesto for New Times*. Too often their own analyses appear to assume that in order to achieve a non-reductionist analysis it is sufficient to assert the autonomy and even sometimes merely the pertinence of other phenomena apart from that of production. Here, as should be apparent by now, it is thought necessary to go much further.

6. There is no connection between Legal Realism and Scientific Realism. In essence Legal Realism is a position that insists that to understand the law one has to look beyond its 'black letters' and investigate the whos, whats and wherefores of its actual use. (The most accessible account for social scientists is that provided by Hunt, 1977.) Because most legal realist work assumes the correctness of an empiricist metatheoretical stance, it should not be thought that it has anything in common with what has been called here 'scientific realism'.

PART I
Metatheoretical Starting Points

1 Realism, Non-humanism and Deconstruction

Two aspects of the metatheoretical stance taken here distinguish it from that adopted in postmodernist texts proper and, therefore, impose limits upon the degree of deconstruction to be undertaken in what follows. First, the present text is ontologically realist rather than idealist in that it assumes that social reality, including its discursive dimension, exists independently of the perceptions, actions or whatever of human subjects. Second, it is epistemologically realist rather than empiricist in that it assumes that theory precedes but does not displace observation in the order of scientific inquiry (Bhaskar, 1978; Benton, 1977; Keat, Urry, 1975). Additionally, it also assumes that reality may be apprehended, at least referentially, by the social sciences, although, because of the mutual irreducibility of the two, there can be no certainty as to the correctness of this apprehension (Trigg, 1981, p. vii). Thus knowledge of the social is both possible and accompanied by a specific scepticism that is an inevitable as well as a required feature of its pursuit. Finally, the ontological stance taken here is also a non-humanist one; that is, it assumes that the primary objects of social scientific enquiry are not, in the first or the final analysis, either human beings or combinations of them. Rather, they are *sui generis* social entities (Durkheim, 1964a; Gane, 1988; Pearce, 1989).

Non-humanism, the Human Subject and the Task of Sociology

In its non-humanism resides the principal difference between the present stance and that more commonly adopted by realist authors (e.g. Bhaskar, 1978, 1986; 1989; Sayer, 1984). The existence of this difference is a product of the view taken here that the independence of the sociological and psychological realms of enquiry is real and not simply an illusory side-effect of the division of intellectual labour. And it is something, moreover, that cannot be avoided by

25

taking as one's starting point what are supposed to be ontologically and disciplinarily neutral (but in fact irredeemably humanist and therefore psychologistic) notions such as 'action' (Parsons, 1949). This view is derived from Foucault's (1974) seldom acknowledged insistence that the conditions that make it possible for a particular discourse to exist also determine to a significant degree what that discourse can and cannot be about (see below, pp. 30–2, 61–4). Thus Foucault's concept of 'discursive formation' may be taken as sanctioning not, as is all too often supposed, a denial of any autonomy to subjects, but rather the exclusion of any reference to concrete individuals as such from the domain of sociological inquiry, on the ground that they may be properly understood only by resort to the discourses made possible by the discursive formation that allows one to talk, at all, about 'the psychological'.

That said, it should not be taken as suggesting either that no aspects of individual practice are sociologically pertinent, or that the psychological and sociological spheres are not imbricated with one and interpenetrative of one another empirically. What it does suggest, however, is that there are aspects of individual practice which have a psychological pertinence that is distinguishable from their sociological pertinence: the sociological and psychological spheres have first to be understood separately before their concrete imbrication may be elucidated. Moreover, it also suggests that this has to be done in the terms of both disciplines rather than in terms suggested by a necessarily incoherent and insufficient social psychology, whether its starting point is 'action', 'interaction' or whatever, and whose troubled existence (Parker, 1989) serves most importantly to register the unsurpassability of the discursive gulf between sociology and psychology.

As an elaborated consequence of this set of assumptions, a further one may be descried in the set which structure this text. It is the view that, as Comte immodestly argued, sociology is 'the queen of the sciences'. Here this will be taken to mean only that sociology's task is in the end a synthetic one. In my view this task has been lost sight of often and regrettably, whilst Marxists have refused fully to accept and non-Marxists have too enthusiastically followed up the discovery of the third dimension of sociality, that is, 'ideology' (Marx), 'meaning' (Weber), 'representations' (Durkheim), or 'values' (Parsons). Whole 'sociologies' (for example Symbolic Interactionism, Ethnomethodology and, thanks to his extraordinary faith in the powers of reasoning by analogy, Lévi-Strauss's variant of structuralism) have grown and prospered on the basis of a confusion, never made by the founders, between the discovery of this dimension and that of the whole subject matter of sociology. Moreover, and this is the connection between this point, realism and non-humanism, if the understanding that sociology seeks is to be genuinely synthetic it must involve more than an amalgamation, no matter how complex, of the economic, the political and the ideological.

Thus the ultimate task of sociology is nothing less than the supercession of the ontological constraints that necessarily marked the formation of the social sciences, including sociology itself, and which Foucault (1970; 1974) began to specify. As Foucault and indeed his 'structuralist' precursors emphasised, critical to this enterprise is the displacement of the figure of 'man' as the object of ontological and hence social scientific concern in favour of non-human forms of being. This is a displacement that Weber and all who have followed him have refused to make (hence the insufficiencies of notions like 'ideal-type' (Weber, 1978), 'emergence' (Parsons, 1949) and 'structuration' (Giddens 1985)), as well as one that the functionalist usurpers of Durkheim's patrimony have brought into disrepute. Only those capable of responding to the ontological challenge posed by 'structuralism' – that is, some postmodernists and some Marxists – have proved to be at all interested in promoting, let alone achieving, this displacement.

Discourse and Social Science

What must now be specified is the more substantive role expected of the concept of discourse in the achievement of this displacement. Discourse analysis has been defined in the following usefully descriptive manner by a theorist working within a rather different tradition to that which has produced post-modernism:

> Discourse analysis is a method of seeking in any connected discrete linear material, whether language or language-like, which contains more than one elementary sentence, some global structure characterising the whole discourse (the linear material) or large sections of it. The structure is a pattern of occurrence (i.e. a recurrence) of segments of a discourse relative to each other. (Harris, 1963, in Burton and Carlen, 1979, p. 16)

The point of using the concept of discourse in an effort to conceptualise the relationships between human subjects and other aspects and dimensions of sociality is that the diverse 'patterns of occurrence' that the various discourses represent may be understood to constitute such subjects, to interpellate them and to allow their interpellation. Thus the subject represents not their origin but a site where they intersect, an 'inter-discourse' wherein the various positions given in discourse are juxtaposed. Moreover, such sites need not even be human (this point will be followed up in Chapter 7). But when they are, as Hirst (1979, p. 67) correctly emphasised in his well-known critique of Althusser's discussion of these issues, the infant is only capable of knowing anything insofar as it has already been interpellated. Of more direct relevance here, however, is the suggestion that ideology should be defined as the realm of discourse, wherein different discourses or sets of discourses are distinguished from one another by the objects they define for themselves, by their differing conditions of existence and by the consequently diverse subjectivities they project on to those inter-discourses they interpellate.

The Limits of Postmodernism
Acceptance of this train of thought does not indicate, however, acceptance of all the consequences thought by some to follow from it. As has been implied already and contrary to Hindess and Hirst (1977, Chapter 1), recognition of discourse as a dimension of the real does not signify the dissolution of epistemology and the consequent abandonment of any striving after the apprehension of extradiscursive reality. Indeed, from the realist position taken by this text, it is difficult to see how the discovery of the impassability of discourse represents anything other than an apprehension of the real. This is a view that Freud, who is otherwise a postmodernist hero, would have shared. Janet Malcolm has put Freud's position particularly clearly:

> Implicit in the idea of transference as distortion is the assumption of some true, or truer, state of things that is being obscured. If the patient's 'menacing illusion' (as Freud called it in *An Outline of Psycho-Analysis*) of being in love with the analyst is just that – an illusion, which the analyst must 'tear the patient out of', showing him 'again and again that what he takes to be new real life is a reflection of the past' – then how is one to regard the 'reality' to which the patient is returned. What is the nature and who is to be the judge of the 'real relationship' between patient and analyst? Freud never much interested himself in this question.
>   His discovery of the illusory relationship was, after all, the news and the actual relationship between doctor and patient was not (Malcolm, 1982, pp. 39–40).

The fact that psychoanalysis, or any kind of analysis for that matter, may be interminable does not mean that it does not apprehend realities. To imagine that it could be terminable, even by the recognition of its interminability, implies a static preconception of reality, indeed one full of just such an essence as the human nature that discourse analysis has otherwise, and correctly, been used to dissolve. Thus, it sometimes seems that those mesmerised by discourse do not realise what they have done, for all the certainty of their style. For example, they do not realise that they have necessarily reconstructed as well as deconstructed 'reality' and, as an aspect of it, the subject too. The subject as an 'inter-discourse', as what Kristeva calls 'the contradiction that activates practice', is still a subject for all that. Although it is not necessarily human, when it is it nevertheless confronts an external reality and seeks knowledge of that reality on the basis of one or other epistemological position, preferably a realist one. If the subject has not been dissolved, nor has epistemology and, therefore, the possibility of the apprehension of a reality additional to discourse.

Using the concept of discourse to specify the structure of the ideological realm enables one to understand its reality and its autonomous determinative capacity. This is something which is, quite simply, impossible otherwise thanks to the prevalence of such anachronistic dichotomies as 'base/superstructure' and 'thought/ behaviour', which tend to diminish the significance of the ideological realm. By contrast, ideologies as discourses have real effects, for example as interpellations on, in and through inter-discursive subjects. These effects would not occur in their absence and they must therefore be understood in this sense as inherently autonomous. However, for reasons that will be indicated below, I understand this autonomy to be variable and relative rather than constant and absolute. All discourses certainly exhibit some pretty random running about, as is etymologically suggested. Individual signs themselves are, I have no doubt, characterised by a certain Derridean *'différance'*, or deferred meaning, as elements in and of discourse (Derrida, 1977; 1978). The connections between signifiers and signifieds are often loose, and as a consequence varying, even contrary, readings of a particular text are almost always possible. Such divergent readings subvert and thereby raise questions about the fixity of the sets of oppositions whereby the discourses that organise the text are constructed.

However, despite the near universal textual presence of tropes of various kinds, which serve as constant reminders of this looseness, the autonomy that it allows is not equally characteristic of all texts.

In certain types a relative closure of the inevitable gap between signifiers and signifieds and therefore the appropriateness of dialectical (in the pre-Marxist sense) over rhetorical responses to them is structurally overdetermined (Perelman 1963; 1980). All discourses, like all economies and polities, have certain conditions of existence, which don't simply account for their presence and sometimes secure their reproduction, but also determine what is sayable in terms of them. What this allows is that in the case of some discourses, not only does the object they have defined for themselves produce a relative closure of the signifying hiatus, but so too do the discursive and non-discursive conditions of their existence.

At the one extreme are literary texts where a special effort is made to take advantage of and to enhance the slippage that allows variations in readings. This is, as the Russian Formalists suggested, in order to 'defamiliarise' or to make strange and thereby newly if varyingly visible what might otherwise be taken for granted and neglected (Bennett, 1979, pp. 20–5). For this reason, the connotative play of words and the tropes within a poem, for example, may be as or more deserving of attention than what the same words commonly denote. At the other extreme, however, are scientific texts, including those of the social sciences, and somewhere in between are legal ones. In such texts even the self-defined objects of the discourses that make them possible are the *familiarisation* of the world for a particular set of readers with terms derived from a particular lexicon, whose value depends upon the stability of the set of significatory oppositions upon which it rests, whether or not the confidence placed in it latterly turns out to have been justified.

A Non-representationalist Account of Reference

In my view, what underlies the postmodernists' refusal of the discursive particularities of science and especially of social science and of the law (that is, those – and there are plenty of them – that have survived the supposed collapse of what Lyotard (1985) has termed '*les grands recits*'), as well as what explains the rampant eclecticism with which the resulting cognitive vacuum has been filled (for example in Lyotard, 1985, 1987), is a failure to break finally from the humanism that was inherent in the phenomenological positions from whence they all began their various journeys.

In order to have made such a break they would have had to have elaborated an alternative metaphysic. This they have steadfastly refused to do, because of their hostility towards any instance of intellectual if not political positivity or, relatedly, towards the restoration of any form of totalising reason. This, in turn, appears to reflect their fear of complicity with a world of power that they consider evil or banal or usually both. Hence, for example, Foucault's angry refusals to account for his various switches of interest and approach, hence Derrida's determination to stand his ground at the point of '*différance*', and hence the general refusal of postmodernists to define what they stand for. In each case elusiveness appears to be valued both for reasons of self-defence and for its own sake.

This refusal to elaborate an alternative metaphysic, which would have to be fully non-humanist, has one particularly important source, which, I suggest, is what defines and indeed explains the limits of postmodernism – the, in a sense, prior refusal to provide an account of linguistic reference. Wittgenstein and the Pragmatists have been used to provide accounts of linguistic reference or, better, of its motility by some postmodernists. However, whatever else one might want to say in support of such borrowings, one thing one cannot say is that they may be justified on the basis of an unambiguous sharing of what is otherwise the postmodernist preference for non-humanist modes of thought. The critical category of 'use' invites, even if it does not quite require, the presence of subjects and their reasons for acting. And this is an invitation, for example, that the 'linguistic' school in Anglo-American philosophy has almost always accepted. Without a non-humanist account of reference there is no coherent way of distinguishing different sorts of texts from one another (for example poems from scientific treatises). There is no way of justifying the invocation of different criteria when reading different sorts of texts, no way of judging the truthfulness of any text, and, finally, no way of writing texts that are themselves other than metaphysical.

This, of course, is ostensibly the point. I say 'ostensibly' because few practising deconstructionists have managed or even attempted to abide by so stringent a nihilism (Norris, 1982, 1988). Moreover, there is something ironic and even slightly tragic about the very promulgation of the position. As has often been noted, in itself and especially in its cruder manifestations, the position rests upon a claim to know an epistemological truth; that is, that epistemology offers no satisfactory route to the truth. More importantly, as only those also working within the same tradition can recognise, because of their interest in what Saussure termed *parole* rather than *langue*, Foucault and Derrida made critical, if largely unknowing, contributions to the overcoming of the lack of a post-representational account of reference at the same time as they propounded their various nihilisms.

These contributions are those allowed to the structuralist tradition by Saussure's (1974, p. 75) largely unnoticed denial that linguistic change is a purely linguistic matter and his very strong assertion that it is primarily a social matter. The significance of this has long been obscured by his even stronger assertion that *langue* rather than the intrinsically more social *parole* should be the object of linguistic study. The opportunity represented by the former assertion may only be taken advantage of properly (that is, non-positivistically) in the presence of the verificational scepticism central to scientific realism; that is, in the presence of, according to my variant, its insistence on the mutual irreducibility of discourse and all else in the world, which means that we can never be even probabilistically sure that we know anything (note that this does not mean that we cannot know anything but only that we cannot be sure to *any* degree as to the correctness of what we know). Where such scepticism is present, it has the effect of reversing – from negative to positive – what might be called 'the significatory polarity' of the central Foucauldian and Derridean concepts; that is, once the impossibility of verificational certainty is accepted, the significances of the family of concepts that Foucault created around that of discourse and of Derrida's technique of deconstructive reading are both transformed.

They need no longer serve solely as the means for iconoclastic attacks upon the presumptions of Reason, but rather may serve instead as the means for providing a rigorously non-representationalist understanding of the content of any instance of reason. Foucault's family of concepts, especially some of the more neglected 'rules of formation of a discursive formation', enables one to understand why particular discourses have the referential content they have, as well as why referential adequacy has a varying pertinence to their practice and assessment.[1] And, moreover, it enables one to do this sociologically rather than psychologically as in Critical Theory (see Dews, 1988, p. 28). Similarly, when used in association with a non-humanist variant of 'scientific realism' and these Foucauldian concepts, Derrida's technique of deconstructive reading, which is freed thereby from simply and repetitively demonstrating '*différance*', enables one to determine the degree of scepticism with which one should approach particular signs or chains thereof as one interrogates different types of text. For example, it provides a means of drawing critical attention to the presence and effects – in the form of reinforcing or subversive subtexts – of tropes of one kind or another where there should be concepts.

Deconstruction in Social Science

As has already been mentioned, in contrast to literary texts, the mode of enlightenment operant within scientific and social scientific texts is not 'defamiliarisation' but, on the contrary, the familiarisation of a particular community with certain terms so that they become its *lingua franca*. The shared 'purposes' and 'rules' of scientific communities, as understood by means of Foucault's concept of 'discursive formation', require that any variation in the meaning of such terms should be, if not as restricted as possible, then certainly as conscious and explicit as possible. Otherwise the sharing of thoughts and results that is the *sine qua non* of scientific activity is impossible. The fact that scientists often fail to meet this requirement and that wordplay, tropes and rhetoric play important roles in scientific presentations, in no way undermines its critical nature. Indeed it strengthens it, in that this requirement is what allows the activity of critique and so is one of the principal barriers between science and the submergence of its essential significatory oppositions – in their absence, breakthroughs would not be recognisable – beneath the torrents of rhetoric.

Thus whilst the deconstruction of literary texts may be an activity that is almost without limits, the same cannot be said about the deconstruction of social scientific ones. The limits are set by the discursively imposed requirements just mentioned. This means that the deconstructive response initiated by the discovery of figures of speech and significatory ambiguity within the explanatory structures of social scientific discourse should aim at isolating and removing them and their further effects, as well as at the reconstruction of the affected parts, rather than at the celebration of the freedom inherent in language. Entrapped by an underlying representationalism, pre-deconstructive techniques of critical reading in the social sciences either ignored the connotative aspects of conceptual language, supposing that they could be clearly distinguished from the denotative ones by a supposedly independent and verifiable reference to the real, or simply accepted them as good faith, literature-like attempts to defamiliarise and so draw attention to the obvious. The position taken in what follows is: first, that the denotative and connotative aspects of language cannot be so clearly distinguished; second, that the presence of ambiguities and tropes of various kinds in social scientific discourse is a sign of problems, commonly those associated with scientific underdevelopment rather than obviousness; and third, that the eradication of any such phenomena is not simply a prerequisite for but also a critical part of theoretical reconstruction: the gaps that are exposed thereby demand and in part determine the form taken by the required closure.

An Example: Deconstruction and the Law

When practised as suggested here, deconstruction should be able to shed the connotation of 'trashing' that it has gained, for example, through certain Critical Legal usages. Regrettably, these have caused it to be associated with the denunciations of law that, as in other areas where deconstructive techniques have been applied, too often and too easily accompany demonstrations of intellectual incoherence and indeterminancy. The point that I wish to insist upon is that legal texts, like social scientific ones, involve not simply statements of abstract doctrine, but also statements about the extra-legal world, about things that happen in that world. To use what I regard as an acceptable (that is, descriptive rather than explanatory) metaphor, these two sorts of statements are related to one another, as Saussure suggested, like the *recto* and the *verso* of a sheet of paper: they may be distinguished but they cannot be separated. Like the Legal Realists, one should always bear in mind 'the facts of the case', as well as the fact that such 'facts' are never perceived innocently. However, in contradistinction to the Legal Realists, what should and now can be investigated are not so much the formative experiences of individual judges, jurors etc but rather the myriad other ways in which the world, including its discursive dimension, impinges upon the legal domain and vice versa.

Simple enough points, but ones that are hard to bear in mind, or so it appears, when one shares, as it seems the 'trashers' do, mainstream legal theory's obsession with doctrine, as defined in narrowly legal terms. If one does bear them in mind, which is where the Foucauldian concepts come in, one is in a position to understand at least three things: (1) How the play of signification (that is, the relations between texts and sub-texts) is or is not constrained; (2) How the degree of play may vary from one sub-discourse to another within a single legal system; (3) How the degree of play may vary with respect to a single issue over time within a particular legal system. In sum, once one has socially located a particular legal sub-discourse, one is also in a position to identify those extra-legal discourses and extra-discursive structures with which it is most likely to be imbricated and which therefore are also most likely to have constrained how it may be read.

Thus one challenge to theory is to so conceptualise the law that the nature and causes of this play, of its referential content, of the manner in which both are constrained, and of the way in which all of this changes may be understood socially and sociologically rather than doctrinally and idiosyncratically, as tends to be the post-modernist mode. Put more concretely, the challenge is to understand how it is that legal inconsistency usually does not matter, and how it is that this depends upon whether or not it creates problems at the level of any dominant or hegemonic ideology. I have responded to this concrete challenge elsewhere (Woodiwiss, 1987b, 1990a). However, as should be clear by now, the position taken by the present author is that any such response requires the simultaneous completion of a radical rethinking of sociological categories that includes but goes far beyond simply rethinking 'law'. This is the task that will be addressed in the chapters that follow.

Notes

1. According to Foucault, 'serious talk', such as is exemplified by social science and the law, is made possible by the availability of determinate but loosely structured combinations of objects of concern, concepts, themes and types of statement, which he terms 'discursive formations'. Although such formations are far more loosely structured than the discourses they make possible, they are sufficiently determinate to allow the differentiation of varieties of serious talk and of serious from non-serious talk within a particular realm of discourse. What gives them their determinate quality are the particular conditions which, in turn, made/make them possible. These 'rules of formation of a discursive formation' include, so far as the objects they allow to be addressed are concerned: the social and/or institutional contexts wherein they emerge, most often as the loci or sources of concern of some kind; the social identities of those who have or gain 'authority' to pronounce on such problems and their causes; and 'the grids of specification', the intellectual templates, so to speak, which are used to separate off the particular objects of concern from the many others with which each is intertwined in reality. Although few other readers appear to have noticed this, the presence of such 'rules' suggests that a context wider than that represented by a particular discursive formation has to be investigated before any such formation may be understood. An investigation of this kind would have to concern itself with extra-discursive as well as discursive phenomena and so would have to be a sociological one (see below, Chapter 2).

PART II
Rethinking Production

2 Against Metaphors

Later in this text new and non-economistic concepts of production, law and class will be proposed. In order to grasp the significance of these proposals as part of a quest for a sociology in a new key, their presentation will be framed in a prefatory way by discussing the first of them in the context of one of the more general concerns of practising social scientists – the so-called 'macro/micro problem', because this problem provides the occasion when they are most likely to have to consider the ontological coherence of their approaches. Regrettably, as will be demonstrated below, it also provides the occasion when the usually unconscious representationalism and the necessarily conjoint humanism underlying their approaches assert or reassert themselves under the cover of one metaphor or another.

In broad terms what will most clearly differentiate the alternative approach proposed here is the way in which the problem is posed. Most often, and most elaborately by Giddens (1985), the problem is posed in basically social psychological and humanist terms as one that involves relations between individuals (or agents) and society (or structure), where the latter is most often understood as a more or less stable crystallisation or 'sedimentation' of relations between the former. Here, by contrast, it will be posed in more strictly sociological terms as one that involves the relations between different structures (political, economic and ideological) at different levels of abstraction (for example social formation and workplace; cp Alexander et al., 1987, intro.).

Production and the Incommensurability Problem
To begin with, something will be said about how the difficulties of traversing the macro-micro divide have been dealt with or, better, avoided thus far in industrial relations texts. Reading such texts, one notices the presence of a number of strategies for dealing with this divide: exclude one or other side whilst invoking the necessity

39

of an academic division of labour; leave it to the narrative structure by using it as a criterion for deciding on chapter divisions and by appending a short and often somewhat awkward conclusion; or finally and more fruitfully invoke another distinction, that between the formal and informal aspects of industrial relations. The last abstractly suggests the possibility of a two by two table except that no one shows much interest in the informal/macro quadrant, which in turn suggests that the real concern behind the distinction is the differentiation of particular aspects of the micro sphere rather than the understanding of the macro-micro relation itself. In sum, each of the first two strategies represents an effort to find a way round the problem rather than face up to and overcome it. In essence it seems that the source of the problem here as elsewhere is a general and manifestly debilitating sense of a certain analytical incommensurability as between the two levels – one consisting of agents and the other of structures. This incommensurability is at least made explicit, if not taken sufficiently seriously, by the proponents of the formal/informal differentiation of the micro level.

The critical edge to what has just been said is certainly not unique to the present author. The fact remains, however, that until recently no comprehensive effort had been made to face up to this or any other local version of the incommensurability problem. One highly pertinent recent effort is that of Armstrong, Goodman and Hyman (1981). Drawing on the multi-faceted critical literature of the 1970s, and in line with the then current theoretical literature (for example Knorr-Cetina, Cicourel, 1981), Armstrong et al. seek to consolidate a shift in attention from the macro to the micro which both asserts the autonomy of the latter sphere and involves a rethinking of its relation to the former (see also Henry, 1983). Reflecting the critical literature, the 'new' analytical language they propose is primarily that of Weberian or Symbolic Interactionist sociology, and illustrates well what Knorr-Cetina (1981) has called a new 'methodological situationalism':

[Our aim is] to illustrate and examine the values, notions of fairness and legitimising principles which underpin the continuous processes of workplace industrial relations and which flexibly define the terms of those relationships. The workplace is seen, therefore, as a stage on which the cross-currents of interests, supported by varying degrees of power, are mediated by appeals to value systems and moral perspectives and expressed in the debate between workers, their representatives and management.

These values, which are rooted in ideologies in the wider society beyond the workplace, form the 'currency' with which goals are sought and in which attempts both to maintain and to change current rules and practices are presented. Less emphasis is therefore placed on structural and organisational features than on the dynamics of exchange between participants (Armstrong et al., 1981, p. 15).

What is also apparent in the above is the clear analytical decision that a focus on values or ideologies is the way out of the incommensurability problem; that is, since values form the 'currency' of the workplace, not only do holdings of this currency determine the balance of power but also any outside influences have to be exchangeable with the particular currency of the workplace, if they are to affect what goes on within it – if they are to be 'cashable'. Corroborative though this decision may be, in a general sense, of that to be taken below, and successful though Armstrong et al. undoubtedly are on their own terms, their approach will not be followed here. The general reason for this is that the analytical language they deploy assumes the possibility of the very type of psychologically based sociology that was earlier rejected. For this reason Armstrong et al.'s position, despite its advances, also represents a retreat, specifically a retreat from the insight into what might be called the 'discursive stratification' of the workplace suggested by the formal/informal distinction. This insight is taken here to be that such 'stratification' indicates the existence of a boundary that should be respected and investigated (cp Henry, 1983) rather than, as is more often the case, one that should be blurred.

The more specific reasons for not following Armstrong et al. are threefold and all relate to the point made at the start of this chapter concerning the difference between the way in which the micro/macro problem is posed here and in most of the recent literature. First, the humanism of Weberian and interactionist sociologies makes the direct articulation of their concepts with those of the non-humanist, 'structuralist' tradition preferred here a source of incoherence (epistemologically and ontologically) rather than enrichment. Second, this incoherence arises because 'humanism' analytically privileges human subjects and in this instance as in most others ascribes to them certain intrinsic 'interests' that supposedly determine their actions. The privileging of human subjects creates additional problems in the present context because they tend to become the sole conduits of influence from the outside to the inside. Hence the presence or absence of, for example, a trade unionist, a factory inspector or whoever, and/or the occurrence of certain actions on their parts, whose relationships to the 'structural and organisational' context are untheorised, tends to be taken as explaining the particularities of a workplace value system. By contrast the approach advocated here will allow for and explain the effects of ideological influences that are not necessarily consciously mediated by human beings; for example as well as legal differences in workplace value systems, it will allow for and seek to provide a means for explaining the determinant presence of all those ideological 'structural and organisational' differences that are commonly termed 'national'.

Third, Armstrong et al. will not be followed because, as a further linked consequence of their humanism, they have no way of understanding the dynamics of workplace value systems, as it were, on the latter's own terms. Thus they cannot understand these dynamics as those of words, of language and of discourse. Rather they are understood via a central, economic metaphor, which, as the earlier quotation indicated, is the notion of 'currency'. Not only does this metaphor substitute for explicit analysis, but it also has the particular disadvantage, perhaps unintended, of corroborating what from the Marxist point of view is the fictional account of the workplace as a market, as primarily a site of bargaining and negotiating rather than of exploitation. In conclusion it should be noted that the presence of another metaphor – 'the workplace is seen as a stage' – which sociologists call the 'dramaturgical metaphor', is what makes these three theoretical moves possible.

Despite the distance between this text and that of Armstrong et al., the latter nevertheless will be followed insofar as it sees the solution to the ideological dimension of the 'incommensurability problem' as lying in disaggregating what is termed in this text 'the ideological sphere'. Indeed it will also be followed in its insight as to the 'currency' *dealing* aspect of the practices that empirically characterise this sphere in the workplace. The difference will be that their metaphorical mode of reasoning will be replaced by a non-representationalist one that not only develops the implications of the formal/informal distinction but also sustains Armstrong et al.'s insights.

As has already been made clear, central to the position to be elaborated here is the concept of 'discourse'. In order to specify further the contribution expected of the concept of 'discourse', and to define the position of this text more precisely, a brief critical account of previous Marxist attempts to theorise the ideological dimension of production will now be provided.[1] In passing, the account will demonstrate the intellectual havoc wrought by representationalism and its supports, even amongst those trying hardest to escape from its confines so that they might be able to talk about what they felt sure existed but could not represent because they could not see it – with or without their specially constructed theoretical spectacles.

Classical Marxism and the Discourses of Production

In Marx's own work there are two principal occasions on which he addresses or rather approaches the phenomena suggested by the notion of the 'discourses of production'. The qualification here is necessary because on both occasions Marx comments on the role of ideology in production in order to establish the plausibility of a more generally applicable and unfortunately economically reductionist conception of this role, and then rapidly moves on to elaborate this latter conception. The first is in *The German Ideology* (1970) where he differentiates three aspects of production – productive forces, the division of labour and 'internal intercourse'. He says little about the last of these beyond indicating that it refers to the ideas which facilitate the maintenance of sets of particular production relations and legitimise them, but which also in time come into contradiction with the same production relations. In so far as the nature of these ideas is specified, then, it is as one or other of the variant forms of property that distinguish the tribal, ancient, feudal and capitalist 'nations' from one another.

Some of the successors to the Frankfurt School have made much of the clear separation of the productive forces from the forms of internal intercourse and used it as a basis for the construction of a non-reductionist Critical Theory (Held, 1980). However, although there is some justification for this reading in *The German Ideology* itself, such a premature separation of what Habermas has termed the 'productive' and 'communicative' spheres impoverishes our conception of production and therefore makes the task of understanding the relation between it and the wider society more difficult (Woodiwiss, 1978). Marx's own use of 'internal intercourse' similarly is of little help for present purposes because of its exclusive concern with ownership relations, which may be most easily understood to reproduce particular sets of production relations from outside, since the word 'internal' more obviously refers to 'intercourse' within a 'nation' than within production. This said, the less obvious reading has some justification and will be developed below.

Before any such development is possible, however, another general problem, additional to reductionism, must be overcome. This is the problem of what Larrain (1983) has usefully called the 'negative' quality of the concept of ideology found within *The German Ideology*. 'Negative' in the sense that, again on the easiest interpretation, the meaning of the famous proposition that 'the ruling ideas of a period are the ideas of the ruling class' would lead one to think that 'the ruling ideas' are necessarily misleading for the proletariat. Marx himself moved some way towards overcoming this problem on the second of the occasions on which he approached the area of interest here, namely in the discussion of the 'fetishism of commodities' contained in Volume I of *Capital*. Unfortunately, his reductionism prevented him from going further and fully realising the theoretical benefits that can accrue given the possession of what Larrain has called a 'positive' concept of ideology. Such a concept is one whereby the ideological realm is understood as real rather than fictional and therefore as unavoidable as well as not inherently delusory. The principal benefits of interest here are those that follow from the possession of such a positive antidote to any recidivist tendencies towards reductionism, which in addition provides a means of transcending the individual/society, or, in more contemporary terms, the subject/structure dichotomy.

Marx introduces his discussion of 'the fetishism of commodities' with the following well-known passage:

> A commodity appears, at first sight, a very trivial thing, and easily understood. Its analysis shows that it is, in reality, a very queer thing, abounding in metaphysical subtleties and theological niceties. So far as it is a value in use, there is nothing mysterious about it, whether we consider it from the point of view that by its properties it is capable of satisfying human wants, or from the point that those properties are the product of human labour. It is as clear as noon-day that man, by his industry, changes the forms of the materials furnished by Nature, in such a way as to make them useful to him. The form of wood, for instance, is altered, by making a table out of it. Yet, for all that, the table continues to be that common, every-day thing, wood. But, so soon as it steps forth as a commodity, it is changed into something transcendent. It not only stands with its feet on the ground, but, in relation to all other commodities, it stands on its head, and evolves out of its

wooden brain grotesque ideas, far more wonderful than 'table-turning' ever was (Marx, 1965, p. 71).

Since this and the paragraphs that follow are such familiar and much discussed passages (for example Fine, 1984; Geras, 1971; Rose, 1977), they will not be subjected to a detailed analysis here. The point of general theoretical interest is that what is present here is the proposition that an economic process, exploitation, produces *as a necessary consequence* a gap between reality and appearances, which appearances constitute the ideological sphere, wherein are fetishistic objects (for example wages) that are thought of as existing separately from the process of exploitation (that is, a process is lost in a result). This allows them to appear as if they were the product of another process, namely exchange. What differentiates Marx's position here from that in *The German Ideology*, or indeed in the 1859 *Preface*, is the explicit recognition that the existence of the ideological sphere is necessary and unavoidable. What he does not appear to have been able to recognise is that, in principle, the fact of the ideological sphere's existence may be distinguished from any supposed need to delude associated with capitalism, or any other antagonistic mode of production.

As several commentators (for example Hirst, 1979; Rose, 1977) have pointed out, the proximate sources of this resistance are the reductionism and, relatedly, the representationalism implicit in the identifications of the economy with reality and of ideology with the realm of appearances. And, as Hirst and Rose have emphasised, what the latter correctly terms 'the figure of fetishism' additionally prevents any transcendence of the subject/structure dichotomy, since pre-constituted subjects are required as the 'bearers' of fetishistic representations. This, as anticipated in the introduction to the present text, makes humanism the ultimate source of this instance of resistance to recognition of the inherent autonomy of the ideological realm:

> Commodities cannot themselves go to market and perform exchanges in their own right. We must, therefore, have recourse to their guardians, who are the possessors of commodities. Commodities are things, and therefore lack the power to resist man. If they are unwilling, he can use force; in other words, he can take possession of them. In order that these objects may enter into relation with each other as commodities, their guardians must place themselves in relation to one another as persons

whose will resides in those objects, and must behave in such a way that each does not appropriate the commodity of the other, and alienate his own, except through an act to which both parties consent. The guardians must therefore recognize each other as owners of private property. This juridical relation, whose form is the contract, whether as part of a developed legal system or not, is a relation between two wills which mirrors the economic relation. The content of this juridical relation (or relation of two wills) is itself determined by the economic relation. Here the persons exist for one another merely as representatives and hence owners, of commodities. As we proceed to develop our investigation, we shall find, in general, that the characters who appear on the economic stage are merely personifications of economic relations; it is as the bearer of these economic relations that they come into contact with each other (Marx, 1965, pp. 178–9).

Interestingly, in this passage (as in that quoted from Armstrong et al. above), the presence, in this case implicit, of the dramaturgical metaphor suggests a similar level of theoretical underdevelopment.

The debilitating effects of the representationalism and reductionism crystallised in the figure of fetishism were either not realised or were inappropriately countered by subsequent generations of Marxists. These failures have been clearly and concisely described recently by Laclau and Mouffe (1985) and so need not be redescribed here. Acceptable though this aspect of Laclau and Mouffe's work may be, the same cannot be said for their explanation of these failures as the product of an immanent but thwarted 'hegemonic logic' that eventually gained fuller expression in Gramsci's work. However, this is not the point at which an argument with them should be pursued, since their effort to deploy a concept of discourse (the *terminus ad quem* of the 'hegemonic logic' whose difficult birth they describe) in a critical onslaught on the Marxist tradition in general will be at the centre of the following chapter. What will be provided here is an account of the consequences of the failure to escape the limitations inherent in the figure of fetishism for contemporary Marxist writings on industrial relations.

Contemporary Marxism and the Discourses of Production

In the conclusion to what is undoubtedly the most developed effort to understand the ideological dimension of industrial relations in recent Marxist literature, the inherently representationalist figure of fetishism is clearly present and therefore explains the underdeveloped theorisation of the role of ideology in industrial relations which is also summarised in the following extract:

> We have argued that the social conflicts which ideologies of fairness mediate and qualify are too intense and too pervasive to be contained by such stratagems. But in any case, the key implication of our discussion of the structural contradictions inherent in the existing political economy is that the effects of *any* normative framework will be uneven and contradictory. Norms of fairness, as this study indicates, even though couched in terms wholly conducive to the stability of the social order and the interests of those in positions of privilege and power, nevertheless can provoke and legitimise actions with quite contrary effects; and this is likely to occur even if the prevailing ideology is internally consistent. The argument, then, is that such consequences reflect not merely 'normative disorder' but far more fundamental societal characteristics. Strategies which rest essentially on the paternalistic manipulative or authoritarian intervention of those in controlling positions in management or government fail to transcend these contradictions. In the last analysis, the practical and the normative problems in industrial relations can be resolved only by the creation of social relations of production whereby economic activity is consciously and collectively controlled by the members of society generally. To achieve such a society, in the face of existing structures of material and ideological domination, is inconceivable except through the activity and struggle of the mass of producers. Where social conflicts and system contradictions interpenetrate, and the oppressive character of the social structure becomes increasingly transparent, the possibility of such a challenge to capitalist social relations is increased. This point evidently raises immense issues which can ultimately be resolved, not by theoretical discussion but by practical action. For the present, though, we may safely conclude that the notion of a 'reconstruction of normative order' in industrial relations which leaves intact the basic structure of the political economy is a singularly futile goal (Hyman, Brough, 1975, pp. 252–3).

As the extract indicates, the economy is clearly privileged relative to the ideological sphere, which only has the degree of autonomy that the figure of fetishism allows. It can have 'uneven and contradictory' effects but no final, determinative power. More specifically this confinement of the efficacy of the ideological is reflected, reinforced and made inescapable by the description of the ideas of 'fairness' etc to be found in the workplace as 'norms', that is as guides to action, where that action is ultimately determined by 'structural contradictions inherent in the existing political economy'. The particular significance of this is that ideas when so conceptualised have no existence except in relation to action, which in turn suggests that they have no existence separate from human subjects, whether individual or collective, who are necessary as the authors of actions. The analytical consequence is that Hyman and Brough have no way of understanding the effects of ideological influences that are not consciously mediated by human beings, and which may enter the workplace through or even simply with the words they utter and the texts and discourses made pertinent by the wider structures of society.

Despite the criticisms that have just been made, Hyman and Brough's approach is considerably in advance of that produced later under the heading of 'labour process theory', at least as far as the present topic is concerned. The latter approach draws its inspiration from Braverman's (1974) *Labour and Monopoly Capitalism*, which, despite what has just been said, represents the most serious and sustained attempt to theorise what happens in production since that by Marx himself. Unlike Marx's effort, however, it contains no acknowledgement whatsoever of the existence or the importance of the ideological sphere, except in the residual form of a subjective side to work, 'mental labour', which the logic of capitalist exploitation gradually but relentlessly extirpates. This is an omission that continues to characterise labour process theory, despite general acceptance of Lee's (1980) point concerning the ideological dimension of its central theoretical category 'skill', and the pressure to acknowledge the wider significance of ideology expressed in the comparative sections of Littler's (1982) influential study.

The one exception to what is unfortunately a rule is the work of Burawoy (1979; 1985). But before it can be discussed something has to be said about Althusser's efforts to escape from the limitations imposed by the figure of fetishism, since, as Burawoy states, a reading of them allowed him to move towards developing an alternative to Braverman. The general structure of Althusser's project and indeed the source of its limitations are apparent in a well-known passage in his early, programmatic essay 'On Contradiction and Overdetermination' (Althusser, 1969, pp. 99–101). In this passage there is clear evidence of a profound equivocation in Althusser's thought which takes various forms: between a concern to avoid a conception of the social formation as an 'expressive totality' bound together by any single essence, and an insistence on 'economic determination in the last instance'; between a series of 'relatively autonomous instances' (polity, economy and ideology) and a conception of them as deriving from 'the main contradiction'. Unfortunately, the basic equivocation was later firmly embedded in the heart of Althusserian theory through the formulation of the notion of 'structural causality' (Althusser, 1970), whereby two of the relatively autonomous instances are understood to be not only the product of the third, the economy, but also to reproduce it by securing its conditions of existence. In other words, Althusser does not escape the return to fetishism, which is not surprising since it is symptomatic of the tenacious hold reductionism has had on Marxism, even after it has been generally accepted that last instances never come. This said, his return is not a simple repetition, since he goes further than any Marxist had gone before in attempting to specify the particular and autonomous way in which ideology has its effects, namely through adding the concept of 'interpellation' to Marxist theory (Althusser, 1971).

Although Althusser borrowed the concept of 'interpellation' from Lacan, who in turn had developed it in the course of his Saussurian re-reading of Freud, Althusser's use of it is significantly different from Lacan's, and in two important and unfortunate ways (Hirst, 1979), which explain why he could not avoid fetishism and remained in the grip of representationalism. First, the subject that ideologies seek to interpellate is assumed to pre-exist them, to be a unity, and to be pre-symbolic and therefore pre-ideological, in violation of Althusser's own supposed non-humanism. Second, the conception of language at work in the text, as in those of Marx discussed above, is itself a 'representational' one. The problems created by these differences are as follows: the first facilitates and thus helps to preserve a distinction between personal and class interests (that is, if subjects exist prior to interpellation this must allow the possibility that they are capable of articulating a strictly personal interest); and the second achieves the same for the idea that both sets of interests have fixed referents in the extra-discursive dimensions of reality.

In sum, the potential that the Saussurian concept of language possesses with respect to the gaining of a new understanding of the discursive dimension of production remains unrealised because of the respect mistakenly accorded the original Marxist figure of fetishism, which critically depends upon just such a notion of a clearly discernible, objective class interest as Althusser retains. Thus the failure to acknowledge anything but the most relative form of autonomy at the structural level as between the ideological, political and economic spheres (the latter being determinant in the last instance) is repeated in his conceptualisation of the nature of the otherwise liberatory notion of interpellation. The latter is dependent upon a representational theory of 'the imaginary' (a term Althusser perhaps mistakenly uses in place of another Lacanian term, 'the symbolic'), which makes the content as well as the truth or falsity of the material interpellated a function of who (that is, what sort of subject) produces the material, a bourgeois 'ideologist' or a proletarian 'scientist'. In sum, Althusser would have been unable to escape from reductionism even if he had wanted to because of his unwitting but apparently politically overdetermined commitment to a representational theory of language. Moreover, this also explains a further inability which he shares with fully humanist writers – Marxist and non-Marxist – namely, that of being unable to find an alternative way of posing the problem of the macro–micro relation to that which depends upon the traditional differentiation of the subject and structure.

The net result is that one finds in Althusser the same inability to understand the effects of ideological influences on the workplace or wherever that might enter without being mediated through the consciousness by human subjects and that has been noted with respect to Marx, Hyman and Brough and Armstrong et al. Not surprisingly, Althusser too uses a dramaturgical metaphor, when he explains the analytical purpose of his model of 'structural causality' as that of providing the analyst with a *mise en scene*.

Burawoy and the Limitations of the Politics of Production

With Althusser as a major source of inspiration, it is hardly surprising that Burawoy's attempt to overcome the extreme reductionism of Braverman's *Labour and Monopoly Capitalism* should fail for the same reasons. Nevertheless, Burawoy's work is also worthy of attention since it too is no mere instance of repetition. Instead it offers a way into the heart of the concerns here. Why this is so is readily apparent in the preface to his book *Manufacturing Consent* (1979), where he states:

in contrast to the conventional wisdom among Marxists and non-Marxists, I propose to demonstrate how consent is produced at the point of production – independent of schooling, family life, mass media, the state, and so forth. [2]

Burawoy additionally suggests the particular relevance of his project for that of the present text, when he says that 'the activities on the shop floor cannot be understood outside the political and ideological realms of the organisation of production'. Unfortunately, a strong feeling of disappointment also makes itself felt early on, since in his discussion of his 'premisses and concepts' Burawoy makes it clear that the non-economic aspects of what he terms 'the relations *in* production' have the same function, and I use the word advisedly, as the non-economic relations *of* production; that is, that of guaranteeing the reproduction of the economic relations of production. Inevitably, this functionalism is justified by reference to Marx's discussion of the fetishism of commodities (ibid., p. 16).

There follows an extremely condensed discussion of the nature of ideology and of its relationship with something called 'lived experience', which is ascribed to Poulantzas but in fact sounds more like it was derived from the work of E.P. Thompson (1978). Condensed or not, this discussion produces a distinction between what is regarded as the raw material of ideology and ideology itself, which is the raw material worked into a form such that it can serve as 'a cement for social relations'. Thus he says:

> People do not carry ideologies around in their heads. They carry theories, knowledge, attitudes in the form of consciousness (Burawoy, 1979, p. 18).

While this distinction is what later allows Burawoy to talk in an original way about the production of interests as well as of ideology or consent in the workplace, what should be noted immediately and critically is that this 'raw material' is not understood in any important sense as being linguistic and that there are therefore definite limits beyond which he cannot take his insights. Of course, attitudes etc are expressed, and again I use a term advisedly, according to Burawoy, through language. However, as this formulation implies, attitudes are, somewhat bizarrely if typically (cp Stedman-Jones, 1983, p. 21), regarded as more real, whilst language is seen as the epiphenomenal and presumably neutral means whereby they are communicated. I have already implied that this position will be reversed below. In the absence of such a reversal the constraints inherent in the figure of fetishism will once again impose themselves. Indeed this process starts in the first chapter, when Burawoy states that the capitalist labour process has an essence, which is the 'simultaneous *obscuring* and securing of surplus-value'. I have added the emphasis in order to indicate that reductionism, as is so often the case, is here accompanied by a retreat from the positive concept of ideology.

However, before the reimposition of orthodoxy completes itself, Burawoy's distinction between ideology and its raw material proves to be sufficient to free him from dependence on the dramaturgical metaphor. Instead he invokes that of 'the game'. Although the use of any metaphor indicates a certain under-theorisation, the ludic metaphor nevertheless restores a notion of 'rules' to industrial sociology which had been lost to Braverman's followers with the demise of the formal/informal distinction. Indeed Burawoy reinforces the possibility of a certain 'discursive stratification' carried by the notion of 'rules' by using a further metaphor, that of the 'internal state', to refer to the structure of power relations within the workplace, whereby unions and management participate in the 'obscuring and securing of surplus-value'. As it turns out, this last metaphor is also and unfortunately one of the principal ways in which Marxist orthodoxy reasserts itself in Burawoy's text.

More importantly, the ludic metaphor also allows Burawoy to deliver with respect to his promise 'to demonstrate how consent is produced at the point of production'. The prime source of the inspiration that produced the metaphor was Burawoy's sustained empirical observation of what he calls 'making out'. According to the workers he observed, 'making out' means trying to shift the terms of the wage/effort bargain to one's advantage by fair means or foul. Significantly, and here there is a clear echo of the notion of 'informal rules', management in general colludes in this practice. Thus it is understood by both sides to be an ambiguous practice in its wider effects. When successful, workers gain the satisfactions associated with gaining some control over the exercise of their labour-power: a certain camaraderie, a feeling of being 'one up' on management and an increase in their wages. For Burawoy the last of these outcomes is the least important with respect to the manufacture of consent, since the former satisfactions account for the intrinsic interest of the game. From management's point of view any means of increasing effort are acceptable provided they are not in the end subversive of industrial order. In Burawoy's opinion subversion would only be the consequence of 'making out' if one of three crisis situations developed: profits were threatened, the game became too easy or too hard, or for some reason workers lost interest in it. Under such circumstances, what he terms 'the radical need' for self-management that is latent in worker satisfactions might escape the constraints that normally turn their pursuit into a means for manufacturing consent and instead manifest itself in a revolutionary uprising.

If 'making out' echoes the notion of 'informal rules' then the aforementioned notion of an 'internal state' along with that of an 'internal labour market', which Burawoy uses in the familiar sense, echoes that of 'formal rules'. As with the formal/informal distinction, Burawoy's distinction seeks to differentiate those aspects of the workplace which owe more to the external and social environments rather than to the psychological environment from those which owe less. What is problematic about his distinction is that, unlike the formal/informal dichotomy, it does not signify what might be called a 'global' difference between different dimensions of workplace activity, but singles out a particular 'region' of this activity, the ideological, as being theoretically and empirically unique as compared to the political and the economic. Whilst the latter are very much the product of processes originating outside the workplace the former is not, except in a crisis. This claim provides the means whereby Burawoy obscures the insight as to 'discursive stratification' suggested by his two key metaphors, as well as the occasion for him to exhibit his variant of the humanism that always seems to accompany the attempt to transcend the macro–micro dichotomy in the presence of the figure of fetishism – he posits 'the instinct for control' (Burawoy, 1979, p. 157)! Moreover, the claim that the ideological dimension of the workplace is uniquely self-subsistent is also very difficult to defend theoretically and empirically. In the absence of his belief in such an unlikely instinct, it seems implausible that one aspect of 'the relations *in* production' should be insulated to a unique degree from influences arising at the level of 'the relations *of* production', let alone from those arising outside the workplace.

Finally, can it be plausibly suggested that the metaphor of work as a game is universal and owes nothing, for example, to ideological influences originating outside the plant? Whatever might be the empirical answers to this question, it would seem advisable not to pre-empt them (as regards Japan, for example). Moreover, such preemption may be avoided without much difficulty provided one refuses Burawoy's notion of workplace ideology's uniqueness and provided one refuses yet another even more deeply embedded metaphor, namely the geological one, whereby the economic, political and ideological spheres are thought of as so many levels. This, of course, is the metaphor that informs one of Burawoy's theoretical starting points, namely Althusser's concept of 'structural causality'.

It is now possible to resume the critical discursive means and conditions which explain Burawoy's failure to achieve satisfactorily his goal of demonstrating how consent or indeed conflict is produced at the point of production. The conditions involved, in the sense of theoretical premises with uncontrollable effects, are: the geological metaphor, which in Burawoy's variant allows the internal homogeneity of each sphere to be transferred across the macro–micro divide; and the figure of fetishism, which allows the functionalist and reductionist understanding of the inter-relationship of the different spheres to be similarly but less unequiv-ocally sustained over the same divide. The means involved, in the sense of theoretical innovations over which control is claimed, are: the ideology/raw material dichotomy, which is what allows the possibility of the equivocation just mentioned; the game metaphor, which seeks to capture the nature of the relative autonomy of the ideological sphere, at least in its workplace form; the 'instinct for control', which is posited as an essential aspect of human nature in order to explain why the relative autonomy represented in the game metaphor is irrepressible, notwithstanding the determination in the last instance intrinsic to both 'structural causality' and fetishism. In sum, despite his very precise focus upon the phenomena of concern here, Burawoy's work is of little direct use in trying to understand them, not least because he has excluded from investigation not just ideological influences that are not humanly mediated but any that might originate outside the workplace.

It is this same rigour, however, that makes Burawoy's work of considerable indirect use, since the causes of his 'failure' are so clear and their correction is therefore made that much easier. Thus it will be argued here that the two immediate preconditions for building on the insight contained in Burawoy's two key metaphors are the refusal not only of the figure of fetishism, but also of the geological metaphor. The basis upon which these refusals may be made irre-versible must remain for the time being unelaborated beyond repeating that it has to do with adopting a non-representational concept of language and with taking the linguistic nature of ideology seriously.

The refusal of the geological metaphor is no easy matter since it involves being able to sustain the argument that the metaphor involves a mistaken reference to extra-theoretical reality. This is not so difficult when, for example, the concepts 'economy', 'state' and 'ideology' are taken to refer to particular institutions *in toto*, such as factories, parliaments and the mass media respectively. This is not what Burawoy does, however, since here he completes a process that Althusser and Poulantzas (1975) began and takes the same concepts to refer to particular structures and practices within concrete institutions, namely the internal labour market, the internal state and the game of 'making out', respectively. Accepting this advance, it may still be argued that he is mistaken, since the phenomena referred to by the concepts of 'the internal labour market' and 'the internal state' clearly have ideological dimensions too. Consequently and by contrast, like E. P. Thompson (1975) but with a different significance, it will be argued here that the three general concepts refer to extra-theoretical realities that are imbricated with and interpenetrative of one another. However, as against Thompson and the arguments he mounts in his essay 'The Poverty of Theory' (1978), the reason Burawoy cannot acknowledge these relationships is because of the underdevelopment of the theorisation of ideology that allowed the ludic metaphor in the first place, which, in turn, is the result of a mistaken dependence upon a representationalist theory of language and a derived approach to theory that must now be corrected if the incommensurability problem that has thus far vitiated all efforts to overcome the macro–micro divide is, finally, to be overcome.

Notes

1. According to context, the terms 'production', 'economy' and 'the economic' will be used either to signify the analytically separable processes whereby material objects of whatever kind are transformed, whether for immediate use or sale, or to refer to the analytically distinguishable substantive realm wherein such processes occur and wherein they are imbricated with ideological and political processes.
2. Burawoy's later text *The Politics of Production* is not discussed here since the theoretical position taken in it is substantially the same as that elaborated in *Manufacturing Consent*, except

that the notion of the 'internal state' is rejected. Whilst this greatly enhances the utility of his ideas on the political dimension of production, it does not invalidate the more general criticisms that have been made of his approach on the basis of its treatment of the ideological dimension. The criticisms of Burawoy developed here are almost exclusively theoretical. For substantive criticisms see Thompson (1983).

3 The Discourses of Production

Refusal of the primacy of the subject, which is so critical to the mode of overcoming the incommensurability problem proposed here, is not exactly the metaphysical move in the traditional, somewhat negative sense that it might at first appear. It has behind it, for example, the authority and achievements of contemporary linguistics, which would not exist had it not been for Saussure's refusal of the primacy of the subject. This is just as well, since it is a refusal which has profound sociological consequences. It creates the possibility not only of the discovery of new entities, which may or may not be coextensive with the old 'peopled' ones (for example companies, unions, workplaces), but also of the discovery of new 'life' within them. Only the second of these possibilities will be pursued here. It should be said in advance, however, that what will be argued below has some highly critical implications for the conventional conceptualisations of entities such as 'classes', which will be spelt out in Part 4.

The Theory of Signification
It is one of the great ironies of the history of sociological thought that it was a sociologist, Emile Durkheim, whose insistence on the separability of 'social facts' from what might be called 'individual facts' was a critical event in the construction of the discipline of linguistics, which in turn has had profound consequences for the credibility of the claims made on behalf of humanism as an appropriate metatheoretical starting point for social science. The irony lies in the fact that because of Durkheim's 'functionalisation' and his subsequent eclipse by the Weberian, Marxist and empiricist schools of sociological thought, sociology has been very resistant to considering what might be gained by taking seriously Saussure's discovery of the irreducible sociality and autonomy of language.[1] Indeed many sociologists actively and contrarily prefer the social but still anthropocentric (that is, humanist) philosophical theory of

57

language to be found in the work of the later Wittgenstein and as developed by Winch (1958), wherein reference is typically swallowed by intention and a difference is produced thereby between Wittgensteinian and traditional representational theory. Additionally, the Symbolic Interactionist tradition emerged in part out of the school of linguistics initiated by C. S. Pierce, which although it led to a more general semiotics which today is assumed to share the same referent as Saussurian semiology nevertheless may be clearly distinguished from it. The critical difference is the absence in Saussurian linguistics of an account of extra-linguistic reference; that is, the difference between Saussurian and Piercian linguistics may be illustrated by stating that the former, unlike the latter, could not explain by itself why many linguists today think of semiotics and semiology as synonyms.[2]

For Saussure language is undoubtedly a self-sufficient system but it is not a self-subsisting one. What Saussure never forgets, although many of his 'structuralist' and 'post-structuralist' followers apparently do, is that language is not simply a discrete social fact but also the property of what he called 'a community of speakers' (Saussure, 1974, p. 78). And as such it is subject to *sociological* and other constraints as to what it might signify. Although Saussure himself does not explicitly make the point, it will be contended here that it would be consistent with his theory to extend it and argue that what is sometimes regarded as 'the third term' of an analytical linguistic trinity, 'reference', is explainable non-representationally by resort to social factors, some but not all of which may be language-borne, and not to purely linguistic ones; that is, it is not language itself, but society in general that aligns language with the extra-linguistic world. But first the manner in which language as such contributes to the creation of what commonsense knows as 'meaning' must be specified in order to secure this text's refusal of reductionism.

As is well known, Saussure deploys two sets of oppositions (*langue* and *parole*, 'synchronic' and 'diachronic') in order to demarcate the object of linguistic study, namely the socially embedded, structural and tangible aspects of language that explain its persistence and hence its capacity to serve as a medium of communication. What persists and how is specified and explained by two further sets of oppositions: 'signified' and 'signifier', 'syntagmatic' and 'associative' (which today is usually termed 'paradigmatic'). A 'signified' is defined as a differentiated item of thought, a mental image, whilst a 'signifier' is a differentiated graphic or sound image. Together the signified and the signifier produce a sign, which according to Saussure is an 'unmotivated' or arbitrary combinatory. Abstractly, it might be thought that a sign as such could exist in a single human mind, but in fact it never does since it is only possible as the property of a community of language users. What explains its presence in such a community is also what explains its presence in as well as its visibility outside particular minds. It is its use in discourse, at least in so far as this is determined by the syntagmatic and paradigmatic relations specific to a particular language. To elaborate: a sign gains 'value' or meaning syntagmatically according to its linear position in discourse (for example as determined by syntactical relations); it also gains value paradigmatically according to what signs could have been substituted for it but were not (for example as determined by the nature of a particular lexicon).

In sum, then, language-use is determined by specific structures (for example syntaxes and lexicons) that are extra-individual ontologically and thus are a dimension of a separate and distinctively social world. Further and perhaps ironically it is precisely because of its sociality that language-use is beyond purely linguistic control; as the circumstances (mental and physical) of its users change so does language and therefore what they communicate. Saussure himself did not say much about how and why language changes but he did insist that the fixity of even the denotative meanings contained within a particular *langue* was never more than relative and that it was conditional on other things remaining equal (Saussure, 1974, p. 75). Most importantly, the *sine qua non* of a theory of linguistic change is present at the very core of Saussurean theory, namely the ultimately arbitrary nature of any signified/signifier combination. It is this notion that allows that what may be signified by a particular signifier might differ over time, across space and between groups, all within the same society. Further discussion of the significance of this will be presented below in the course of a critical examination of the recent work of Laclau and Mouffe. For the time being what is of greater importance is that Saussure has provided us with the means to refuse the representational theory of language and in so doing has deprived Marxism's economic reductionism of one of its principal props. Ideology may now be described as a 'second-order, linguistic sign system'; as such and in so far as such entities as syntaxes and lexicons are not the product of economic forces (contra Macdonell, 1986), ideology must be understood to possess a necessary and irreducible autonomy in relation to the economy as well as in relation to human beings.

The 'Restricted' Concept of the Mode of Production

Leaving aside for now Cutler et al. (1977), who have used a concept of discourse, possibly derived from Saussure, to mount a critique of epistemology in general as well as of the overall structure of Marxist theory, hitherto no one has used the notion of the inherent autonomy of language as part of an effort to reform the Marxist theoretical system as a whole. This said, some reformative work has nevertheless been done that makes it possible to acknowledge this inherent autonomy. The work I have in mind is that of Harold Wolpe (1980).

In the course of a survey of recent writings on the concept 'mode of production', Wolpe distinguishes two principal variants of it: one he terms 'extended' since it covers the forces and relations of production and their conditions of existence; the other he terms 'restricted' since it covers only the forces and relations of production. The first is by far the most common and is inherently reductionist. As has been noted earlier with respect to the Althusserian notion of 'structural causality', which it underpins, it conceptualises the relation between the forces and relations of production and their political and economic conditions of existence as necessarily one of reproduction. The second is very rare. Somewhat ironically it appears briefly in Hindess and Hirst's first book (1975). Wolpe's elaboration begins by distinguishing the forces and relations of production from their conditions of existence and reserving the term 'mode of production' for the former. It proceeds by stating that, nevertheless, if a certain combination of forces and relations of production is to be sustained certain political, ideological and indeed further economic prerequisites are necessary; for example, in the case of the capitalist mode of production these prerequisites include a state, a legal system that contains a concept of private property, and a set of markets that allows the more or less 'free' circulation of commodities. However, Wolpe's elaboration of the 'restricted' concept concludes by indicating that to specify these prerequisites is neither to specify how exactly they will be met (what precise form the state, the property concept or markets should take), nor to prejudge either that they should in fact be met or the degree to which they will be met – the state need not necessarily be 'capitalist' nor ever be effectively so; the property concept similarly need not be capitalist nor ever fully so; markets need not be 'free' nor ever totally so (cp Jessop, 1982, Chapter 5).

In sum, the conditions of existence of the capitalist mode of production need not necessarily appear simultaneously with the mode of production itself, nor need they ever be fully or unambiguously met, even once capitalism has become the dominant mode of production. The conditions of existence of capitalist production can only be more or less fragilely secured at the level of the social formation, which need not be coextensive with the nation state. All of this is not to deny that the capitalist mode of production has the particular dynamic or the crisis tendencies that Marx ascribed to it. Rather, it simply allows the denial, as against Althusser in 'Contradiction and Overdetermination', of the view that the economy is necessarily the site of the 'main contradiction' and that only it and not the other spheres might be the focus of a process of overdetermination and hence the site of a possibly terminal social crisis.

In the preceding section it has been argued that the consequences of completing the removal of the human subject from its privileged position in the discourses of the social sciences involve recognising the separate reality and autonomy of language and therefore of the ideological sphere, and hence allowing the correctness of Wolpe's restriction of the concept mode of production to the denotation of the forces and relations of production. It is now time to complete the theorisation of ideology and so specify the ground upon which the refusal of the geological metaphor may be achieved. These are the final preparations required before the concept of 'the discourses of production' may be presented.

Towards a Theory of Discourse

For Saussure language in use or *parole* could not serve as the object of study for linguistics since, contrasted with *langue*, it was an individualised, contingent, intangible and therefore transitory phenomenon. Eventually, however, literary critics (for example Barthes, 1972; Jacobson, 1960), psychoanalysts (Lacan, 1977) and others (for example Foucault, 1967) turned their attention to *parole* in the hope of discovering behind it additional structures to that of *langue*; structures that could facilitate the completion of the analysis of meaning, and that would allow semantics to take account of the connotative as well as the denotative dimension of language. Knowledge of *langue* provides information as to the so-called 'literal' meanings of words, whilst it was the shared hope of the aforementioned that knowledge of these other structures would provide information as to the connotative and therefore more social meanings of words.

Using the Saussurian terminology that is common to all these writers, what one is confronted with in *parole*, or discourse as it is now generally known, is a chain of signifiers rather than one of signs (Barthes, 1972, p. 115). The suggestion therefore is that one may work back through an additional set of syntagmatic and paradigmatic relations to discover the signifieds added socially to signifiers. The earliest work along these lines (for example Jacobson, 1960) was primarily concerned with poetry and therefore with discovering the particular mechanisms whereby connotative signifieds could diverge from denotative ones and yet still be understandable by readers, indeed to an enhanced degree. These mechanisms he found exemplified in the familiar tropes of metaphor and metonymy, the former working along the paradigmatic and the latter along the syntagmatic axis (cp Lacan's discovery of the similarity between the concepts of 'condensation' and 'displacement' that Freud uses for the interpretation of dreams, and those of metaphor and metonymy respectively).

Barthes (1972) attempted to go a step further and specify the structures, or 'myths' as he calls them, which such a process of 'decoding' uncovers, and whose existence explains the presence and effectiveness of both the tropes mentioned above and the additional connoted signifieds that all discourse carries. The problem with Barthes' position from the present point of view is that, rather surprisingly, he initially tied it to a reductionist Marxist conception of the social totality (*vide* the negative connotations of the term 'myth'). In order to avoid these connotations, the term 'ideology' in its positive sense will be preferred here to 'myth'. In this way it is hoped that Barthes' insight as to the sociological constraints on connotation may be sustained below alongside his (Barthes, 1975) subsequent and correct emphasis on the autonomy of discourse.

In the meantime, the lesson to be drawn from the work of such as Jacobson and Barthes is that no language use may occur without the possibility that it might carry additional freight loaded by the fact that most such use is structured by other social constructs and not just by *langue*. Moving on, the means necessary for the specification of these other constructs may be found in the work of the eclectic (Dreyfus, Rabinow, 1982) and consequently often divergently read Michel Foucault (Pearce, 1988). It is Foucault who has provided the means for thinking about the connotating structures and the sociological constraints upon them, which sit most happily with the positive concept of ideology.

Discourse and Discursive Formation

Irrespective of its own eclectic genealogy, Foucault's concept of 'discursive formation' may be read as consistent with the non-humanism, realism and Marxism of the present text. Contrary to many readings (for example Cousins, Hussain, 1984; Laclau; Mouffe, 1985), this concept is not understood here as a synonym for and/or an improvement on that of discourse, but rather signifies the conditions of possibility of a discourse:

> Whenever one can describe, between a number of statements, such a system of dispersion, whenever, between objects, types of statement, concepts, or thematic choices, one can define a regularity (an order, correlations, positions and functionings, transformations), we will say, for the sake of convenience, that we are dealing with a *discursive formation* – thus avoiding words that are already overladen with conditions and consequences, and in any case inadequate to the task of designating such a dispersion, such as 'science', 'ideology', 'theory', or 'domain of objectivity'. The conditions to which the elements of this division (objects, mode of statement, concepts, thematic choices) are subjected we shall call the *rules of formation*. The rules of formation are conditions of existence (but also of coexistence, maintenance, modification, and disappearance) in a given discursive division (Foucault, 1974, p. 38).

Foucault goes on to specify the critically important but often neglected 'rules of formation' that apply to the objects addressed or referred to by discursive formations as: their 'surfaces of emergence' (for example social institutions); their 'authorities of delimitation' (for example the professions); and their 'grids of specification' (for example the body). As is made clear in the above quotation it is simply the aggregate of these and the other rules of formation that accounts for the structure and fate of a particular discursive formation, rather than any shared immanent logic. What is clear from the elaboration provided in the four chapters that follow in Foucault's text is the fact that for him, as for Saussure (see pp. 58–9 above), the determinants of these rules are social in the general sense – that is, in Foucault's terms they are 'non-discursive' as well as discursive. In terms of the argument developed in this text rather than Foucault's, whilst what discourses might signify is determined by the pertinent sets of linguistic and discursive relations, what they *refer to* is determined by those additional discursive and non-discursive structures which determine the nature of the institutional settings, the corporate groups and the intellectual templates whereby their objects are defined.

However, Foucault's contribution to the present argument does not stop here since, apart from enabling one to understand that a discourse has discursive and non-discursive (language-borne as well as extra-linguistic) conditions of possibility and existence, the concepts of 'the rules of formation' and 'discursive formation' also allow us to define what is meant by discourse in a way that clearly differentiates what it signifies as a connotative, ideological practice from what it signifies as a denotative, linguistic one. In order to suggest that ideological discourse adds meaning to *langue* Foucault describes their joint product not as a sentence but as a 'statement'. He then defines this as a series of signs, which (a) assumes the particular subject position given by the relevant discursive formation, (b) projects a certain dynamic on to the set of signifiers that constitute it, and (c) possesses a definite materiality by being recognisably different from other statements. A discourse is thus 'a group of statements in so far as they belong to the same discursive formation' (ibid., p. 117).

A Theory of Articulation: Knots and Nodes

Laclau and Mouffe's recent work is the most important attempt so far to apply some of Foucault's insights to traditional Marxist concerns. Unfortunately, for reasons that will be set out below in the course of a critical analysis of the central chapter of their text, it offers little direct help or guidance in the search for a new social theory. Indeed, as has already been mentioned, their history of Marxism with its two contending logics (that of 'the social' and that of 'hegemony') leaves no space for a third position, which does not replace Marxism but which rethinks it in terms of discourse theory and therefore better deserves to be called 'an articulatory practice'.[3] However, as with all the texts discussed so far, Laclau and Mouffe's is no mere repetition and is therefore of considerable indirect use since criticism of it provides a further opportunity to advance towards the specification of this third position.

What makes their refusal to contemplate even the possibility of a third way particularly surprising to the present author is that they build their argument in part on the basis of a discussion of some of the very same industrial relations texts that have been discussed here (for example Braverman and Burawoy). The view that the greatest significance of such texts and the several cognate ones they also discuss is that they exhibit signs of the presence of an emergent logic of hegemony can only be sustained if the latters' negative comments on economic reductionism alone are registered. A less selective reading of these texts, such as that presented above in relation to Burawoy, makes it perfectly clear that many of their authors continue to find reductionism quite acceptable and only requiring qualification, if at all, by some notion of 'relative autonomy', which remains very under-theorised and therefore very unreliable. Such texts deserve to be struggled with on their own ground, as the method of critique requires. They ought not to be press-ganged into serving on any passing ship.

Laclau and Mouffe begin the construction of their own position by locating the source of Marxism's problems with ideology in economic reductionism and in the resulting theoretical dominance of the category of 'totality'; that is, fatefully, in issues of substantive theory rather than metatheory (see above p. 6). This is the category that supports the logic of 'the social' that they wish to displace by the logic of 'hegemony'. To do this, however, requires the elaboration of an alternative conceptualisation of the nature of social connectedness, one that doesn't assume it, as does 'mediation', but on the contrary one that problematises it. This, they suggest, may be found in a concept of articulation, which they then elaborate and use as a means for refusing the acceptability of any pre-existing notion of the social totality.

The first phase of their elaborative work takes them on what they call a 'detour' through some of the works of Althusser and Hindess, Hirst et al. The former is subjected to a critique which is similar to that outlined above, whilst the latter are subjected to one that does not seem to be pertinent in the current context since it arises out of the anti-realism that both sets of authors share.[4] However, the ending of this detour is pregnant with intimations of what is to come in that it raises the suspicion that a certain circularity might characterise the journey as a whole. The ending in question is:

> ... *a certain notion of totality* could be reintroduced, with the difference that it would no longer involve an underlying principle that would unify 'society', but an ensemble of totalizing effects in an open relational complex (Laclau and Mouffe, 1985, p. 103, emphasis added).

The detour completed, the means for constructing this notion of totality are specified as follows:

we will call *articulation* any practice establishing a relation among elements such that their identity is modified as a result of the articulatory practice. The structured totality resulting from the articulatory practice, we will call *discourse*. The differential positions, insofar as they appear articulated within a discourse, we will call *moments*. By contrast, we will call *element* any difference that is not discursively articulated (ibid., p. 105).

In order that the significance of this analytical vocabulary should be properly grasped, further specifications are provided. These begin with a clarification of what is meant by the term 'discursive formation'. This is said to be close to but not the same as its Foucauldian meaning. However, the difference between the two meanings is somewhat more radical than they imagine. They think that to see a discursive formation 'as an ensemble of different positions' (ibid., p. 106) is simply to look at it from 'the perspective of the regularity of dispersion' (ibid., p. 106). This, however, is to go beyond Foucault's perspective, since such an ensemble is precisely what a discourse is. Thus Laclau and Mouffe seem not to have developed the concept of discursive formation, but like Cousins and Hussain (1984, p. 94), to have confused it with that of discourse. This in itself might not have been too damaging, but they go on to use the terms interchangeably and indirectly to suggest, unintentionally, that there is a deeper difference between them and Foucault than they imagine.

Although the fact of their confusion may not be something that they are conscious of, it gradually becomes apparent that it is not accidental. Although it is very difficult to see exactly how – the link in the text is a very preremptory expression of criticism of hermeneutics and structuralism – this confusion appears to be produced by a desire to depart from Saussurian orthodoxy. The evidence being that Benveniste's (1971, Chapter 4) argument for the necessity of the relation between the signified and the signifier is preferred to Saussure's argument for the arbitrariness of this relationship. The reason for this preference, in turn, becomes clear in the second of Laclau and Mouffe's clarifications, their rejection of the discursive/non-discursive distinction accepted by Foucault and the author of the present text: they totally reject the possibility that the discursive might be in any way determined by the non-discursive and that therefore the 'nodal points' that are the points of relative discursive fixity in discourse are in any way the product of non-discursive factors (Laclau and Mouffe, 1985, pp. 112–13).

The arbitrary nature of the signified/signifier relation is what for

Saussure (1974, pp. 75, 76) allows non-linguistic forces to affect language:

> Language is radically powerless to defend itself against the forces which from one moment to the next are shifting the relationship between the signified and the signifier. This is one of the consequences of the arbitrary nature of the sign ... As it is a product of both the social force and time, no one can change anything in it, and on the other hand, the arbitrariness of its signs theoretically entails the freedom of establishing just any relationship between phonetic substance and ideas. The result is that each of the two elements united in the sign maintains its own life to a degree unknown elsewhere, and that language changes, or rather evolves, under the influence of all the forces which can affect either sounds or meanings. The evolution is inevitable; there is no example of a single language that resists it. After a certain period of time, some obvious shifts can always be recorded.

It is likewise with the discourse/discursive formation distinction. Although the relation inside this distinction is not arbitrary, far from it, it is also not tightly determinist since differing discourses are made possible by the same discursive formation. Hence, for example, the variety of schools of thought within different disciplines. More important in the present context is the point that the discursive formation is produced by rules that depend on non-discursive as well as discursive phenomena, so that differences in the former are as likely to be responsible for differences between discursive formations and between schools contending within the bounds of a particular discursive formation, as differences in the latter. It therefore seems that in this regard at least Foucault, so far from exhibiting a 'linguistic fault' (Brown and Cousins, 1980), may be read as a correct as well as an orthodox Saussurian. He completed the latter's work by providing a means through which the changes in connoted meanings that transform what is denoted by a particular signifier may be understood.[5] It is this notion, then, that the discursive may be determined by as well as imbricated with the non-discursive that Laclau and Mouffe wish to reject and which explains not only their semi-conscious preference for Benveniste over Saussure but also their unconscious confusion of discourse with discursive formation.

Laclau and Mouffe's departure from the orthodoxy that Saussure founded, however, does not stop with the preference for Benveniste but continues to the extent of claiming some kinship with the thought of Wittgenstein and Merleau-Ponty. To assess the significance of this move, which again is deeper than they realise, but this time has unwanted consequences, attention must shift to their discussion of what they call, somewhat airily, 'the more common misunderstandings' of 'the theory of discourse'. They are correct when they say that the theory has no necessary relation to idealism in the dispute with realism over the existence of a world external to thought. They are, however, themselves the victims of a most uncommon misunderstanding if they suppose that any variety of what is commonly known as 'discourse theory', apart from their own non-Saussurian one, has much in common with either Wittgenstein's or Merleau-Ponty's thought. As a result Laclau and Mouffe unintentionally contribute to the currency of the first of their 'common misunderstandings'. The locus of this unintended contribution is their belief that the avowal of materialism is an unfailing antidote to idealism, which leads them to say, in claimed agreement with Wittgenstein and Merleau-Ponty:

> the practice of articulation, as fixation/dislocation of a system of differences, cannot consist of purely linguistic phenomena; but must instead pierce the entire material density of the multifarious institutions, rituals and practices through which a discursive formation is structured (Laclau and Mouffe, 1985, p. 109).

All of which sounds very like saying that if agents move words around they also move the world around, since it is through 'the practice of articulation' that the piercing is done. This is very hard to read as anything other than an idealist statement, especially when they later describe their position as espousing 'the primacy of the discursive' (ibid., p.149, n. 19). It indeed bears a very strong resemblance to similar statements found in the writings of Wittgenstein and Merleau-Ponty and as such to positions that are located somewhere along a continuum, at one end of which is Hegel's definition of the 'Zeitgeist' and at the other Pierce's definition of an 'index', these being examples of the rationalist and empiricist poles of idealist thought. As these resemblances also suggest it is also very hard to read Laclau and Mouffe's statement as anything other than a humanist one, since it would appear to be only humans who are capable of moving words around.

Ontologically, Laclau and Mouffe are anti-realist, but they seem to be unaware that they must therefore be idealist. What they seem not to have realised is what Trigg (1981) makes very clear, namely that no simple claim to materialism can reverse this. Thus what is being argued here is that Laclau and Mouffe are mistaken if they think that as anti-idealists they can hold both that discourse has a material character and that 'literality is, in actual fact, the first of metaphors' (Laclau and Mouffe, 1985, p. 110). The latter statement repeats their idealist theory of reference, whilst the former seeks to deny that it is idealist. Thus they may best be categorised as 'irrealists' (Bhaskar, 1986, p. 9) or as unwilling 'objective idealists', since whilst their anti-realism leads them to deny that objects outside of discourse may be known, their materialism leads them to claim that the objects that exist in discourse are real. There is, therefore, an incoherence here, which may only be corrected by either retaining the theory of reference and acknowledging its idealism or abandoning it altogether on the grounds that its claimed materialist character does not prevent it from being axiomatically idealist on the grounds of its anti-realism.

Ultimately, since they wish to be neither realist nor idealist, the source of their confusions would seem to be their decision to seek a third way in the realm of ontology, where only two exist, rather than in the realm of epistemology, where at least three ways exist – idealism, empiricism and realism. It should be remembered that it is precisely their refusal of the epistemological third way – realism – that forces them to attempt to find one in the realm of ontology. Ontologically one has to make a basic choice between, as Trigg puts it:

> those who wish to 'construct' reality out of men's [sic] experiences, concepts, language or whatever, and those that start with the idea that what exists does so whether men conceive of it or not (Trigg, 1981, p. vii).

This is the choice that places one on one side or the other of the idealism/realism divide. This is the choice that no additional ontological choice, whether it be for or against materialism, for or against humanism or whatever can substitute for. Even if, as Trigg further argues, the latter set of choices can result in unintended consequences for the basic position one thinks one holds; for example theism and anthropocentrism tend to make a text idealist even though the author thinks of her or himself as a realist. Similarly, the ontological choice is one that no epistemological choice can substitute for, although again some such choices can also have unintended consequences; in this regard Trigg stresses that the verificationism characteristic of empiricism can lead through its stress on intersubjectively verifiable experience to idealism (cp the Piercian theory of language alluded to above).

Whatever the actual reasons for their confusions, it is hard to resist the conclusion that Laclau and Mouffe end up advocating an idealist theory of discourse. The resemblance between their position and idealism is neatly illustrated by their use of the Hegelian term 'moments' to denote the 'elements' articulated in discourse. Ironically, it also connotes exactly the Hegelian notion of interconnectedness, 'mediation', that their concept of articulation is intended to displace. The way-stations on the circular tour that the incompleteness of this displacement suggests may be summed up as: the confusion of the concept of discourse with that of discursive formation; the rejection of the Saussurian notion of the arbitrariness of the signified/signifier relation; the rejection of the discursive/non-discursive distinction; and finally the incoherence that is a product of their mistaken view that a claim to materialism can reverse the idealism that is the unwanted consequence of their anti-realism.

These, then, are the knots that stand out more in the text than the 'nodal points' it was designed to recommend as the core of a set of methodological protocols. What happens at each of these stops increases the likelihood that the 'certain notion of totality' they are moving towards will turn out to be idealist, albeit in a novel way, since on each occasion the possibility that the extra-discursive world might have effects on discursive practice, whether humans are aware of it or not, is denied in one way or another. Thus what is here considered to be the sociological and therefore multi-dimensional problem of 'hegemony' is thought by Laclau and Mouffe to be analysable by the deployment of a conceptual scheme – 'difference', 'equivalence', 'negativity', 'antagonism' – which relates to only one of the pertinent dimensions, the language-borne one of discourse. Nevertheless the conceptual scheme and the notion of 'nodal points' that it makes possible remain useful for describing the topography of particular interdiscursive sites, specifically those that relate to the formation and transformation of individual and/or group identities where these are produced as part of a process of conflict. Provided, that is, that one accepts that the relative fixity of any set of nodal points is the product of the non-discursive as well as discursive forces brought into play by the rules of formation of the discursive formation.

As a product of an idealism Laclau and Mouffe's text is of no further direct use in this one, since here the concern is to understand the imbrication and interpenetration of the ideological and the other spheres of social life, not to privilege and isolate it. Moreover, as such a product their text is necessarily marked by the co-presence of a humanism that is otherwise denied – perhaps because humanism is understood to inhere only in the claim that human subjects are the origin of the social and not also in the wider claim with which it is identified in this text, namely that humans are the sole active substance of sociality? Certainly this co-presence will tend to occur whenever, as in Laclau and Mouffe's text, the separate existence and the comprehensibility of the non-human social world is denied. In the presence of such a denial the world may only be understood through the investigation of *human* experience. In this way the ontological ground comes, willy nilly, to be thought of as occupied solely by human subjects or aggregates of them, and any structuring to be merely a transitory crystallisation or 'sedimentation' of the interactions between these subjects, much as it has by generations of humanist sociologists. Almost inevitably, the next step is the recommendation of hermeneutic modes of interpretation and thereby the restoration of a representationalist conception of language and language-borne phenomena such as discourse. It remains to be seen whether or not Laclau and Mouffe will finally take this fatal step; fatal because thereby they would cut themselves off from much that is valuable in their own texts. (Unfortunately, the signs are that they may be about to do just this, see below p. 171.)

In sum, as well as serving as the source of a recuperable schema for the analysis of certain discursive phenomena their text may serve as a navigational buoy warning of the presence of a substantial hazard and demarcating the other side of the channel, otherwise demarcated by economic reductionism, through which those who seek a third way with discourse have to pass. (The locations of the two hazards have recently been confirmed in the debate between Geras, 1987, and Laclau and Mouffe, 1987.) I will leave to others the task of relating the irrealism of Laclau and Mouffe's text to the criticism of the political recommendations that it contains. The task that remains to be completed here is the specification of what is meant by the phrase 'the discourses of production' and of what the significance of this is for a non-idealist conception of an articulatory theoretical practice.

Non-humanism and the Subject Revisited

Before the meaning and significance of this phrase is finally specified, a clarificatory comment must be made concerning where this
train of thought leaves the individual human subject. This is particularly necessary since non-humanist thought is often regarded as
involving either the analytical annihilation of the subject or its
demotion to the status of a mere 'bearer' of social relations.
Whatever may be the justice of these criticisms with respect to
other instances of non-humanist thought they are not applicable in
the present case. To argue for the removal of the subject's privileged
metaphysical status, as has been done here, is not to argue for its
sociological annihilation. Likewise, to argue that the subject *ab
initio* (contra Althusser) is constructed in and by discourse, through
multiple interpellations, as has been assumed here, is not to argue
that such a construct is all the subject is.[6] For Lacan, whose concept
of the subject lies behind that operant in this text, the subject's
'desire', as inaugurated by its founding 'lack', may be shaped by its
entry into the realms of the 'imaginary' and the 'symbolic', but the
crossing of these thresholds expunges neither the 'lack' nor its structural effectivity, nor indeed its biological conditions of existence.
What it does lead to, however, is the recognition that the individual
human psyche is a distinguishable object of study from social relations, the means for whose study are the product of a similarly
distinguishable discursive formation.

That said, at the social level subjects are nevertheless of interest in
so far as they engage in calculations and calculated practices, which
bear some resemblance to those traditionally ascribed by Weberian
sociology to 'the actor', but which here are to be understood rather
differently; that is, not as the direct and individually created
products of changing, extra-discursive means and conditions of
'action', but as the products of their positioning by discursive structures ('preconstructeds', Pecheux, 1982) through which the means,
conditions and indeed problems of 'action' are presented to them,
as well as of their physical positionings as embodiments of extra-
discursive political and economic structures. Taken together, these
three modes of positioning largely define the responses possible by
the same subjects, most often to the exclusion of responses determined by conscious or unconscious 'personal' concerns. Moreover,
in so far as the discursive structures are second-order linguistic
systems and hence are carried by language, they require the existence of subjects, as indeed do the other structures, not simply as
their 'bearers' but as an integral part of their existence; that is, in a

relation that Miller (1977/78) characterises as an instance of *'suture'* or a lack that produces its own fulfilment.

In sum, the individual subject will be conceptualised here not simply as a 'bearer' of discursive and other positionings originating inside and outside of the workplace but also as a presence within the discourses of production and the other sets of positions, as a potentially critical source of support for or resistance to particular efforts at signifying or other practices, and as the maker or breaker of signifying and other chains. In the realm of ideology, for example, the subject is a signifier in the social world and as such needs to be decoded paradigmatically and syntagmatically before its signified and therefore its wider discursive significance may be understood.

The Discourses of Production

In more traditional terms the subject may be viewed, therefore, as almost literally the 'inter-face' between the 'formal' and 'informal' workplace discourses. In concrete terms this means that the views and any changes to them of workplace participants are potentially active determinants of the discourses of production not because they are personal or idiosyncratic, but rather because they may reinforce or restrict the discourses already dominant within the particular workplace. Whether or not this potentiality is ever realised, of course, depends upon how else a particular subject is positioned politically and economically.

Views that are purely personal or idiosyncratic comprise what I regard as the 'informal' level of workplace discourse and as such are unlikely to have any effect on the discourses of production. They may merely serve to mark their proponents as oddities or agitators. This is because the discursive formation that creates the conditions of possibility and existence of any particular set (*usually* national) of formal discourses of production is not likely to provide much support for the discourse of a loner. Factories, the legal profession, managerial bodies and trades unions are examples of the concrete sites wherein one discovers the rules of formation of the object of the discursive formation that allows and sustains the formal dimension of the discourses of production, and they have no space (almost literally) for the loner. The discourses of production are therefore a specific set of structures, wherein the formal discourses are dominant, bounded by specific conditions of entry and exit and as such not equally susceptible to interventions originating in other discourses, especially when these are made possible by unrelated discursive formations (for example those that allow one to speak of neurotics or Trotskyists).

Finally, although the variant of non-humanist analysis practised here allows a role to human subjects in the determination of the structure and dynamics of the 'discourses of production', it is a defining difference between it and that of such as Armstrong et al. that the discourses articulated by subjects are not the only or even the most important determinants of the 'discourses of production'. Arguably more important in contemporary British society, for example, are the discourses articulated in a series of texts currently beginning with the contract of employment and followed by collective agreements, pertinent statutes relating to health and safety, holiday entitlement, etc, factory rules and even articles of apprenticeship. The fact that all of the latter texts, except aberrantly those relating to health and safety, currently have a place in the first suggests that the contract of employment is not simply 'the cornerstone of the edifice of labour law', as Kahn-Freund (1954) famously suggested, but is also the veritable incarnation of the discourses of production, and has been so at least since the abolition of the Master–Servant laws (see below p. 133).

The contract of employment defines the boundaries of the discourses of production by its inclusion of the powers to hire (entry) and fire (exit), and of the others signified by the term 'managerial prerogative'. It is comprised of an articulatory constellation of 'nodal points', which by using the analytical schema proposed by Laclau and Mouffe (see above, p. 70) may under certain circumstances become visible as an aspect of a set of antagonistic social relations. It must therefore be acknowledged as the principal source of the strength or weakness of the discursive ties that bind capital and labour together. It is not just the critical discursive link between capital and labour, but also the critical interface between the discourses of production and other discourses, and indeed (contra Laclau and Mouffe) between the discursive and the non-discursive realms; that is, absent certain non-discursive political and economic conditions of existence, it can have no determinant effect (see below, pp. 117).

'Hiring', 'firing' and 'the managerial prerogative' denote the basic and asymmetrical configuration of the employment relation under capitalism. Such terms as 'collective agreements', 'statutes', 'factory rules' and 'articles of apprenticeship' in themselves denote the outcomes of conflicts which are to varying degrees external to a particular workplace but which add a connotative dimension to the terms that are fundamental to the employment contract. More specifically, in so far as they are the products of a democratic political process they tend to reduce the asymmetry denoted by the employment contract through the narrowing of employer rights that they generally connote and thereby provide means of enforcing. Today neither hiring, firing nor the rules governing the direction of production nor indeed the defining of skills are completely unqualified by statutes, agreements or whatever that redress the balance, albeit slightly, in labour's favour. In this way discourses originating outside production, and indeed sometimes apparently utterly separate from it, may come to exercise a powerful influence within it. This, then, is *one* of the ways in which national differences in the discourses of production may be explained; that is, by the effects of legislative or bargained interventions on what is denotatively and connotatively signified by 'the contract of employment'.

Finally, what the signs comprising the contract of employment refer to extra-discursively in any particular nation-state may be explained by consideration of the rules that produce the objects of the discursive formation and that therefore connect the contract with its discursive/non-discursive conditions of possibility/ existence. Examples of the rules of formation in this case would be: their 'surfaces of emergence' (that is, the politico-economic locations of capitalist enterprises – public/private/cooperative, agricultural/industrial, etc); their 'authorities of delimitation' (that is, the nature of the legal profession and latterly employers' associations, trade unions and industrial relations professionals); their 'grids of specification' (that is, the prevailing notions of industrial community – familialist, militarist, communitarian, etc). In sum, as the articulatory tendons between the contract of employment and its discursive/non-discursive conditions of existence, the rules of formation that together produce the contract's underlying discursive formation also explain why the contract has the referent that it does and not that referred to, for example, by the sign 'the unconscious'; that is, the discursive object referred to by the sign 'contract of employment', for example, did not emerge in family settings, was not authoritatively delimited by the medical profession, and did not concern the body or the soul. That said, it must not be forgotten that knowledge of what any sign's referent is, extra-discursive though some of its aspects might be, is not the same as knowledge of the referent itself, which requires a separate and wider sociological enquiry.

Thus the sign 'contract of employment' refers to the taking-on and the laying-off of labour as well as the general structure of work discipline and the nature of the job-structure. Indeed it is constitutive of these realities. However, it is not exhaustive of them, since they are constituted politically and economically as well, as is the workplace itself. This is why (contra Armstrong et al.) the concept of the discourses of production only overcomes one aspect of the incommensurability problem, since the latter recurs in the political and economic spheres also and these recurrences require separate treatments which fortunately they have already received in the works of Foucault (see below p. 112) and Marx respectively (see below, 177).

To conclude, the concept of the discourses of production and the empirical investigations made possible by it promise to dissolve the ideological dimension of the incommensurability problem signified by the macro–micro divide thanks to the recognition that it carries of the constancy of ideological phenomena across the divide. Thus there is a reciprocal transudation between workplace discourses and others (cp Armstrong et al.'s 'currency' metaphor). Further, human subjects may be the only conduits of this transudatory movement, but that is often all they are, since a determinant role has to be allowed to laws, political ideologies, the particularities of national ideological formations, the relations between them and the wider structures that account for their pertinence in production. All of the latter affect and so enter the discourses of production under different and determinant conditions as connotating, non-human and in the case of laws enforceable 'preconstructeds'. Such, then, are the results for the theorisation of production relations that are made possible by taking seriously the independent sociality of language. In Chapter 6 these results, plus those produced in Part 3, will be combined to provide a schematic explanation as to how labour law came to enter the discourses of production in England and the United States, and in so doing to prepare the way for the reconstruction of the subject of class.

Notes
1. For an indication of what sociologists of many different schools could gain from an encounter with Saussurian linguistics and its derivatives see Rossi (1983). For an example of what neo-Weberian thought has gained see Abercrombie et al. (1986).

2. For an elaboration of this point see Jackson (1985, pp. 144–7). It is this difference and what I consider to be the incursion into the realm of sociology that Piercian semiotics represents that lie behind my doubts concerning the advisability of Lipietz's (1985, cp 172ff) attempt to develop the concept of 'fetishism' by resort to semiotics.

3. 'Articulation' is also a central term in Laclau and Mouffe's text, but as will be argued below they give it an idealist inflexion that is unacceptable here.

4. This shared anti-realism itself perhaps arises because of their shared ascription of primacy to the signifier. In this they follow Lacan without realising that the theory of language he develops is one tailored to the needs of psychoanalysis rather than, for example, to those of sociology. As a consequence they appear to regard Lacan's 'critique' of Saussure as one of pan-discursive significance rather than of a very specific significance. Some (for example Archard, 1984) think that Lacan also shared this misrecognition of the significance of his work. However, it seems to me that his critical and famous proposition that 'the unconscious is structured *like* a language' (emphasis added) ought to be interpreted as a metaphor rather than as a statement of fact, as marking the commencement of a novel effort at theorisation related to a specific domain rather than as a critique of all pre-existing theory.

5. A major point of difference between the two being that for Foucault as opposed to Saussure the sources of such change were not purely extra-linguistic but included the 'second-order linguistic phenomena' signified by the term 'discourse'.

6. Pecheux's (1982, pt. 3) concept of 'the preconstructed' is useful as a means of understanding more precisely how interpellation occurs, although his work as a whole suffers from his inability to escape the restraints imposed by the presence of the figure of fetishism that he inherited from Althusser.

PART III
Rethinking Law

4 The Egalitarian Premiss

Legal discourse itself, let alone jurisprudence, in democratic capitalist societies is now and has long been defined by the privileged position ascribed within it to a humanist conception of liberty. In so far as it is not, as I hope to show, simply agents, human and non-human, that are subject to the juridical process, to accept such privileging is unknowingly to confine oneself to a metaphorical understanding of the law and is evidence therefore of conceptual underdevelopment. The purpose of this chapter, then, is to demonstrate that liberal and socialist contributions to jurisprudence, even as theoretical discourses, implicitly and simultaneously constitute and validate different sets of social relations. Furthermore such social relations are as subject to the juridical process as are agents. In Chapter 5 an attempt will be made to produce a concept of law that may be used to explain how this occurs.

Because it shares with the liberal tradition an underlying ontological uncertainty as to the nature of its object(s) of study, Western socialist and especially Marxist jurisprudence has been similarly uncertain as to who or what is subject to legal discipline. Nevertheless, it has pretty rigorously differentiated itself from its liberal counterpart, in such a way as to make criticism of it by far the most promising route for arriving at a non-metaphorical understanding of law. Because of this, the present part will not give as great a prominence to the chasing down of alien and subversive metaphors as the others do. Rather, in order to take the argument forward more rapidly, it will proceed by distinguishing the social relations implicit in liberal legal discourse (that is, those making for material inequality) from those implicit in its socialist counterpart (that is, those making for material equality), as a preface to outlining the concepts necessary for a non-humanist and non-representationalist understanding of the law, only noting in passing some of the problems created by alien metaphors.

81

Equality and Liberal Jurisprudence

The present dominance of liberal jurisprudence and its implicit preference for unequal social relations does not mean that the concept
of 'equality' has not affected legal discourse in democratic capitalist
societies. Indeed, this concept has been extremely influential, especially in the United States, not only in jurisprudence but also in tort
and labour law. Nevertheless, the continued privileging of liberty in
conventional jurisprudence has always meant that the equality it
recommended, and even established, could never be material
equality. Instead, the meaning of 'equality' has repeatedly been
specified in terms which cause the least possible damage to the
coherence of liberal jurisprudence and existing juridicial and other
social relations, and which therefore allow the smallest number of
opportunities for their disruption and displacement by an alternative jurisprudence, let alone an alternative set of social relations,
premissed on material equality.

From my point of view, this liberal interest in equality nevertheless represents a move towards increasing sophistication in
jurisprudential reasoning as the latter has sought to come to terms
with the 'realities' of democratic capitalist societies. However, it
should be emphasised that this judgement is very likely a minority
one in wider legal circles, where classical (that is, pre-democratic)
liberal positions still claim considerable support. Most dramatically,
Hayek – the favourite philosopher of contemporary Anglo-American
'conservatism' – has devoted a considerable proportion of his
prodigious output to the elaboration of the classical liberal conception of law. However, to anticipate the results of my argument a
little, there is a possibility of paradox here.

Hayek is popular amongst contemporary 'conservatives' because
his anti-collectivist jurisprudence may be used in conjunction with
Friedman's equally classically liberal Smithian economics to justify,
in the name of liberty, a reduction in the level of state intervention.
The possibility of paradox is revealed when one remembers that, for
example, alongside 'rolling-back' the state, the present British
government is also engaged in a strenuous effort to regulate industrial relations and the activities of trades unions in particular by
legal means, and that the law is generally considered to be a mode
of state intervention. For Hayek (1980), and the contributors to the
Institute of Economic Affairs' Symposium (1981), however, there is
no paradox. For them, the law is distinguishable from the state and
in a sense prior to it. The consequence of this differentiation is that
it is possible to argue coherently that society should be free of state

interference, that everyone should be under the law, that trades unions in Britain should not enjoy legal immunities and that the state should legislate to remove this anomaly. In making this argument, Hayek is recognising that law exists, as Marxists would say, as an element in an hegemonic ideology. But he is neglecting the point, which Marxists never would omit, that while law may not be reducible to the state it is also neither thinkable nor possible without it. In this neglect, liberalism, become a form of conservatism, shares with its revolutionary ancestor the same blindness to the structure of its dominance that Karl Polyani (1957) long ago recognised in his *The Great Transformation*. However, this is not the place to pursue the silences of conservative thought (see instead Skillen, 1977, Chapter 3).

Despite, or probably because of, its venerable origins, the moral, or ideological, force that the notion of 'the rule of law' continues to exert depends upon a generally persisting conviction that it represents a veritable incarnation of the inviolability of the individual's liberty. This conviction persists even amongst those who have otherwise devoted themselves to denying, disproving or displacing claims as to the actual and/or exclusive dependence of 'the rule of law' on the premiss of the inviolability of individual liberty, whether supported by theological or naturalistic arguments. The legal positivists sought to deny any such dependence (Annette, 1979; Austin, 1913; Bentham, 1970; Halevy, 1972). The practitioners of sociological jurisprudence and legal realism were concerned to disprove it (Gilmore, 1977, Chapter 4; Hunt, 1977; Twining, 1973). And, finally, contemporary legal philosophers like Rawls (1971) and Dworkin (1977), as well as sociologists like Unger (1976), have committed themselves to displacing liberty as the sole premiss upon which 'the rule of law' and its understanding should depend by placing some conception of equality and therefore some acknowledgement of law's more obviously social role alongside it. Notwithstanding their various arguments against the claims made on liberty's behalf, and whether or not they regard the idea itself as a fiction, all of those just mentioned argue for the maintenance of its privileged, if no longer exclusive, position at the centre of legal discourse. Thus they also argue, though typically less consciously, for the acceptability of at least some forms of inequality. Here, the text of particular interest is Dworkin's *Taking Rights Seriously*, where the positivists' assumption as to the self-sufficiency of legal rules is refused and the latters' dependence upon the principle of liberty is exposed and contested. In place of liberty, he proposes 'equality of concern and respect in the design and administration of political institutions' as the principle to be invoked to resolve difficult cases in a democratic society (Dworkin, 1977, p. 180). In making this suggestion, Dworkin develops the ideas contained in the much discussed, revised version of social contract theory presented by John Rawls (1971).

Rawls and Dworkin on Equality

What Rawls argues is that any group of people ignorant of the social significance of their own particular attributes, meeting together at one of those imaginary social contractarian congresses and wishing to act both rationally and in their self-interest would adopt two principles of justice: (a) that each person should have the maximum degree of political liberty compatible with like liberty for all; and (b) that inequalities of power, wealth, income and other resources should not exist except in so far as they work to the absolute benefit of the worst-off (Dworkin, 1977, p. 150). The second right limits the first and is, thus, logically, if not discursively, prior to it. Individuals may only exercise their liberty not only so long as it does not interfere with that of others – the traditional liberal position – but also so long as it does not reduce the power, wealth, income, etc of the worst-off. This dualistic conception of natural rights clearly represents a significant qualification of the original liberal premiss, sufficient for example but perhaps *only* to provide a jurisprudential rationale for juridical decisions allowing reverse discrimination where gender and/or racial discrimination has been proven.

The continuing liberalism of Rawls' position is indicated on the one hand by the juridicial consequence that the concept of liberty may be used to protect the power, wealth, etc of the powerful and the rich, as well as of the less powerful and the poor, and on the other by the *lack of coincidence* between the logical and discursive ordering of the propositions. What determines the discursive ordering is the view that it is self-interest that gives content to rationality and, therefore, that it is liberty that allows inequality to exist in the first place as its rational consequence. Within Rawls' definition, inequalities caused by gender or racial discrimination may be shown to reduce the absolute quantum of power, wealth, etc of the society as a whole and, therefore, to require positive rectification. However, inequalities caused by ownership and non-ownership of the means of production are very unlikely to reduce the absolute power, wealth, etc of society as a whole, since, for example, capitalism's *sine qua non* is the continuous and increasing accumulation of wealth, which, willy nilly, is likely to benefit the worst-off in an absolute sense. Thus, the Rawls–Dworkin reformulation of natural rights theory fails to overturn the liberal premiss because liberty and therefore inequality is still privileged relative to material equality. Not only is equality defined immaterially as 'a right to equal concern and respect in the design and administration of the political institutions that govern them', but as a consequence inequality is defined in such a way as to exclude one of its major forms – ownership and non-ownership of the means of production. Moreover, the rectification of two of its other major forms, gender and racial inequality, is made dependent upon an unreliable statistical test (Barnett, 1982). This point leaves politically progressive jurists in some difficulties when faced by arguments such as those of Posner in his *The Economics of Justice* (1981) with its Hayekian 'wealth maximisation theory of justice' and its consequent critique of such as the Supreme Court's *Bakke* decision, which favoured some forms of 'positive discrimination'.

Some critical writers have simply dismissed the Rawls–Dworkin approach on the grounds that, like all liberal approaches, it ultimately cannot escape being an apology for the status quo (Woolf, 1977; Daniels, 1975). However, it is a qualified and, indeed, unwilling apology (cp Buchanan, 1982), which by virtue of its established practical significance in the struggles for gender and racial equality and its unwitting demonstration of the problems the privileging of liberty creates for those struggles, should embolden all who have an interest in an alternative jurisprudence.

In order to construct a new and more radically progressive jurisprudence that will also help to rid social theory of its dependence upon representationalism, one must first understand two things. First, why liberty became a revolutionary principle and, second, what was the role played by the rule of law in defending the revolution made in its name. The most complex answers to these questions are those provided by Unger (1976), Hay et al. (1975) and Thompson (1975). It is to Unger's rather Weberian work that I will now turn. And this for several reasons: because of its immense influence in American Critical Legal Studies, the explicitly jurisprudential nature of his argument, the clarity with which he illustrates the relevance of equality/inequality to such arguments, and, finally, because of the incoherence of his position.

Unger on Liberty

Unger summarises his understanding of why liberty and its rule of law became revolutionary notions in words that indicate the centrality of the issue of equality to his thought:

> The basic issues of jurisprudential and political speculation arise from the twofold experience of the unjustifiability of the existing rank order and of the corruption of moral agreements or traditions by the injustice of their origins. In so far as people have this experience, they struggle to avoid or diminish enslavement to each other in the rank order and to establish the most far-reaching power, the power of government, upon a basis that overcomes the arbitrariness of ordinary social hierarchies.
>
> A major form of this struggle is the striving toward the rule of law (Unger, 1976, p. 176).

However, unlike most liberal philosophers, Unger does not believe that the 'unjustifiability of the existing rank order' ceases to be relevant once the rule of law has been established and the antithetical monarchial principle of authority qualified. For him, the persistence of inequality provides the context within which law exists, as well as the strongest reason for its supercession:

> Unless people regain the sense that the practices of society represent some sort of natural order instead of a set of arbitrary choices, they cannot hope to escape from the dilemma of unjustified power. But how can this perception of immanent order be achieved in the circumstances of modern society?
>
> The mere existence of moral agreement within a particular association would not bring about this end. First, it would be necessary for the subversion of inequality to proceed to such a point that people would be entitled to place greater confidence in collective choices as expressions of a shared human nature or of the intrinsic demands of social order rather than as a product of the interests of dominant groups. Second, it would be indispensable that this experience of increasing equality also make possible an ever more universal consensus about the immanent order of social life and thus help refine further the understanding of what equality means. The first condition without the second is empty. The second without the first is dangerous because it threatens to consecrate the outlook of the most powerful and articulate elements in the society.
>
> Such a reconciliation of immanent order and transcendent criticism would imply a greater replacement than we could now comprehend of bureaucratic law or the rule of law by what in a

sense could be called custom. This customary law would have many of the marks we associate with custom: its lack of a positive and a public character and its largely emergent and implicit quality. Yet it would differ from custom in making room for a distinction between what is and what ought to be. It would become less the stable normative order of a particular group than the developing moral language of mankind (Unger, 1976, pp. 240–1).

In these passages, which strikingly illustrate the profound jurisprudential effects that can flow from taking Weber seriously (cp Hunt, 1978, Chapter 5), Unger goes beyond Rawls and Dworkin, and breaks with liberalism. However, it must also be said that it is only because Unger shares with Rawls and Dworkin a belief in the possibility and desirability of some equalitarian improvement that he can refuse Weber's pessimism and break with liberalism. The problem faced by Unger, although he does not seem to realise it, is that having made the break he may be lost. His 'ideal of a universal community', where 'the sense of a latent or natural order in social life must be harmonised with the capacity to let the will remake social arrangements' sounds very like the classical Marxist utopia of communism. However, the liberal, and particularly Weberian, social theory that Unger remains committed to (1976, p. 266) is not merely attached to a social pessimism that denies the possibility of such a utopia, but is permeated by it. For liberty to be fully realisable only under conditions of material equality, for the state to disappear, for law to be replaced by custom, inequality itself must be surpassable, and this is a socialist rather than a liberal belief.

Weber was not a social pessimist just because of some biographical misfortune, but because he had good reason to think that rationality was most probably the Occident's fate. Rationality, in turn, could have this effect because in its economic form, for example, it assumed inequality. The productive superiority of capitalism over other economic forms arose, in Weber's view, out of the entrepreneur's untrammelled power at the point of production, his freedom to adjust means in relation to calculable ends. Thus, to refuse inequality would involve refusing rationality, which in turn would mean becoming once again dependent on nature or, in other words, materially poor. For Weber, inequality was not surpassable, and, in refusing the line of argument behind this position, Unger ceases to argue a liberal position and enters unknown territory. Not realising that he has surpassed liberalism he concludes with these words:

> ...the richness of immediate concerns combines with the longing for universality in thought to give the mind an enthusiasm that prompts it to boldness, opens it up to the unusual and to the commonplace, and awakens it to the unity of things.
>
> The great social theorists had this experience when they went from the speculative generalities of their predecessors to the narrower conjectures of a social science. Now it is for us to imitate our teachers by travelling in the opposite direction, back along the road by which they came (Unger, 1976, p. 268).

But, if one does travel back along the road of 'narrower conjectures' towards the 'speculative generalities' Unger would rediscover, one passes through the oppositions of 'individual' versus 'society' and 'subjective' versus 'objective' until eventually one reaches what he unapologetically calls 'human nature' – the essence of humanity, the origin of the originating subject, the incorrigible *saboteur* of both the feudal order, and the 'natural order' Unger otherwise desires. Thus the very terms he uses, let alone those he forgets, declare the impossibility of him reaching his destination. For Unger, the material equality that characterises his longed-for 'universal community' is immanent within 'human nature' and represents the creation of the conditions necessary for the final resolution of the tension between the 'individual' and 'society'. But the social condition actually prefigured in the social theory he deploys, as a consequence of the privileging of human nature and its derivatives – liberty, rationality, etc – is *inequality*.

Socialist Jurisprudence

In his ultimate incoherence and wishful thinking Unger shares much with the Marx of the *Economic and Philosophical Manuscripts* (1964). However, as Marxism has developed, it has sought to escape the self-contradiction contained in the proposition that communism is an immanent presence within some eternal human nature. Instead, it has gradually moved toward a conception of communism as a structure beckoning humanity and promising a new subjectivity (cp Buchanan, 1982). As was pointed out earlier, it was only with Althusser that Marxists became able, with the help of Lacanian psychoanalysis, to attempt to jettison the notion of human nature as an eternal category and as the origin and sole substance of

society. However, from Marx's *German Ideology* (1968) on, the sociological priority of social conditions over individual ones has been
accepted. For this reason, Marxism has been able to argue consistently that material inequality is surpassable, because it is a product
of transitory social structures rather than of an eternal human
nature. What allowed Marxism finally to attempt to deny any place
at all to human nature within its theoretical structure was that line
of theoretical development from the concept of 'labour power',
through that of the 'labour theory of value', to that of 'mode of
production', which allowed the writing of *Capital* (1965) and
thereby created a basis for understanding the changing content of
human subjectivity.

The consequence of these theoretical developments for Marx's
own assessment of those natural 'equal rights' that form the basis of
that aspect of subjectivation attempted by law in capitalist societies
is most famously demonstrated by his acerbic *Critique of the Gotha
Programme*, where he comments on the inclusion of the phrase, 'the
proceeds of labour belong undiminished with *equal right* to all
members of society' as follows:

> Here obviously the same principle prevails as that which regulates
> the exchange of commodities, as far as this is exchange of equal
> values. Content and form are changed, because under the altered
> circumstances no one can give anything except his labour, and
> because on the other hand, nothing can pass to the ownership of
> individuals except individual means of consumption. But, as far
> as the distribution of the latter among the individual producers is
> concerned, the same principle prevails as in the exchange of
> commodity-equivalents: a given amount of labour in one form is
> exchanged for an equal amount of labour in another form.
>
> Hence *equal right* here is still in principle – *bourgeois right*,
> although principle and practice are no longer at loggerheads,
> while the exchange of equivalents in commodity exchange only
> exists on the average and not in the individual case.
>
> In spite of this advance, this equal right is still constantly stig-
> matised by a bourgeois limitation. The right of the producers is
> proportional to the labour they supply; the equality consists in
> the fact that measurement is made with an equal standard,
> labour.
>
> But one man is superior to another physically or mentally and
> so supplies more labour in the same time, or can labour for a
> longer time; and labour, to serve as a measure, must be defined by

its duration or intensity, otherwise it ceases to be a standard of measurement. This *equal right* is an unequal right for unequal labour. It recognises no class differences, because everyone is only a worker like everyone else; but it tacitly recognises unequal individual endowment and thus productive capacity as natural privileges. *It is therefore a right of inequality, in its content, like every right.* Right by is very nature can consist only in the application of an equal standard; but unequal individuals (and they would not be different individuals if they were not unequal) are measurable only by an equal standard in so far as they are brought under an equal point of view, are taken from one *definite side* only, for instance, in the present case, regarded *only as workers* and nothing more is seen in them, everything else being ignored. Further, one worker is married, another not: one has more children than another, and so on and so forth. Thus, with an equal performance of labour, and hence an equal share in the social consumption fund, one will in fact receive more than another, one will be richer than another, and so on. To avoid all these defects, right instead of being equal would have to be unequal' (Marx, 1972, pp. 164–5).

In the light of this argument Marx concludes that the appropriate distributive principle in a communist society would not be equal rights, but 'from each according to his ability, to each according to his needs', or as he says 'unequal rights'. However, as he also implies in this passage, the only condition that can justify unequal rights is material equality or the striving after such equality.

Thus, the premiss of a progressive juridical strategy and of a future system of democratic *customary law* should also be material equality. The terms custom and law have been coupled here against the Marxist grain, since it is agreed with Hirst (1979) that the autonomy of procedure and enforcement capability characteristic of the law but not usually of custom are essential if there is to be any justice in large, complex post-capitalist societies, irrespective of the ideologies dominant within them. Moreover, whilst natural or equal rights should be excluded from socialist juristic discourse because they drive one towards the same essentialist and inequalitarian conception of the originating subject found in Unger as well as in the *Gotha Programme*, this should not happen to rights as plain entitlements. If there is to be law there must be rights, not simply because such secularised rights, as 'nothing more than capacities sanctioned by law' (Hirst, 1979, p. 104), are necessary to the specification of many juridical relations, but also because under any rule of law they allow individuals and groups or organisations the possibility of defending and advancing themselves. The democracy in making and exercising rules that is contained in the concept of custom needs to be augmented by that of democracy in entitling access to adjudication contained in the concept of rights. And finally, both require that autonomy of procedure, reasoning and enforcement that is contained in the concept of a rule of law if they are to be completed. In this case the law includes unequal rights in favour of, in Marx's sense, 'needy' subjects regardless of whether their need arises from lack of ownership in the means of production, gender and/or racial discrimination, the presence of dependants, or whatever.

What in turn legitimates 'need' as a source of rights is the privileging not of an individual subject's freedom or liberty, but of a society's freedom from want. Whereas the privileging of liberty drives one back to the originating subject, the privileging of material equality drives one back to the structure of a subjectivating society. Thus it is once again agreed with Hirst that:

> Legal rights reflect no inherent ontological attributes; rather, they serve certain socially determined policy objectives and interests. The rights sanctioned in law need not correspond to the forms of consistency demanded by any ontological doctrine of the subject (Hirst, 1979, p. 104).

It cannot be agreed, however, as he continues (cp Lyotard, 1986, p. 100) that 'they have no inherent unity or a single point of reference'. If the 'socially determined objectives and interests' are to be related to the reproduction of socialism/communism then some 'single point of reference' if not an 'inherent unity' has to be found in material equality. Otherwise law could become a source of social disruption rather than justice. Under the premiss of material equality there may be liberty to enjoy one's rights, but in the case of individuals this freedom is allowed only in so far as it does not detract from material equality. Freedom is thus restricted to freedom to develop oneself; as Marx put it so alluringly:

> In communist society, where nobody has one exclusive sphere of activity but each can become accomplished in any branch he wishes, society regulates the general production and thus makes it possible for me to do one thing today and another tomorrow, to

hunt in the morning, fish in the afternoon, rear cattle in the evening, criticise after dinner, just as I have a mind, without ever becoming hunter, fisherman, shepherd or critic (Marx, 1968, p. 45).

In other words, and even in advance of the achievement of 'communist society', freedom does not include the liberty to aggrandise oneself, to become wealthier or more powerful than others. To summarise, in freedom under the rule of material equality, individually, one may become more competent but not superior (Norman, 1982) and socially, inequality not equality is what requires justification. Since competence in scarce or democratically decided upon socially valued areas of expertise would provide one of the main bases upon which inequalities could be justified, the old canard about a system premissed upon material equality being necessarily one of absolute equality may be shrugged off.

Liberal Jurisprudence and Labour Law
Not surprisingly, when one considers the jurisprudential dimension of labour law, a very similar differentiation of positions may be observed between those who privilege liberty, those who qualify it with some conception of equality and those who would replace it with material equality. In labour law, however, perhaps because of its typically statutory, and therefore inescapably social, rather than common law origins – as well as, in England, because of the impact of such Marxist-influenced jurists as Kahn-Freund – the second position is much more common than in jurisprudence in general. There nevertheless remain those who, like Hayek (1980) and the contributors to the Institute of Economic Affairs Symposium of 1978 (1981), adopt what Kahn-Freund has called, following Fox (1966), a 'unitary' approach; that is, one that assumes the complementarity of labour and capital in industrial relations. They begin with the assumption that the individual contract of employment is the core of labour law and then argue in the classical liberal manner that, since like all other contracts it is premissed on the general social contract, the parties to it are equal. Jurists who take this position are consequently suspicious of all statutory interventions, since they consider them likely to undermine freedom of contract (that is, liberty) or more typically these days to unbalance the relationship between supposedly equal parties. For example, both the *Taft Hartley Act* (1947) in the United States and the British *Employment Act* (1980) were justified on the ground that they

partially restored a balance that had become too favourable to labour. In a utilitarian fashion, such restorations, and the even more drastic proposals of Hayek, are in turn justified on the basis that they will preserve or restore prosperity. Writing at the beginning of the still current depression, Hayek argued that:

> There can be no salvation for Britain until the special privileges granted to trade unions three-quarters of a century ago are revoked (Hayek, 1980, p. 58).

More typical of British liberal jurisprudence are those who, like Kahn-Freund himself, adopt what he called a 'pluralist' approach; that is, one which recognises the unequal and inherently contestatory nature of industrial relations. Kahn-Freund was a German social-democrat, who was both a legal scholar and a judge in the Berlin Labour Court of the Weimar period. He had to leave Germany in 1933 and eventually settled in Britain. As a social-democrat, as one who had read Marx, Weber and the German sociological jurists, he was profoundly critical of the law he administered in Berlin. He thought that its overall intent, including its provisions for works councils, was not simply corporatist but actually fascist (Kahn-Freund 1980). Thus, at the time he arrived in Britain, Kahn-Freund was profoundly suspicious of labour law because it represented an obstacle to the achievement of socialism. Once in Britain, he noted the industrial strength of the unions, the absence of the law from industrial relations and the continuance of democracy. Eventually, he connected these points together in a causal chain, shed his belief that industrial conflict would not exist under socialism and began to argue for the universal necessity of labour law as an aid to the maintenance of a balance between permanently contending parties:

> The principal purpose of labour law, then, is to regulate, to support and to restrain the power of management *and* the power of organised labour (Kahn-Freund, 1977, p. 4, emphasis added).

The idea that, despite its necessity, labour law can only aid and not in itself secure the required balance is a very important one in Kahn-Freund's work and one of the chief indicators of his continued sociological awareness. For him, like the present author, law can only be 'a secondary force in human affairs', and this is what both distinguishes his position in general terms from that of the classical liberals and accounts for his lack of surprise at the failure of the Conservative government's *Industrial Relations Act* (1971).

In Kahn-Freund's view, the law can only effectively intervene in human affairs if what is socially desired is not being otherwise obtained, if the existing arrangements between 'social powers' are insufficient, or if nationally specific reasons require it. For this reason, he thought that the 1971 *Industrial Relations Act* failed because it was inappropriate in the context of Britain's then still largely intact and socially well-embedded 'voluntarist system' of industrial relations with its defining legal 'abstentionism'. What, however, most precisely distinguishes his position from that of the 'unitarian' liberals is his conception of the employment contract. It is here that his appreciation of the insufficiency of liberty as *the* juridical premiss is clearest. Although he, like them, regarded it as 'the cornerstone of the edifice' of labour law, he also considered it to be a possibly misleading 'figment of the legal mind'. It is the 'cornerstone' because:

> Everything hinges upon what is called the 'contract of employment' or 'contract of service'. By virtue of that contract the employer has a legal right to the employee's services, a right which he can enforce in a court of law by means of an action for damages in the event of breach, and by virtue of that contract the employee obtains a legally enforceable right to his wages or salary. Breach of contract by either side thus leads to the application of civil sanctions (Kahn-Freund, 1953, p. 33).

Kahn-Freund is, however, anxious to point out that the equality the law assumes to be present in a contract is not characteristic of the employment contract:

> Typically, the worker as an individual has to accept the conditions which the employer offers. On the labour side, power is collective power. The individual employer represents an accumulation of material and human resources, socially speaking the enterprise is itself in this sense a 'collective power'. If a collection of workers (whether it bears the name of a trade union or some other name) negotiate with an employer, this is thus a negotiation between collective entities, both of which are, or may at least be, bearers of power. But the relation between an employer and an isolated employee or worker is typically a relation between a

bearer of power and one who is not a bearer of power. In its inception it is an act of submission, in its operation it is a condition of subordination, however much the submission and the subordination may be concealed by that indispensable figment of the legal mind known as the 'contract of employment' (Kahn-Freund, 1977, p. 6).

Nevertheless, the law can and almost inevitably does, in the case of labour law, set out to equalise this relationship:

> The main object of labour law has always been, and I venture to say will always be, to be a countervailing force to counteract the inequality of bargaining power which is inherent and must be inherent in the employment relationship. Most of what we call protective legislation; legislation on the employment of women, children and young persons, on safety in mines, factories, and offices, on payment of wages in cash, on guarantee payments, on race or sex discrimination, on unfair dismissal, and indeed most labour legislation altogether must be seen in this context. It is an attempt to infuse law into a relation of command and subordination (Kahn-Freund, 1977, pp. 6–7).

Kahn-Freund, however, does not allow this basic thrust of the law to cloud his view of the nature of the employment contract. Like Dworkin and Weber, but unlike Unger, Kahn-Freund is unable to forget the pivotal assumption of liberalism, namely that economic rationality presumes inequality. Consequently, there is a limit to the equalisation that law can bring to the employment contract:

> Capital resources cannot be utilised by anybody (whether the body be private or public) without exercising a command power over human beings. This is, or ought to be a commonplace. In any event I have not heard of any legal system which has sought to replace the relation of subordination by a relation of coordination. Except in a one-man undertaking, economic purposes cannot be achieved without a hierarchical order within the economic unit. Let me say it again, and let me repeat it in view of what I shall have to say now: there can be no employment relationship without a power to command and a duty to obey, that is without this element of subordination in which lawyers rightly see the hallmark of the 'contract of employment' (Kahn-Freund, 1977, p. 7).

In the United States, Selznick (who also holds a 'pluralist' position) regards law like Kahn-Freund as a secondary force in human affairs, but like Dworkin and Unger he regards it as possessing none the less a special role within them: that is,

> ...the protection of just those substantial rights which the ideal of legality is meant to protect. These include primarily all that we term civil rights, the rights of members of a polity to act as full citizens and to be free of arbitrary official power (Selznick, 1980, p. 12).

Selznick adopts a position closer to Unger's than Dworkin's in his insistence that the law does not simply provide a means whereby these rights may be protected, but represents an immanent form of social order that could displace the existing inegalitarian one. Drawing on the work of Durkheim, Mead, Piaget and Weber he argues that the increasing legalisation of all aspects of social life in industrial societies exemplifies their 'maturation' as societies within which a 'morality of cooperation' could become predominant. Within the sphere of labour law the primacy of the right to private property became increasingly anachronistic in the light of this emerging morality. Not only did private property necessitate the subordination of employees, but this subordination was increasingly hard to justify as individual ownership was replaced by joint stock ownership and competitive enterprises were replaced by oligopolistic ones (Selznick, 1980, pp. 67–72). However, other developments have created the basis upon which a new and more inclusive legal framework for industrial relations may be created, one which is consistent with the morality of cooperation. These developments have been: the bureaucratisation of the workplace as a consequence of the quest for orderly management; and the requirement to take account of human needs as a consequence of the quest for productivity. In making industrial life rule-governed these developments have opened the way for its legalisation by such as the American *Wagner Act* (1935). For Selznick the ultimate significance of this development is that:

> Legality has a strong affinity with the ideal of political democracy, and that a legal order should be seen as transitional to polity. It follows that there is latent in the law of governance a norm of participation. Due process strains to take account of all legal interests, provide opportunities for the offering of proofs

and arguments, and deepen the legitimacy of authority. These premisses invite new forms of legal and political participation. Without yielding the position that democratic forms are not to be imposed mechanically on uncongenial institutional settings, the perspective of governance sounds a note of caution and of hope: In the end, the quest for justice may be indistinguishable from the quest for civic competence and personal autonomy (Selznick, 1980, pp. 275–6).

In this concluding passage Selznick appears to travel back from the social egalitarianism implicit in the 'morality of cooperation' towards the individualism of the autonomous subject, and in much the same way as Unger does with respect to his 'ideal of a universal community'. No matter how radical the form that 'pluralism' may take, it remains a liberalism – its privileging of the individual human subject as the origin of society and therefore also the source of its limits must subvert its social desires. If 'the quest for justice ... [is] indistinguishable from the quest for civic competence and personal autonomy', then what makes this a cause for caution as well as hope is that the latter might be impossible and as a consequence so might the former. One of Selznick's starting points is the following quotation from Jefferson, which he admits is pessimistic, and in which the notion of the individual subject as the *saboteur* of all forms of social order is made explicit:

> Free government is founded in jealousy, and not in confidence, it is jealousy, and not confidence, which prescribes limited constitutions, to bind down those whom we are obliged to trust with power ... in questions of power, then, let no more be heard of confidence in man, but bind him down from mischief by the chains of the Constitution (Selznick, 1980, p. 18).

Socialist Jurisprudence and Labour Law
In neither Britain nor the United States has any developed, *theoretically* innovative critique of labour law, such as that prefigured here and attempted elsewhere (Woodiwiss, 1990a), emerged thus far among socialists. The socialist critiques that have been available up till now have concentrated their attention on the misleading accounts of the history and effects of labour law that follow from the liberal assumptions that inform both the law and most of the commentary upon it. In Britain, their starting point appears to be a reassertion of Kahn-Freund's observation concerning the funda-

mental inequality disguised by the form of the employment contract (for example Lewis, 1979). In the United States, such critiques often begin rather more abstractly by identifying labour law, along with law in general, as aspects of a generally repressive liberal ideology that has its roots in an alienation that is intrinsic to capitalism (for example Klare, 1981; 1982). On both sides of the Atlantic, the analyses that then follow tend to confine themselves to indicating the presence of inequalities that are a consequence of political class conflict and/or ideological domination. Consequently, whilst the British critics have produced a socio-political history of labour law, which says little about legal discourse (for example Lewis, 1976; Pritt, 1970; Strinati, 1982; for partial exceptions see: Collins, 1982b; Lewis, Simpson, 1981), the Americans have produced a history of post-1935 developments that says a lot about the specific discourse of labour law, but little about its relations with legal discourse in general and even less about its relations with its socio-political context (for example Atleson, 1984; Klare, 1978; Stone, 1981; for a partial exception see Tomlins, 1985).

Precisely because of the greater attention to theorisation the situation is (was?) somewhat more encouraging in some of the countries of continental Europe. In France, for example, through combining the insights to be found in the *Critique of the Gotha Programme* with those of Althusser, Edelman has been able to put the Critical Legal Theorists' point about legal alienation far more rigorously by arguing that the employment contract does not simply disguise an inequality between employer and employee, but is a necessary product of the separation that defines and differentiates capital and labour-power. In other words, because it is the capital/labour relation in general which is the source of the inequality and not the specific employer/employee relations, *it is the employment contract itself that is unequal rather than any distribution of rights within it:*

> ...We can see now that the power which the bourgeois can accord the union cannot exceed these limits. We can see more clearly that this power can be exercised only on condition that no further issue be made of the labour contract, the right of ownership, and the man into the bargain (Edelman, 1979, pp. 53–4).

In this way, then, the antagonistic class relations of capitalist society are not simply invoked as the context of labour law, as they have tended to be by Anglo-American socialist writers, but are argued to be constitutive of it. There are problems, additional to its dependence on the figure of fetishism, with the overall structure of Edelman's argument, which will be discussed below. However, what is immediately important is that his work enables one to show how the pluralist position, in the end, universalises a set of production relations that are in fact specific to a particular mode of production. By focusing on the terms of the contract, pluralism reinforces the contract's integrity. By simply contextualising the contract, the Anglo-American critical jurists make the means by which labour law might be transformed impossible to imagine, except as part of a revolutionary scenario. Disappointingly, this last point may also be made in criticism of Edelman himself, albeit for different reasons. It will be assumed here, however, that this does not have to be the case.

Edelman grasps that labour law is an ideological construct articulated with particular economic relations. He does not appear to understand, however, that these economic relations need not be a single coherent unity. Consequently, he argues that they and labour law can only change significantly if they change totally. By contrast, if one agrees that law and economic relations are so articulated, but not that the economy is necessarily a unity, then one may argue that labour law also need not be a unity and that significant changes need not be total ones. However, whilst it may be possible that the law and the economy may vary independently of one another, this text does not intend to support what Hindess and Hirst (1977) have claimed is their 'necessary non-correspondence'. On the contrary, it is intended to argue that any effective movement in a socialist direction in either the legal or economic spheres depends upon it being secured in both spheres simultaneously; that is, upon a necessary and enforced correspondence, similar in its closeness to that which, for example, eventually crystallised around capitalist production relations in England and the United States in the middle of the nineteenth century. In order to make this argument with the required rigour, certain conceptions of law as a discourse, of the state and of the relation between them are necessary, but have not as yet been set out in this text. To end this chapter, the work of two Swedish jurists, Abrahamson and Brostrom, will be outlined since they present a substantively if not theoretically similar argument.

The purpose of Abrahamson and Brostrom's *The Rights of Labour* (1980) was to construct a jurisprudential basis for the gradual socialisation of Swedish industry that was prefigured in 'the Meidner Plan'. According to this plan, which has now been passed into law in a less radical form, Wage Earner Funds controlled by the unions would gradually acquire majority shareholdings in the larger companies. In itself, this development would not transform the affected companies into socialist producers' associations, although it would be accompanied by the activation of already existing but hitherto unclaimed participation rights. However, such companies would also not remain companies in the current legal sense, since, for example, the dualistic shareholding structure involves qualifying profitability as the pre-eminent criterion against which responsibility to shareholders should be judged. The problem that socialist jurists consequently face is: how may whatever criteria labour invokes be made legally sustainable? Or in Swedish legal terminology, how may labour gain the position of 'mandator' or possessor of ownership rights?

Very briefly, Abrahamson and Brostrom's answer to these questions is to propose the establishment by constitutional amendment of a set of labour rights, which should be privileged relative to private property rights. The reasoning behind this, following Marx's labour theory of value, is that labour alone creates value, that capital is nothing but stored-up, dead labour. Although the two jurists do not explicitly say this, it seems that the passage of such a constitutional amendment is considered to be a necessary prerequisite to both the establishment of the Wage Earner Funds and the taking up of the participation rights already on the statute book, since without it these might have the same incorporative effects as do the contemporary West German co-determination laws. By contrast, with such an amendment in place, the contract of employment itself would be radically changed as well as the distribution of rights within it. Moreover, remembering Marx's strictures against 'equal rights', such a set of entitlements would be profoundly unequal, since if enforced they would gradually undermine any rights of capital, in the pursuit of the material equality of need-fulfilment. Finally, through privileging in this way the social condition of material equality, on the basis of the conception of the capitalist economy contained within the labour theory of value, such labour rights would represent the valorisation of a particular socio-economic structure rather than that of any notion of human nature.

5 A New Theory of Law

Marx and Engels wrote a great deal about the nature of law, although not as much as about its relation to the wider society. However, as in all areas apart from the economy, they provided little in the way of systematic theory (Cain and Hunt, 1979). Of the many points they made, two appear to have been the most influential. Both, not surprisingly, were very general and therefore have required considerable critical elaboration before anything like an adequate theorisation of law's role in capitalist societies could be developed. The first was that the institutions of the law are elements of the state structure and because the state is but the 'executive committee of the bourgeoisie' they are used by the latter to advance their interests. The second was that legal concepts are ideological categories and that because 'the ruling ideas of a period are the ideas of the ruling class' the use of these concepts causes people to think about their behaviour and act in terms that, again, advance the interests of the bourgeoisie. The first of these ideas was initially taken up and elaborated by Renner in his book *The Institutions of the Private Law and their Social Function*. The second was not taken up until somewhat later when Pashukanis wrote his *Law and Marxism: a General Theory*. Unfortunately, as will be indicated below, the separate development of these two themes has had negative consequences from which Marxist jurisprudence has yet to recover entirely.

Renner: Law, State and Production

Renner's core idea was that although formal legal categories were themselves abstract and neutral, a position shared with the legal positivists, their deployment at the behest of the bourgeoisie meant that their content corresponded to the latter's interests and changed with them. Thus he argued that the basic elements of what was to become bourgeois law reflected the requirements of the earliest widespread form of commodity production; that is, simple or petty commodity production, which is independent production for sale without the use of wage-labour and is most often exemplified by the family farm or the artisan's workshop. With the subsequent rise of capitalism, especially factory capitalism, he argued that these basic elements had their content changed to suit the new demands of capitalist commodity producers. The main points in Renner's analysis are concisely illustrated with reference to the employment relation in the following extract from Kahn-Freund's introduction:

Property, then, the central institution of private law, fulfilled, in the system of simple commodity production, the functions of providing an order of goods, and, in part, an order of power. It did so without any essential aid from other institutions. It was not, however, able, to guarantee for any length of time an order of labour. Outside labour was increasingly used by the independent artisans, and this was regulated not by the law of property itself, but by complementary norms, norms which were at first derived from public gild law, and subsequently from the law of free employment. It is at this point that the order of simple commodity production starts to break up, and the functional transformation of private law, and of the law of property in particular, begins.

The law of property was substantially the same in 1900 as in 1600, but what had become of its social functions. Did it still provide an order of production? No: the producer now worked in another man's house, with another man's tools. The producer was still the detentor of the raw materials, the means of production, the finished products, but they were no longer 'his'. Ownership was no longer capable of expressing the order of goods.

Did it, then, fulfil its function to regulate consumption? No, the man still 'occupied' the house in which he lived, but he occupied it as a tenant. The furniture which he 'held' and used was, perhaps, hired under a hire-purchase contract. The house, the family, had long ceased to be a universal unit of consumption. The children were educated in schools, the sick cared for in hospitals, the old and invalid in homes.

The *universitas rerum* of the 'house', that microcosm of tangible objects which had been the substratum of the property norm, had been torn asunder, but the norm survived the destruction of its substratum. The single pieces – things – which had been the constituting elements of a functional entity had been – in the

Marxist sense – 'expropriated'. Each object – land, house, means of production, commodities for consumption – followed its own destiny.

The things which a man owns are no longer held together by a common function. Nothing except the fact of ownership itself links them together. If and in so far as, they are consumers' goods – a dwelling house and garden, an allotment, furniture etc. – they 'belong' to their owner not only in the legal, but also in the functional sense. But the bulk of all the things which are privately owned have no intrinsic connection with the proprietor at all. They happen to belong to him – legally – they would function just as well if they belonged to someone else. From his point of view their sole object is to be a title, to profits, a title to interest, a title to rent ... The property object has become capital (Renner, 1949, pp. 26–7).

In sum, then, the concept of property was initially very broad. If one owned one's own house/workshop one could determine: (a) what should be produced; and (b) how any surplus created should be consumed. As a result, in Renner's terms, the concept of property contained both an 'order of power' and an 'order of goods'. Subsequently, however, under capitalism the concept of property on its own allowed the owner of the means of production only the right to draw a profit. It soon ceased to define an order of labour since for this a contract of employment was required, albeit initially of the most primitive oral kind. Nor did it define an order of goods, since it was up to wage-earners themselves and the state to determine how goods should be consumed, although they were still bought out of the proceeds of production. In this way, then, Renner argued that law as a 'common will' imposed by the state changes as the forms of production change in an 'evolutionary' and 'organic' way, but with increasing positive help from the state (ibid., pp. 45–8, 292–8). The state therefore mediates between the economy and the law, so that those who dominate the economy, control the state and determine the content of the law, which in turn regulates the economy.

Pashukanis: Law, Ideology and the Market

Pashukanis found little to disagree with in Renner's work except his positivist assumption that legal categories were in themselves neutral containers, which only served the bourgeoisie because of the context in which they were produced and the content that was therefore given to them. Pashukanis was in no way a legal positivist since he shared Marx's conviction as to whose progeny the ruling ideas of a period were. At the centre of his work was Marx's concept of fetishism, which underpins this presentation of its main thesis:

> Whereas the commodity acquires its value independently of the will of the producing subject, the realisation of its value in the process of exchange presupposes a conscious act of will on the part of the owner of the commodity, or as Marx says:
>
> Commodities cannot themselves go to market and perform exchange in their own right. We must, therefore, have recourse to their guardians, who are the possessors of commodities. Commodities are things, and therefore lack the power to resist, man. If they are unwilling, he can use force; in other words, he can take possession of them.
>
> It follows that the necessary condition for the realisation of the social link between people in the production process – reified in the products of labour and disguised as an elementary category (*Gesetzmassigkeit*) – is a particular relationship between people with products at their disposal, or subjects whose 'will resides in those objects'.
>
> That goods contain labour is one of their intrinsic qualities; that they are exchangeable is a distinct quality, one solely dependent on the will of the possessor, and one which pre-supposes that they are owned and alienable.
>
> At the same time, therefore, that the product of labour becomes a commodity and a bearer of value, a man acquires the capacity to be a legal subject and a bearer of rights. The person whose will is declared as decisive is the legal subject ...
>
> If objects dominate man economically because, as commodities, they embody a social relation which is not subordinate to man, then man rules over things legally, because, in his capacity as possessor and proprietors, he is simply the personification of the abstract, impersonal, legal subject, the pure product of social relations, in Marx's words:
>
> In order that these objects may enter into relations with each other as commodities, their guardians must place themselves in relation to one another as persons whose will resides in those objects, and must behave in such a way that each does not appropriate the commodity of the other, and alienate his own, except through an act to which both parties consent. The guardians must therefore recognise each other as owners of private property (Pashukanis, 1978, pp. 112–14).

For Pashukanis, then, the origin of rights was not some primordial social contract, as it is for liberal jurisprudence, but the emergence of commodity production and in particular the fact that guaranteed and predictable exchange is necessary if surplus value is to be realised as profit, if capital is to be accumulated. The conclusion that he drew from this was rather different from that derived above from Marx's *Critique of the Gotha Programme*. In his view all legal concepts based upon and articulating rights are intrinsically bourgeois. More radically still, he argues that in so far as rights are constitutive of law then law in itself is inherently bourgeois and has no place in communist if not in socialist society; as he says: 'We can therefore come to a conclusion opposite to Karner [Renner, A.W.], that "norms change and their social function remains the same"' (ibid., 1980, p. 87).

Although Pashukanis understands, unlike Renner, that ideology itself is constitutive of society and that legal categories are not disembodied fictions available for any interpretation, he shares with Renner an analytically disabling reductionism carried over from Marx's initial positions. The difference being that whilst Pashukanis reduces directly from the form of law to the economy or more precisely the market, Renner reduces from the content of law indirectly through the state to the economy or in his case production relations. The reason Pashukanis performs his particular reduction may, not surprisingly, be found in his dependence on the concept of 'fetishism' (cp Fine, 1984) that Marx deployed in *Capital*, which, as has been indicated already, presents ideology as a set of illusory representations generated by a real essence, namely the economy. A critique of representationalism might have allowed Pashukanis to avoid reductionism and thereby have enabled him to combine his insistence on the intrinsic effectivity of ideology with Renner's insistence on the independence of at least the forms of legal ideology; that is, his epistemological realism could then have resulted in the preservation and transformation of the product of Renner's positivism.

However, it did not and the points behind raising the possibility are twofold: first, to bring out what remains positive about these two classics after all the criticisms have been made; second, to suggest that the reason for this non-event is deeper than it might at first appear. What remains positive are the notions of law as real and law as possessing at least some measure of autonomy. The only problem is that the two notions existed separately and in opposition to one another. The reason for this separation and opposition is not only their origin in different insights of Marx's, but also their shared supposition of a preconstituted subject as the object of law. Pashukanis considered law a fetish and therefore as constraining in relation to this subject, whilst Renner considered it to be neutral. Either way, the preconstituted subject provides an otherness and a set of criteria against which law may be judged as good or bad. The difference between Pashukanis and Renner is in the end that the former judged the law to be bad, whilst the latter judged it to be good, each in relation to their particular and barely articulated conceptions of human nature. If one thinks of human nature as essentially flawed, as it seems Renner did, then law must be good, since humanity's constraint is necessary. If, on the other hand, one thinks of human nature as intrinsically good, as it seems Pashukanis did, then law must be bad since humanity's constraint is unnecessary.

It is only through refusing the notion of an originating subject that rights as 'capacities sanctioned by law' (Hirst, 1980, p. 104) may be distinguished from natural rights and thereby preserved as a necessary element in socialist legality. In the same way, this refusal will allow a conception of law as real and as possessing some independence. This is the refusal, as was made clear earlier, that since Althusser's *For Marx* (1969) has powerfully affected contemporary Marxism and thereby allowed, after a considerable lapse of time, the critical continuation and elaboration of Pashukanis and Renner's work. Of course, the denial of the humanistic originating subject is not the only difference between contemporary and classical Marxism that is relevant to the analysis of law. Also pertinent are the reformulation of the two propositions from which they started: that is, that the judicial system is part of the state apparatuses and as such an instrument of the bourgeoisie, and that the law is an aspect of the dominant ideology and hence serves only the interests of the bourgeoisie.

The State and the Ideological Realm in Democratic Capitalist Societies

Although the state and ideology are still theorised by Marxists as securing the conditions of capital's existence, these relationships are today most frequently understood as tendential rather than necessary. This is because, whether one looks at Poulantzian (1980), neo-Gramscian (Buci-Glucksmann, 1980), Capital Logic Theory (Holloway, Picciotto, 1978) or especially at the 'post-Marxism' of such as Laclau and Mouffe (see above, pp. 64–72), the state and ideology are understood to be relatively autonomous in relation to the economy. The basis upon which this new understanding has been reached in relation to ideology has already been set out at some length in the introduction and Part II of the present text. Little has been said about how it has been reached in relation to the state. At the end of his definitive review of the pertinent studies, Jessop has summarised the achievements of recent Marxist state theory with the following list of substantive propositions:

> Firstly, the state is a set of institutions that cannot, *qua* institutional ensemble, exercise power.
>
> Secondly, political forces do not exist independently of the state: they are shaped in part through its forms of representation and forms of intervention.
>
> Thirdly, state power is a complex social relation that reflects the changing balance of social forces in a determinate conjuncture.
>
> Fourthly, state power is capitalist to the extent that it creates, maintains, or restores the conditions required for capital accumulation in a given situation and it is non-capitalist to the extent that these conditions are not realised (Jessop, 1982, p. 221).

Thus, in their different ways, each school may be seen to have converged on a conceptualisation of both the state and ideology as arenas of struggle, which, whilst they are predominantly structured to the advantage of the embodiments of capital, are not entirely or automatically so structured, and therefore do not totally exclude the embodiments of other classes or social groups from either state power or ideological effect. One result of this has been an additional convergence between Marxist and non-Marxist conceptions of the nature of contemporary democratic capitalist societies. The nature of the social relations implicit in and valorised by Marxist and non-Marxist jurisprudence may be very different, but this does not mean that nothing the latter have had to say about the law is of interest to Marxists. On the contrary, because the last convergence casts a more favourable light on some non-Marxist rather than Marxist means of understanding such societies, the presumption must be that those who have continued the liberal tradition have much to say that is of interest. The problem is to decide what this is and how it may be synthesised with that which retains its validity in the Marxist tradition.

Consistency and the Law

Both the liberal and the Marxist traditions have long agreed that legal discourse in democratic capitalist societies is marked by an internally dominant concern to achieve consistency. What they disagree on is why this should be. The liberal suggestion is that it reflects the law's social neutrality, whilst the Marxist one is that it reflects the law's capital-serving role. Thus the particular point at which the intellectual dissonance caused by the combination of empirical convergence and continuing theoretical divergence is most apparent is not, as it happens, one that is only newly visible. However, it is nevertheless the case that the goal of synthesising the otherwise very divergently produced explanations involved has only recently become an achievable one. And again, as in the previous part, it will be argued here that this is because of the theoretical possibilities created by non-humanist and non-representationalist modes of theorising as well as, more substantively, by the concept of discourse itself. The consistency of democratic capitalist law is, then, what this chapter will now attempt to understand anew, whilst at the same time creating the means whereby the non-human objects of legal discipline may be discovered.

The clearest and strongest contemporary source for the liberal claim that consistency for its own sake is the dominant internal object of the law may be found in the work of Christie (1969; 1982). Arguing in a refreshingly unapologetic way within the terms of positivist discourse, Christie is concerned to elaborate a conception of law that is logically more defensible than the normative ones that have found favour with such as Dworkin. He begins his argument by stating that the only allowable legal substances are 'those marks on paper called statutes and cases', and that:

> ....the primary social purpose of the judicial process is deciding disputes in a manner that will, upon reflection, permit the loser as well as the winner to feel that he has been fairly treated ... this goal requires that courts grant the parties the right to present proofs and reasoned arguments to them *and* that the courts squarely meet the proofs and reasoned arguments addressed to them by the parties (Christie, 1982, p. 61).

Given his critical intent, the problem he has to overcome is: how can the judicial process just described move from 'those marks on paper' to making decisions in new cases without invoking such 'chimerical' entities as 'rules of law', Dworkin's principle of 'equality of concern and respect' or even 'the rule of law'? Christie's answer to this question is to propose the following model of and for legal argument:

> The model requires that anyone who wishes to use a statute in the course of legal reasoning gives what he believes to be the paradigm case or cases covered by the statute. 'Presenting a paradigm case' does not mean divining the 'true meaning' of the statute – the model makes no such demand – but only presenting a case as to which it is asserted that, whatever else *may also* be covered by the statute, this case *is*. The party must then argue that the instant case is or is not significantly different from *any* such paradigm case (Christie, 1982, p. 65).

The insistence on 'presenting a paradigm case' and specifying 'significant differences' as the critical moments of juridical argument thus produces consistency as the constitutive object of law. In terms of the present text the problem with Christie's argument is not so much that what he is describing is abstract and an ideal rather than the actuality, since a defensible form of the former produced within the dominant legal discourse is precisely what is being sought. Rather, it is that he positivistically believes that the pursuit of consistency exhausts the juridical process (cp Langdell, below p. 137). In the end, this is because he shares the humanism of Weber and of course liberal jurisprudence generally, only in his case the critical quality is not the subject's rationality but its *desire* for consistency, which on an humanistic reading of Freud is said to originate in a need to avoid anxiety. Thus, ultimately and teleologically, the law achieves autonomy because it more than any other social institution realises a critical human need:

> ... for some of us and on occasion even for most of us, the short-term interest in not appearing ridiculous by behaving inconsistently forces us, however reluctantly, to practise what we preach, that is, to behave consistently (Christie, 1982, p. 33).

Powerful though the discursively produced strain towards consistency may be in relation to the law, it is only ever imperfectly achieved because of the specificity of the objects its component discourses define for themselves and because of the differing polit-

ical, economic and indeed other ideological conditions of their existence. For example, the term 'contract' is used in family,
commercial and labour law, but clearly the discursive and extra-
discursive realities addressed by these different branches of law are
very different, which results in the 'patterns of occurrence' in which
the term appears and therefore its meanings exhibiting considerable
differences. Moreover, these differences will be overdetermined by
additional differences at the level of conditions of existence; that is,
the relevant political, economic and other ideological conditions
may exhibit differentially developed oppositions and/or conflicts
that will further affect the 'patterns of occurrence' within which the
term occurs. It is for these reasons that the 'chimera' Christie seeks
to exclude and their attendant and necessarily 'rhetorical' arguments must inevitably be part of the juridical process – they record
the existence of such oppositions as well as the outcomes of their
attendant conflicts.

Nevertheless, despite the practical impossibility of achieving a
total closure of the signifying hiatus and the hoped-for level of
consistency, the point remains that the autonomy of law is much
less than that of literature. There are reasons for this that remain to
be discussed, which go beyond the general ones given above and
whose provision will facilitate the completion of the explanation as
to why consistency is the primary, internally produced discursive
object of law. (It should be noted in advance that, again, these
reasons represent an acceptance by a Marxist of an originally non-
Marxist idea.) Put briefly, these further reasons revolve around the
special relationship that exists between the discourses of law and
the apparatuses of the state. The point is made by Edelman as
follows:

> 'The doubly speculary structure of ideology', that is, this double
> mirror-structure assures the functioning of juridical ideology. On
> the one hand, the subject in law exists in the name of the law,
> that is, the law gives him his power. Better, law gives right the
> power to give itself a power. On the other hand, the power law
> has given right returns to law. The power of right is none other
> than the power of subjects in law. The Subject recognises itself in
> the subjects. The power, ownership, recognises itself in the
> power, the State. Ideologically, the State operates the place that in
> the Middle Ages devolved on to the Church. The constitution of a
> State subject in law assures the functioning of juridical ideology
> (Edelman, 1979, pp. 33–4).

It is elaborated upon by Poulantzas (1980, pp. 76–92) when he argues that what in turn gives this mutually necessary relationship between law and the state its particular character is the fact that within it the law also represents 'the code of organised public violence'; that is, the state as possessor of 'a monopoly of legitimate force' normally determines whether punishment is to be meted out or not through the processes and in terms of the discourses of law. However, as he further says, 'the activity, role and place of the state stretch a very long way beyond law and judicial regulation', with the consequence that in some situations and especially 'exceptional' ones (Poulantzas, 1974) the law is inoperative. For this reason, then, notwithstanding the autonomy of its discourses, the law as an institution in the state is subordinate to the state as an ensemble of institutions. In sum:

> State-monopolised physical violence permanently underlies the techniques of power and mechanisms of consent: it is inscribed in the web of disciplinary and ideological devices; and even when it is not directly exercised, it shapes the materiality of the social body upon which domination is brought to bear (Poulantzas, 1980, p. 8).

In so strongly asserting the significance of the originally Weberian conception of the state as the possessor of 'a monopoly of legitimate force' for an appreciation of its role in capitalist social formations, Poulantzas is developing an explicit critique of a very influential idea contained in the later work of Foucault. This idea is crystallised by Foucault in the following terms:

> It is the economy of discourses, I mean their *intrinsic technology*, what they need in order to function, the tactics they launch, the power effects that underpin them and that they carry – it is that and not the system of representations that determines the fundamental characteristics of what they say (Foucault, 1979, p. 92 – emphasis added).

In other words Foucault is attempting to specify what he previously took for granted, namely how exactly discourse has its effects. His answer is, through its 'power' or through the discipline it imposes upon those it interpellates. The conclusion that he ultimately draws from this is that power is very dispersed, that it is wherever discipline is and therefore wherever discourse is. He argues that failure to recognise this dispersal of power has led not simply to a neglect of a critically important 'micro-physics of power', but also to many theories of power, such as that contained in Marxism, remaining trapped by an overcentralised and legalistic/juridico-discursive conception. It is this radical decentralisation of power that Poulantzas objects to and why he lays such emphasis on the state's monopolisation of legitimate force as indicating the necessity of centralisation, the critical importance of law and the materiality of their joint dominance through their possession of enforcement powers over 'the social body'.

It will be agreed here that the state/law relation is a special one, wherein the state's monopoly of force and the law's codification of the use of this force both justifies a relatively centralised conception of power and in part explains why the closure of the signifying hiatus should be particularly marked within the discourses of law. However, although Marxism is committed to the privileging of the state and law in matters of power because of its acknowledged discursive structure, irrespective of any unacknowledged monarchism, there seems to be no reason to accept Poulantzas' total rejection of Foucault's 'micro-physics of power'. At least two of Focault's contributions in this area ought to be retained in any attempt to construct a non-humanist sociology. The first is his profoundly important realisation that power, like language and discourse, may be conceptualised as an inherent property of social relations rather than as the product or property of individuals or institutions. The second is his suggestion that discourses have their effects through the discipline that inheres in successful interpellation achieved against the resistances produced in subjects by the always present other discourses (see Minson, 1980).

Transpositioning: State Power, Discourse and the Disciplinary Role of the Law

The view taken here is that, without the conception of power as 'discipline-against-resistance', one is left arguing either that discourses have their effects spontaneously by their very presence, or that, as Poulantzas implies, they have their effects only at the behest of the state and law. In the latter case, discursive change must always be *waiting* on changes at the level of the state and law, changes that are themselves understood regressively as reflexes in relation to developments in the economy, 'in the social division of labour and the relations of production' (Poulantzas, 1980, p. 86). In the former case the process of discursive change becomes very hard to understand if one cannot examine the intrinsic technologies of discourses as they clash as a necessary aspect of the continuous process that is interpellation. The final benefit seen here in the notion of 'discipline-against-resistance' as the power of discourse is one that, although it follows from the associated recognition of the dispersal of power, paradoxically resides elsewhere. Specifically, in the contribution it makes to understanding the reasons for the relative closure of the signifying hiatus in legal discourse and for the privileging of this discourse in relation to others. As Palmer and Pearce argue in their Marxist reading of Foucault:

> There is nothing in Foucault's position to lead to a denial of the existence of the juridical relation ... Foucault's analysis operates at a different level: the liberties only function, he says, because the disciplines create citizens in the appropriate mould, and therefore the existence of the juridical relation is only formal. The question then becomes this: is this 'formal' existence merely epiphenomenal and therefore deprived of any efficacity? ... What space does this leave for the juridical relation within Foucault's conception of power? It is this: that *the juridical relation operates as the point at which a given individual shifts his position within the disciplinary network, in other words that in the juridicial relation is defined the moment at which the disciplinary network needs the reinforcement of exclusion. The moment at which surveillance takes the form of incarceration* (Palmer, Pearce, 1984, pp. 376–7, emphasis added).

Noting that Palmer and Pearce are specifically discussing the criminal law, nevertheless two very important general points may be developed which follow from their reading and which make it possible to build on Kahn-Freund's point about the law being 'a secondary force in human affairs' (above p. 93). First, the privileging, if this is now the right word, of legal discourse may be explained rather than asserted. And this on the basis that it does not displace or substitute itself for the other discourses, but *provides a means whereby the objects of legal interest may be shifted from position to position within a particular disciplinary network*. In other words, it is necessary to the reproduction of the whole disciplinary network in a way that the others are not. Second, the relative closure of the signifier/signified gap and in turn the demand for consistency and calculability may be understood practically rather than abstractly as a necessary consequence of the *transpositioning* place of law within a disciplinary network, regardless of whether the required change of position is between or within discourses.

The meaning of 'transpositioning' will be specified further and elaborated on below, but first the concept's genealogy will be outlined in a little more detail. First, the conclusions reached by two other contemporary, British Marxist theorists will be briefly excerpted and contrasted. Hugh Collins concisely encapsulates the problems posed for Marxists by trying to overcome difficulties within an unregeneratedly reductionist framework in the following words:

> The idea that laws reflect existing patterns of social arrangements is an interesting and suggestive theory. Yet terms such as 'determines', 'expresses', or 'arises' tend to restate the problem of defining how the base influences the superstructure rather than providing an adequate solution to it (Collins, 1982b, p. 24).

His own solution is:

> The special quality of law ... is that, once a formal legal rule has been announced, it often appears to subsume the existing customs within itself, for members of the society look henceforth to the legal rule rather than the customary practices for guidance ...The law is a metanormative phenomenon because it overlays and swallows up existing standards of conduct... The origin of legal rules is found, according to Marxism, in the dominant ideology as it is represented in customary standards of behaviour. The content of the law is determined by this dominant ideology and therefore legal rules are superstructural in form. Nevertheless the metanormative quality of law then places the legal rules in the position of closely regulating the relations of production, to the extent of being the sole institution giving them concrete form and detailed articulation. Thus law is superstructural in origin but because of its metanormative quality it then may function in the material base (ibid., pp. 87–9).

As is clear from the quotation, and as Collins himself acknowledges, all he has done is 'weaken the topological metaphors' (ibid., p. 87) rather than abandon them. Economic determinism remains the inevitable explanatory principle wherever these metaphors occur, no matter in how weakened a form, and has the same empirically and historically unsupportable consequences. As just one example, Sugarman has made the point that in nineteenth–century England,

... the use of legal formalities did not, of necessity, engulf the parties concerned in the paraphernalia of the legal system. The use of legal formalities such as a contract or trust deed might be utilised as tools to secure a good deal of autonomy from the legal order ... (Sugarman, 1983, p. 216).

Despite the theoretical conservatism of Collins' framework, the idea of law as 'metanormative' remains highly suggestive as to how law and the wider structures of ideology are linked. In Collins' own use of the idea its potential is obscured by its combination with a particular reading of what has been termed 'the dominant ideology thesis' (cp Abercrombie, Hill, Turner, 1982), whereby the dominant ideology is considered to be the product of a single class, the bourgeoisie. (It should be noted, however, that there is another reading of the same thesis that does not make this assumption and which sees the dominant ideology as being the product of many classes and other social groups but articulated in such a way as to bespeak the hegemony of the bourgeoisie, see Therborn, 1984, Woodiwiss 1990b.) Collins also, perhaps merely by default, assumes an automaticity in the transformation of bourgeois 'standards of behaviour' into legal rules and as a consequence has no means of explaining the variability as to its significance that Sugarman has drawn attention to.

Nevertheless, on the basis of Collins' lead and forewarned by Sugarman's discovery of law's varying social pertinence, what will now be outlined are the results of an effort to specify the mechanism of metanormative transformation that avoids replication of the one-class version of the dominant ideology thesis, whilst allowing the possibility of hegemony (Laclau, 1977, passim). It does not assume any automaticity in the transformation of ideology into law nor does it assume that the role of law is primarily to regulate production.

The net result, then, of reflecting upon these recent writings is that the traditional Marxist conception of law and its role in democratic capitalist societies may be restated as follows: the law is a set of state-enunciated discourses which interpellates the subjects it addresses in such a way that they will be law-abiding, provided that the same subjects do not successfully resist this disciplining because of prior or other interpellations produced by counter-discourses. In this way, and as was exemplified in Chapter 3 by reference to the role of the labour law in production, the law may be understood to produce a background 'ideology effect' that helps to maintain the security of the social relationships that the state may reproduce and that may also be reproduced in other ways. A second and more innovative conclusion is that, once the law is understood as a set of discourses it is possible to be more specific about the precise means whereby law produces this 'ideology effect', upon which it, in turn, largely depends for its own power. In order to draw these conclusions, one has to define: the mode of interpellation specific to the law; the nature of its 'intrinsic technology'; and the distinguishing characteristics of its discursive structure. The remainder of this chapter will expand upon these points.

As an interpellative structure, the law places the subjects it addresses in particular positions relative to one another and itself according to the schema to be found in its component discourses. These positions are constituted by the rights and duties that define them and which therefore determine the relations that can or should exist between them (for example husband/wife, employer/employee and citizen/state). Now, of course, such positions and such relations are also defined and confined by other discursive and non-discursive positionings apart from those specific to the law (for example in relation to husband and wife, by religion, economic and psychological interdependencies, and even, regrettably, sometimes by physical force). As a consequence, legal discourses possess a varying substantive content according to which sets of non-legal positionings they refer to. The pertinence of these positions being defined in law is that, when the disciplinary balances achieved by these other means break down, they *may* be reinforced, mediated or terminated by invoking the law. More particularly, given the law's intrinsic technology, this reinforcement takes the form of a discursive, and sometimes non-discursive (that is, where some form of physical constraint or distraint is involved), *compulsory transpositioning* so as to effect an exclusion of other mechanisms. By 'involuntary transpositioning' I mean a transformation of rights, duties and therefore social relations more generally that cannot be gainsaid by another state institution, or in terms of any other official discourse, except under conditions laid down by the law itself.

Thus the legal positivists' point about law's prerogative character may be accepted, but without incurring the problems that follow from having, as a consequence, to regard all laws as commands. Once the law is understood to consist of a variety of discourses that vary with the extra-legal conditions to which they refer, the temptation to reduce all laws to a single mode of discourse with a single relation to their subjects may be easily resisted. As a consequence, whilst accepting the prerogative character of the law, various modes of transpositioning may be distinguished according to the basis upon which the legal subject becomes liable to the disciplines that the discourses represent. That is, according to whether this basis is provided by: (a) *proactive positionings*, which are those rights and duties that are involuntarily assumed by legal subjects, as in constitutional and criminal law; (b) *enactive positionings*, which are those rights and duties which have to be consciously accepted and/or actively invoked before they may have an effect, as in much of the civil law; (c) *simul-active positionings*, as in tort law, whereby a judicially fashioned 'general standard of care' is proactively imposed upon all legal subjects, but may or need only be invoked under certain enactive conditions, given the qualifications and exceptions that have been judicially and statutorily attached to it. Further, two sub-types of the primary modes of positioning may be distinguished: (a) *repositionings*, whereby subjects gain positions they had not previously held and so alter their pre-existing positionings – as in attaining the age of majority (proactive), getting married, the purchase of property, the entering of a contract (all enactive) and in offering a service (simul-active); and (b) *depositionings*, whereby the subjects cease to occupy the positions they previously held and so, again, alter their pre-existing positionings – as in imprisonment (proactive), divorce, the sale of property, the discharge of a contractual obligations (all enactive) and satisfactorily performing a service (simul-active). In sum, the interactive, discursive and non-discursive effects of these modes and varieties of positionings make up the legal dimension of the disciplinary network in democratic capitalist societies.

The Need for Closure and Consistency

As was indicated earlier the very possibility of legal transpositioning requires that legal discourse, unlike literature (Derrida, 1977) and dreams (Lacan, 1977), exhibits a relative closure of the signifying hiatus and a consequent consistency in its use of concepts. Without such characteristics, the law could not exist. I would therefore maintain, contrary to Christie (1982) and closer to Weber (1978, Volume 2), that the law is characterised by an inherent strain towards consistency *because of its own systemic requirements as a discourse* in a determinate social location, rather than because of any needs of its human subjects. In sum, for the law to have even its background ideology-effect it must be committed at least to the goal of internal consistency as well as be consistently invoked and consistently enforced according to consistent criteria, even if only in limiting (that is, appealed) cases; otherwise it will be treated with contempt or pass into desuetude.

Having said this, a further point should be made immediately: the position proposed here is very definitely not a functionalist one. It is not part of the present argument that capitalist societies need a mechanism of specifically *legal* transpositioning, nor that the law is necessarily *the* mechanism of transpositioning. This is not to deny that the conditions appropriate to the securing of capitalist production and exchange may strongly suggest an affinity with legalistic forms, as Weber so clearly recognised. However, it is at least conceivable that, for example, religious, political or even military institutional forms and associated procedures might secure them as effectively; *vide* early Meiji Japan (Woodiwiss, 1990b). Without developing the point, it may be suggested that the adoption of a legalistic mechanism of transpositioning was overdetermined by the typically democratic polities of capitalist societies that emerged as the capitalist mode of production attained dominance within the various economies. Simplification of the economic structure would clearly enhance the appeal of consistency and indeed facilitate its achievement.[1] Similarly, the emergence of a democratic polity intensified the demands that any transpositioning should be, if possible, neutral or at least consistent. C. B. Macpherson's (1977) emphasis on the resistances encountered by those who sought to democratise capitalist societies is suggestive here. So too is the temporal proximity of the achievement of 'one *man*, one vote' and the emergence of juridical formalism, as the culmination of a double 'shift of emphasis from property to person' (Stedman-Jones, 1983, p. 103) as the prime object of reference for both political and legal discourses.

Law as the Transpositioning Discourse
In terms of the argument outlined above, law may be defined as that set of discourses which are *the* transpositioning discourses precisely because they are the discourses of closure, consistency and therefore calculability. Other discourses may exhibit more or less closure, etc but their disciplinary effects are not a consequence of their possession of these characteristics. The transpositioning place of law means that its particular and direct effects are rather more restricted and selective than is generally assumed. Developing Sugarman's point (see above, p. 115) and that contained in the

concept of 'enactive positionings', aside from circumstances where proactive positionings are involved, legal discourse only has *direct* effects where legal action is taken, and where whatever is the object or circumstance of transpositioning has been constituted in a legal discourse, whether it be a person, a commodity, a kin relationship or whatever. Outside of such situations subjects are interpellated and their relationships governed by other discourses. This is why Poulantzas's (1979, p. 92) dismissive question, 'If law is so important why is it not taught in schools?' has little force, and why I refer in what follows to the *intermittent* interpellative structure of the law.

Describing legal discourse in this way, as an abstract, *meta-discourse* with a defining impact on other discourses and therefore as an intermittently operative interpellative mechanism in relation to particular subjects, is not to imply that, when the law is invoked or enforced, its intrinsic semantic technology is sufficient in itself. Indeed, given that reinforcement of other discourses is its valued effect, to a greater degree than these other discourses, it requires articulation as an institution with the other institutions that comprise the state, and with the latter's continuing discourse of authority, which articulation accounts for many but not all (contra Goodrich, 1984, p. 187ff) of the characteristics of the discursive formation that allows its possibility. There are two specific reasons for the necessity of this articulation. The first is that only the state's monopolisation of legitimate force and its claim to authority as a continuous presence can make up for its intermittent character and thereby enable it to overcome the resistances it must encounter. The second is that, leaving aside judge-made law, only the state's representative structures, no matter how imperfect, provide a means for giving content to the discourses of the law.

In this way, then, it is possible to construct a concept of law in democratic capitalist societies that dissolves the unhelpful opposi-tions that marked the work of Renner and Pashukanis – oppositions that required one to choose, on the one hand, between ideology and the state when seeking to understand the law, and, on the other, between autonomy and materiality when deciding how it has its effects. By contrast, in the present conception, law as a transposi-tioning mechanism has materiality as a discipline and autonomy as a discourse, while as a particular ideological element it not only has materiality but also a necessary relationship to the state, which stands as the source of the power upon which its success as an inter-mittent, interpellative discourse ultimately depends.

As stated above, what is proposed, here, is a concept of law in 'democratic capitalist societies', and it is to the clarification of this latter phrase that the text will now turn. Building on the insights of Weber and Unger (see above, pp. 87), the phrase refers to all those social formations within which capitalism is the *dominant* mode of production, whether or not it is articulated with such other modes of production as feudalism, slavery or petty-commodity production (Wolpe, 1980, intro.). Its analytical import is twofold. First, it is only in such social formations that law can take the form specified above, since it is only in them that legal discourse exhibits the requisite closure and consistency and the state takes a representative form that monopolises legitimate force and so 'ensures' that consistency of application and enforcement should also be the object of the judicial and police apparatuses. Second, the content of the particular legal discourses and the precise nature of their disciplinary effects will depend upon a number of different factors, some of them familiar to Marxists, some not. These include, on the one hand, which other modes of production capitalism is articulated with, and the level of development of the various class formations; and, on the other, the existence or otherwise of any alliances between the embodiments of class formations and non-class social groups; the forms of representation and intervention specific to a particular state, including its legal institutions; the nature and structural articulation of non-legal discourses; and, finally, the balances of forces obtaining between the contending groupings created by these processes. Some aspects of the relationship of these factors to the emergence of capitalist law will be examined in the following chapter.

Conclusion: Transpositioning and the Discovery of the Non-human Objects of Legal Discourses

To conclude, in the same way that a particular legal system as an ideological and political element represents a condition of the existence of an economy, then so too economic as well as other political and ideological elements represent the conditions of existence of the legal system. It is for this reason that one has to look beyond the law if one wishes to understand fully such signifying chains as are contained in constitutions, statutes and juristic arguments, and such disciplinary effects as are exemplified by decisions to proceed or not, degrees of enforcement and even judgements themselves.

In sum, it is not simply individual agents, human or non-human, that are subject to the juridical process, or even that come before the courts, but also the discourses that bespeak the problems and solutions, hopes and fears of those who utter them. In the same way that the law intermittently adjudicates as between the rights and duties of individual agents, so it also adjudicates on the relative acceptability or otherwise and, therefore, on the wider social influence of particular discourses as well as on particular sets of political and economic relations. Thus, in the light of the concept of law here proposed, the law may be seen as even more important than is traditionally recognised. It does not simply contribute to the securing of social order by disciplining agents, but also contributes significantly to the definition of the nature of that order by allowing the defining and redefining of the social order's structure and content every time a judge makes a decision.

It is, then, because it obscures all of this that one must reject the humanism that underpins liberal jurisprudence. Moreover, it is this same humanism that, more importantly even than the law's capital-serving role (see Goodrich, 1986), accounts for the frequency of the resort to rhetorical ploys, including metaphors, in much liberal jurisprudence and everyday legal disputation. Their use is made necessary by its practitioners' struggles to overcome the limits that are thereby imposed upon their understanding, and by their struggles to maintain that commitment to consistency upon which the law's effectivity, and therefore much of its legitimacy, rests.

The present position may be summarised thus: (1) law in democratic capitalist societies has an effect because it is *the* mechanism of transpositioning (which explains its autonomy); and (2) it has specific effects because of the interaction between the transpositioning demands made on it and its own discursive development (which explains why its autonomy is always relative). In this way the endless post-Pashukanis debate (for example Grau, 1982; Jessop, 1980) over whether the forms of capitalist law should be derived from the circulatory or the productive sphere may be superseded and the essentialism as well as the reductionism present in the texts of all those who have hitherto contributed to it may be avoided.

Whatever consistency legal discourses have in democratic capitalist societies derives not from their relationship to a particular and privileged extra-discursive realm, but from their constitutive characteristics as mechanisms of transpositioning. Further, what particular activities become liable to legal transpositioning is not given in advance and is arranged in no necessary order of derivation. Instead it depends upon the outcomes of unpredictable structural transformations and the conflicts between the embodiments of the structures concerned. Thus aspects of production relations, circulatory relations, as well as kin relations have each become subject to legal discourses, but this does not indicate that they share a substantive unity. For example, the substantive rights currently granted parties to marriages, commercial and employment contracts differ greatly as a consequence of the varying impact of the structural changes that have affected them and the conflicts that have taken place around them. What shared substantive content there may be is the product of these same changes and struggles mediated through constitutions, statutes, etc.

The foundational and constitutive role of 'consistency' is what gives legal discourse its autonomy. However, 'consistency' is never a self-subsisting sign in legal or in any other form of discourse. It is always articulated with other signs which signify substantive rather than methodological principles – for example 'authority', 'liberty' or 'equality' in their multiple combinations and forms – before it can mean anything. Thus what it means, metanormatively, when so articulated will vary according to the ideological background with which it is necessarily imbricated. In other words, it is the necessity of the articulation of 'consistency' with principles and of these principles with wider ideological discourses which ensures that the autonomy of the law is always relative – relative to the extra-legal discourses enunciated by those who are the most powerful and/or the most frequent users of the law. Thus it is the requirement that the law be consistent with the principles structuring the dominant or hegemonic discourses within the wider society that represents an additional and very important criterion against which the consistency of the law may be and is routinely judged.

On this basis, and contrary to many of the substantive readings offered by Critical Legal Theorists, instances of supposed juridical inconsistency may be shown to have been otherwise (see Woodiwiss, 1990a, Chapter 4), or to have involved a repetition of well-established 'inconsistencies' between more narrowly philosophical readings of certain principles and those current in the wider ideology (see Woodiwiss, 1990a, Chapter 8). Law, no more than any other discourse, responds to the promptings of logic alone. Thus, what Dworkin has termed law's 'integrity', as well as what others have termed its 'legitimacy', readily survives, under normal circumstances, both the incompetences of its practitioners and even the infirmities of its own doctrines because it is carried along by and in itself carries the 'coherences' of the wider, dominant or hegemonic societal structures. It is only when circumstances are not normal that juridical consistency/inconsistency becomes an issue. This is because such circumstances usually include structural ferment or actual structural transformations. Under such circumstances, as the Justices of the American Supreme Court somewhat belatedly realised in the 1930s, the best policy is to drift, making as little noise as possible, until a new and clearly prevailing ideological wind picks up (see Woodiwiss, 1990a, Chapter 6).

Notes

1. I owe this point to Maureen Cain.

6 Law and the Development of Capitalism

According to the position set out in the previous chapter, what defines a legal system as 'democratic capitalist' is the juridically recognised primacy of the need for closure and consistency in its component discourses, where these have as their effect the securing of capitalist production relations and where this effect is enforced through the monopolisation of legitimate force by a representative state. What therefore will mark a legal system as non-capitalist is the absence of these three summary requirements. Thus the dating of the emergence of a system of 'democratic capitalist law' necessitates that one demonstrates the absence of these requirements before a certain date and their presence thereafter. This is the task that will be attempted for Britain and the United States, albeit schematically, in what follows.

The task of specifying the nature of the pre-capitalist (feudal) legal system and what gave it its internal discursive coherence, in the absence of a commitment to consistency for its own sake, will not be undertaken here, despite Milsom's (1981) work and Simpson's (1986, pp. 21ff) suggestion that the nineteenth century was a period in which a particular version of common law consensus broke down while the construction of a new version was attempted. Similarly, the specification of the events that mark, and the processes that account for, the monopolisation of legitimate force by the state will also be neglected, in this case because of their familiarity to anyone with even a passing knowledge of political and constitutional history. The final major omission will be the histories of the court system, the legal profession, and the techniques of prosecution, defence and judgement, all of which must be understood as aspects of an account of the pertinent rules of formation if one is to grasp fully not only the developing social role of the law but also its doctrinal evolution (but see Baker, 1979; Milsom, 1981). What will be discussed, then, are only those aspects of these rules that most directly relate to the issues of central concern in this text, namely the relationship between the securing of capitalist production relations and the presence or otherwise of a juridically recognised primacy of the need for closure and consistency in and between the component discourses of the law, that is, certain aspects of, in Foucauldian terms, the changing 'surfaces of emergence' of the objects of concern to the law, and of the changing 'grid of specification' whereby these objects are related to one another topographically.

The Problem of Periodisation in British Legal History

The pre-existing social science literature on the periodisation of legal history is characterised by a very dominant Marxist/Weberian orthodoxy, and one striking challenge, that by Macfarlane (1979). For reasons that have been summarised too many times recently (Berman, 1983, conc.; Macfarlane, 1979, Chapter 2; Sugarman, Ruben 1984), and so will not be repeated here, Marx, Weber and, unfortunately, subsequent generations of social scientists have located the transition between feudal and capitalist societies in Europe and *therefore* (the justification is seldom stronger than this, but see Tigar, Levy, 1977) between feudal and capitalist legal systems somewhere between the middles of the fifteenth and seventeenth centuries. The one major challenge to this double periodisation is that contained in Macfarlane's *The Origins of English Individualism*, wherein a strenuous effort is made to push the period of transition back in time by two or three centuries, at least for England.

As befits an approach committed to the proposition that the law's autonomy is inherent in its nature as, in part at least, a discourse, this discussion of periodisation will start from a position located outside social science (including jurisprudence) and enunciated within the law itself. The legal-historical literature most often pretends to a disinterest in such issues by contrast with its great concern with the histories of certain central, modern concepts. However, in its very constitution as a discipline, legal history unconsciously suggests a very different periodisation to that contained elsewhere in the social science literature, one which locates the occurrence of the transition from one legal system to another in the nineteenth century. In what follows an attempt will be made: (a) to uncover this unconscious periodisation; (b) to provide it with a social-scientific rationale; (c) to compare it critically with that of the Marxist/Weberian orthodoxy and its critic.

The nature of the difficulty faced by the historian of law when confronted by questions relating to periodisation has been well put by Milsom (1981, p. vi):

> It is the nature of law that what is done in the present must be congruous with the immediate past; and it is therefore in the nature of legal history that the evidence is systematically deceptive. The largest changes cannot be obvious to historians because they could not be obvious at the time.

He continues by indicating the significance of the problems thus posed for social scientists:

> Perhaps more than in other kinds of history, the historian of law is enticed into carrying concepts and even social frameworks back into periods to which they do not belong. One of the main things we have carried back is our vision of the law as a system of substantive rules having some existence separate from society and requiring separate adjustment. The legal historian scans his sources looking for changes as he would look for new or altered passages in a modern legal textbook and the social historian is consequently misled.

Apart from its critical implications for the social scientific literature, the latter passage also indicates the nature of the periodisation most often operant within the Anglo-American legal mind, namely before 'law [was thought of A.W.] as a system of substantive rules having some existence separate from society' and after, which may be put summarily as before textbooks/after textbooks. As Milsom (ibid., p. 5) goes on to say:

> Text-books of contract and tort were not written until the nine-teenth century; and nothing in the subject is so hard to reckon with as the implications of that fact.

That this dichotomy is a symptom of a periodisation is suggested by the fact that it is often used to distinguish modern from pre-modern law; that is, legal history until recently seemed almost to be defined by what was left out of textbooks, a suspicion only reinforced by the latter's almost obligatory 'historical introductions'. Reflecting the same unconscious categorisation, the more recent legal histories, in particular, frequently seem to be straining to fill in the gap between where their classical forebears left off and the textbooks begin. The existence of the watershed that the appearance of the first textbooks signified is now widely recognised. Moreover, in the course of writing the history of 'modern' law, legal historians, especially in the United States, have come to see textbooks almost as common law surrogates for codes. Consequently they have emphasised their selectivity and resultant systematicity, contrasting these features with the actual historical and indeed contemporary superabundance of decisions and the inevitable incoherences within and between them. Recent realist critics have responded to this contrast by propounding a scepticism, in terms of which the motives of the systematisers and the social role of a derived juristic 'formalism' are both questioned (for example Horwitz, 1977).

Stimulating as this stance has undoubtedly proved to be, it has unfortunately deflected attention away from the further investigation of the nature and the intrinsic legal significance of the effort at systematisation itself as an instance of a change in a 'grid of specification', and also from considering its implications for the understanding of the structural role of law. It is the latter that is the focus of the current chapter's concern, rather than 'the interest mediating' role that is of concern to the realists. This last is important, of course, but it is different from and does not substitute for a prior understanding of law's structural role. In the absence of such knowledge even contemporary, critical realists are left arguing a position (Horwitz even describes his approach as 'instrumentalist') that is very like that of vulgar Marxism, with all the criticisms this comparison implies and despite its formidable backing in terms of case law scholarship. In sum, despite the general recognition that the appearance of the first textbooks represented some kind of watershed in legal history, the full significance of this development has yet to be fully appreciated. The periodisation of legal history that it allows has been adopted, but it still lacks a social scientific rationale, which is the task to which we now turn (for a detailed critique of Macfarlane, see Woodiwiss, 1987b).

For reasons that have been alluded to earlier (see p. 57 above), Durkheim has been unjustifiably denied, even by his friends (for example Lukes, Scull, 1983), his full due as a significant contributor to the foundation of a rigorous sociology of law (for exceptions see Giddens, 1971; Hunt, 1977; Pearce, 1989). Although I do not share what Hirst (1975) refers to as Durkheim's 'elementarianism', according to which the essences of complex social systems may be found in their simpler precursors, there are nevertheless important things to be learnt from the discussions of the histories of 'property' and 'contract' that are contained in *Professional Ethics and Civic Morals* (1957). In the present context the most important of these is the significance of the reciprocal influence of 'property' and 'contract' on one another and the difference that the emergence of the concept of contract made to the meaning of property in legal discourse. (Durkheim's analysis has recently received unknowing empirical confirmation in the English context in Atiyah's work, 1979, pp. 85–90, 102–12.)

According to Durkheim something very significant happened to the meaning of 'property' in theory during the eighteenth century and in practice during the nineteenth. In the eighteenth century Locke propounded the theory, later accepted by Smith and very belatedly and by then ironically acknowledged by the United States Supreme Court (*Minnesota Rate Case*, 1890), that property is only legitimate if it is founded on labour. In the nineteenth century the emergence of the 'will theory of contract' was both made possible and, as has been explained in some detail elsewhere (Woodiwiss, 1990a, Chapter 2), confirmed by this development long before the *Minnesota Rate Case*:

> ... the bond of contract could not have had a very early origin. Indeed, men's wills cannot agree to contract obligations if these obligations do not arise from a status in law already acquired, whether of things or of persons; it can only be a matter of modifying the status and of superimposing new relations on those already existing. The contract, then, is a source of variations which presupposes a primary basis in law, but one that has a different origin. The contract is the supreme instrument by which transfers of ownership are carried through. The contract itself cannot constitute the primary foundations on which the right of contract rests. It implies that two legal entities at least are already properly constituted and of due capacity, that they enter into relations and that these relations change their constitution; that some thing belonging to the one passes to the other and vice versa (Durkheim in Lukes, Scull, 1983, p. 194).

The point to be taken here from this passage and from Durkheim's discussion of contract in general is that it was only with the emergence of contract and of the contract of employment in particular that capitalism's exploitative production relations (instances of the 'forced division of labour' for Durkheim, 1964a) became possible objects of reference for the legal system, and that the law of the market also became the law of production whether one is talking about the common or civil law systems (cp Fox, 1974, pp. 188–9). To elaborate somewhat, prior to the nineteenth century what will be called 'private property', which (contra Macfarlane) never became 'absolute' in England (see Sugarman and Ruben, 1984, p. 32ff) or on the Continent (see any of the nineteenth-century codes), gradually emerged from the twelfth century onwards as a form of legal ownership distinguishable from feudal 'dominium' (Milsom, 1981, pp. 99ff). However, it was only in the nineteenth century that this process eventuated in the appearance of a specifically capitalist (again not 'absolute') concept of private property thanks to the creation in law of the contract of employment, which belatedly recognised the social dominance of capitalist production relations relative to those of feudalism and simple commodity production.

This was also the development that finally enabled the common law to respond to the jurisprudential promptings of Austin and the provocations of Bentham and, with the help of the positivistic methodologies of both, to abandon its hitherto total dependence on the technique of reasoning by analogy that Weber (1978, pp. 655–6) termed 'merely paratactic association'. Thereafter, to use some additional Weberian terminology, its adepts began to deploy in their textbooks and elsewhere the same techniques of 'synthetic construction' that had produced the 'systematisation' that characterised the continental codes. Reasoning by analogy is only unsurpassable when events occurring within what are (or are thought to be) qualitatively different sets of relations (for example of production) are to be judged against a common standard. Hence the dependence of this mode of reasoning on what Weber himself called 'extrinsic elements', but which are possibly better expressed as 'appearances'. Where, however, such diversity (real or imagined) has ceased to exist or where the law for its own purposes either arranges the diverse set of relations in a clear hierarchy of legal centrality, or segregates them one from another, or both, dependence on 'extrinsic elements' will no longer be the exclusive resort of a system of legal reasoning. It may be supplemented by the deployment of a synthetic logic that starts from what might be called 'intrinsic elements'. Is not such a set of developments what Durkheim describes in the discussions of property and contract summarised earlier? Is there any reason for thinking that what was possible for the German Pandecticists was not possible for the common lawyers?

A Sociological Conception of Ownership and Capitalist Private Property

Before proceeding to justify the negative answer that the second of these rhetorical questions invites, a further piece of theoretical clarification is necessary, and it is one that will simplify the justification of the basis for periodisation just suggested. This clarification relates to the concept of ownership that will be used, which will be that recently proposed by Jones (1982).

Following a critique of pre-existing theories of property (for example the traditional, 'unitary' theory and the more modern 'bundle of rights' theory), which, like the present text, is premissed on an ontologically non-humanist stance, Jones produces what he calls a 'sociological typology of ownership', which allows him to distinguish far more clearly than hitherto between the forms of ownership appropriate to different sets of production relations (for example those of feudalism and capitalism), and the forms of ownership appropriate to differentially structured combinations of the same production relations (for example private ownership and corporate ownership). What enables him to do this is that he works with

a concept of ownership comprising three particular elements; elements which are, depending on the form of their articulation, more or less discrete. These elements are; title, possession and control. The relation of [private] property can be defined as the interrelation of these three elements without reference to the primacy of rights and without introducing the somewhat difficult distinction between rights, subjects and objects. Instead it is their articulation which accounts for specific forms of ownership associated with private and corporate property and not the coincidence or separation of rights and material objects (Jones, 1982, p. 76).

As I read Jones, by 'possession' he means the narrowly economic ability to determine the use or operation, as such, of the production process. By 'control', he means the ability or power to determine the actual deployment of means of production in the production process. Finally, what he means by 'title' refers to the significatory basis upon which claims to any surplus may be made, and so it is not restricted to:

the formal legal right to a claim upon a company or an estate but depends upon the sorts of calculations which govern the circulation of legal titles ... title involves the sort of calculations and conditions that govern the more general provision of finance, the socialisation of debt, the exchange of guarantees and the constitutional position of shareholders (Jones, 1982, pp. 77–8).

In the extracts given above, Jones illustrates the practical application of his concept of ownership by reference to 'private property' in a society where capitalist relations of production are dominant; that is, *that* of interest here. What Jones does not acknowledge, however, is Durkheim's point about the legal existence of such property being dependent upon the later or simultaneous existence of the 'will theory of contract'. The position taken here, therefore, is that it was the articulation of property and contract that allowed the legal recognition of distinctively capitalist modes of ownership and so finally allowed the definition of a distinctive concept of capitalist 'private property', axed, and this is Jones' critical contribution, around the primacy of possession. The latter was the relation recognised by the contract of employment, and, as the now voluminous material (for example Littler, 1982) on the capitalist labour process demonstrates, it was to be some time before this contract was extended to refer to the control relation (*vide*, the typicality of 'indirect' rather than 'direct', or what Marx termed 'formal' rather than 'real', means of control).

The net result of adopting Jones' concept of ownership, with the elaboration just mentioned, is that it allows one to define very precisely what one is looking for as one scans the historical record in search of evidence for the existence of a specifically capitalist form of private property: that is, a concept of property axed not around title, which is what Macfarlane looked for, but one axed around possession. The latter is a concept which recognises that what *primarily* concerns the capitalist is not that s/he has the legal right to buy and sell means of production, raw materials, products etc, although this is a necessary prerequisite, but that s/he has the right to organise and operate the production process without any significant, legally supported challenge or restraint from his or her employees and/or the state. The latter right is what legally allows the capitalist to be a capitalist, that is, to extract 'surplus-value' (Marx) or introduce 'formal rationality' (Weber) into the workplace. The latter right, in sum, is what legally allows 'the production of commodities by commodities' in Marx's sense and so underpins the entire capitalist economy.

The argument that capitalist private property, in the legal sense just defined, could not have existed until the nineteenth century, at first sight appears to pose a tremendous problem since no one doubts that capitalist production relations existed long before the nineteenth century. The problem disappears when, again, it is remembered that, according to the position being enunciated in this text, the sheer existence of an economic relation does not necessarily engender the existence of a legal one. Thus, at least for England, a legal system axed around different concepts of ownership (that is, feudal 'dominium' and petty commodity patriarchy) was initially more than 'good enough' to aid the reproduction of capitalist relations of production despite its far from perfect fit (for a parallel analysis of the criminal law, see D. Hay et al., 1975).

As regards feudal 'dominium', breaks in the tenurial chain of title were achieved without the chain being destroyed altogether. Nevertheless, and despite counter-developments with reference to 'settlements', the effect of these developments was sufficient to enable a market in land to develop, but without justifying any talk of the emergence of 'absolute private property'. Similarly, the loosening and even the escape from feudal possessory relations were achieved without their total destruction. Nevertheless, and this time despite the state's attempts to reimpose them (for example the *Statutes of Labourers* of 1349, 1351 and 1388), these developments were sufficient to allow those at the level of title to have consequences as regards how the land or whatever was worked but without, this time, justifying any talk of the emergence of a concept of capitalist private property. Finally, these developments at the levels of title and possession allowed the imposition of tighter methods of control than were characteristic of the manor or the feudal workshop, and this despite the efforts of guilds, sometimes the state (for example through master–servant laws) and latterly combinations to resist them.

Thus, despite the changing fortunes of those engaged in any or all of the struggles around these three sets of issues, and despite the temporal and geographical unevenness of developments with respect to each of them, *feudal* law gradually *made room for* simple commodity producers and capitalist entrepreneurs, the general trajectory of this adjustment being determined by the interplay between the defensive demands addressed to the courts by the lordly property *holders* and the assertive demands for support addressed to the courts by the newer property *owners*. Hence the latter, whether they were former lords or former serfs, whether their ancestral tenures were free or unfree, asked for support that tended to be confined to the realm of their exchanges of either property or goods and seldom related to issues arising out of production. (This, perhaps, is why the first generation of post-classical Marxists emphasised that capitalist law had its origins in exchange relations in their more substantive accounts of its developments rather than in production as their theoretical commitments might have suggested. Their history did not mislead them on this point, but their theory prevented them from realising its more general significance.) Hence also the shift in what might be called, at the risk of an accusation of teleology, the 'pre-history of contract' from the very specific early forms of tort actions ('debt', 'detinue', 'covenant' and 'account'), to the later (fourteenth to fifteenth century) more general actions ('trespass', 'trespass on the case', *indebitatus assumpsit*) and doctrines ('consideration'), which eventually coalesced in *Slade's Case* (1602) and created the beginnings of a discourse just about recognisable as what today is called 'contract'.

In these ways, and for these reasons, capitalist production relations became established, secure and ultimately socially dominant despite the absence of a specifically capitalist legal discourse, which referred directly to capitalist production relations, was based on a concept of 'private property' axed around possession, and had as its prime discursively defined object the achievement of closure and consistency within and between its component discourses. It is to the ending of this 'anomalous' situation that the first textbook writers, in the context of an increasingly representative state, both contributed and unknowingly witnessed. Elsewhere (Woodiwiss, 1987b, 1990a, Chapters 1, 2) I have described in detail the rise and fall of 'conspiracy doctrine' in the United States as this applied to trade unions, since this trajectory describes very precisely how the law of the market (especially that of contract) hesitantly but, in the end, definitively came both to enter and latterly reorder the discourses of production. In so doing it completed the restructuring (that is, by changing the 'grid of specification' to that of a 'gapless systems of rules') of the common law so that consistency might become its primary, discursively produced object and a new discursive formation might be inaugurated.

The securing of capitalist production relations was most definitely the net effect of the completion of this process, but it should not be forgotten (contra the instrumentalist historians) that the final achievement of this latter effect depended upon the *subsequent* shrinking of labourers' rights as parties to contracts – in Scotland employment contracts became known as 'minute contracts'

(Haines, 1980; Feinman, 1976) – which nicely suggests both their duration and the rights they gave to labourers. However, this too is not something that can be adequately explained by instrumentalists since, as again has been argued elsewhere (Woodiwiss, 1990a, Chapter 4; see also Merritt, 1982) the process by which this occurred, especially in the United States, was far from direct, and was in fact the product of a plethora of legal and other changes that had no immediate or intended connection with industrial relations.

In conclusion, the entry of 'contract' into the discourses of production, as the culmination of the process whereby legal discourse as a whole was restructured, was simultaneously the moment at which consistency became possible as its prime object and that at which its social relativity was made very clear: the object of consistency had to be squared with the requirements of those that most often made transpositioning demands upon the law, namely the owners of capital. That said it should not be forgotten that another very important means by which capitalist production relations were secured was by the gradual democratisation of the state. Indeed the entry of contract into the discourses of production as well, therefore, as the restructuring of legal discourse, was only possible because of this (directly and legislatively in England, indirectly and because of the exigencies arising out of electoral calculation in the United States). Thus the possibility was created also that any subsequent challenges to the substantive consistency of the law need not necessarily benefit only the owners of capital.

The Theory of Legal Transpositioning and the Relative Autonomy of the Law

In one sense at least, Horwitz (1977) is correct in describing the dominant conception of law in the antebellum United States as 'instrumentalist'; that is, in the sense that it was generally conceptualised as a problem-solving discourse. Indeed the description may be extended to England, since, after all, the common law grew out of the 'unsystematised' (in Weber's sense) but clearly instrumental 'forms of action' that Maitland (1936) latterly studied (Milsom, 1968, pp. xxvff). For this reason, its content largely and predictably corresponded to the requirements of those that made demands upon it, and, in so far as these tended to come from the propertied classes, then these classes determined its content. However, the content derivable from such demands was never exhaustive of the law, both because the embodiments of other classes, such as guildsmen, journeymen and even combinations, also made demands upon the law as plaintiffs as well as defendants, and also because legal categories gradually proved to be capable of recognising and giving satisfaction to these demands, at least to some degree. Earlier in this chapter, it was suggested that, as such discursive elements as 'property' and 'contract' became disarticulated from those that had initially expressed the claims of what might be called the 'landlord state', as they accumulated their own sets of treatises and case law, they gradually and unevenly attained a systematicity, an abstractness, and therefore an autonomy, not only from the claims of the increasingly representative and plural state, but also from the claims that lay behind the demands for the recognition of capitalist private property which had occasioned their disarticulation.

Because of these material developments, then, rather than on the basis of some 'transcendental logic of equity' (Thompson, 1975), a system of democratic capitalist law emerged, which, whilst it could never escape determination by or through the structurally predictable but not exhaustive transpositioning demands made upon it (hence the centrality of the concepts of 'property' and 'contract'), nevertheless consisted of a set of discourses with a striking degree of autonomy. This is an autonomy, furthermore, which in one way has increased as the discursive object of consistency has ceased to relate to a set of signs dominated by those of 'property' and 'liberty', unqualified by their articulation with any opposed signs such as 'labour' and 'equality'. The existence of this autonomy is indicated by the possibility that, especially these days, those resorting to law cannot be totally sure of a particular outcome, since they cannot with any certainty anticipate the discursive universe within which their demands will be considered.

Thus, the relative autonomy of democratic capitalist law, which today inheres in part in the unpredictability of its outcomes from the point of view of particular litigants, is in the end not the product of the fact that, given the adversarial system of the common law, counsel can never be entirely sure of the arguments the opposition will raise, the principles they will invoke, or of the assessments the trial or any appellate judge will make of the contending positions, which are its practical and potentially remedial (appealable) causes. Rather, it is the product of the sheer difficulty of knowing what a consistent judgement might be in a particular case, especially once the basic substantive premises and concepts have been qualified (Dworkin, 1986). For this reason what happens in courtrooms escapes, in a certain sense, what happens outside them. Perhaps it was the 'instrumentalism', in the special sense ascribed above to Horwitz, of pre-capitalist law, which made it so predictable in its outcomes (provided the correct 'action' was pursued), and that dissolves what Weber regarded as the English paradox – the apparent contribution of a rationally inappropriate legal system to accelerated capitalist development? And perhaps it would have been the relative unpredictability of the outcomes produced by a more 'systematised' and therefore more autonomous law that would have explained the counterfactual instance?

At first sight, the argument that the relative autonomy of democratic capitalist law may in any sense and at any time inhere in the unpredictability of its outcomes may appear to contradict one of the central theoretical premises of the present position. Namely, that what allows law to occupy the place of a mechanism of transpositioning is its discursively produced object of consistency. However, when the argument is looked at more closely, this does not prove to be the case. First, consistency is argued to be simply the discursively produced *object* of law, which obviously does not mean that consistency need always be achieved. Second, and more profoundly, the consistency striven for is not primarily that of outcomes but rather that of concepts. Leaving aside the differential knowledge, competence and ideological predilections of legal personnel (for these see Goodrich, 1984, pp. 191ff; 1986, passim), the concrete circumstances out of which transpositioning demands arise are so varied that even apparently similar cases will not *necessarily* result in the deployment of the same concepts, let alone the same judgements. To imagine that they would or should is to fall into what from the point of view of this text is the epistemological error of empiricism (Willer, Willer, 1973).

This was, indeed, the position taken by positivistic formalists in general and by American Langdellian jurisprudence in particular during the second half of the nineteenth century. Because such theorists were interested in establishing a scientific jurisprudence, and because they equated empiricism with the scientific method, they formally claimed that the principles they enunciated arose inductively out of the cases classified as relevant. Hence, the pedagogic substitution of books of cases for interpretive treatises in the post-Civil War period. Hence, also, the rise of law schools and departments in universities, bar associations, etc (Chase, 1982; Nelson, 1982; Gilmore, 1977; Stevens, 1983; Sugarman, 1986). However, the critical question faced by all empiricists must also be put to the legal positivists: how can one classify the relevant cases in advance of possession of the concept from which the rules for their recognition may be derived? The answer is that one cannot, and that, moreover, the Langdellians, like most creative empiricists, did not. Rather they worked in a way that has been well summarised by Burton and Carlen in their discussion of British common law reasoning:

> The theory of knowledge evident in the courts is eclectic. It is primarily empiricist in its elevation of the facts of experience as the arbiter in determining the correct decision. Yet, in its insistence on the normative character of the law, the common-law invokes a rationalist method to decide which principle, which legal concept, is to be applied to particular cases. The constant juggling between legal experience and legal reason produces the pragmatist circle of the common-law mode. The doctrine of *stare decisis* (standing by past decisions) requires applying the law 'as it is'. This given object, the law as it is becomes embodied in the *ratio decidendi* (the reason for the decision) of past cases. How is it known which principle of reason is to apply to instant and future cases? The facts of the case guide us. But what facts of the case are relevant? This involves invoking past principles ... Within the space created by this epistemological conundrum is fashioned the site of the judicial agent. Mediating the decisionism entailed in the correct selection of relevant facts and principles is the knowing subject of both rationalist and empiricist epistemologies: the janus-faced judge, at once judge of judicial and epistemological discourse, the guardian of the evolutionary unfolding of verisimilitude (Burton, Carlen, 1979, p. 63).

Thus, the Langdellians and their English counterparts started from the concepts found in the treatises of Blackstone, Kent, Storey, etc, and rationalistically supported their reformulations, elaborations and 'systematisations' by reference to carefully selected or, in the framework of the current text, discursively pertinent cases. Gilmore has made the same point, but from a rigorously empiricist standpoint:

> Langdell has pointed out that the law library was our laboratory and that the printed case reports were our experimental materials. It followed, therefore, that we were to study the cases and that, in our teaching, case-books were to replace treatises. It was,

however, no part of Langdell's scheme that we were to study all
the cases.

[T]he cases which are useful and necessary for (the purpose of
mastering legal principles or doctrines) bear an exceedingly small
proportion to all that have been reported. The vast majority are
useless, worse than useless, for any purpose of systematic study
(Langdell, 1881; as quoted in Sutherland, 1967, p. 174).

Thus the vast majority of all reported cases, past and present
are worse than useless and should be disregarded. The function of
the legal scholar, whether he is writing a treatise or compiling a
case-book, is to winnow out from the chaff those very few cases
which have ever been correctly decided and which, if we follow
them, will lead us to the truth. That is to say, the doctrine – the
one true rule of law – does not in any sense emerge from the
study of real cases decided in the real world. The doctrine tests
the cases, not the other way around (Gilmore, 1977, p. 4).

The Langdellians and the English textbook writers may be criticised
either for their mistaken conception of scientific method or for
their less than rigorous application of it, depending upon one's own
epistemological position, but they nevertheless unconsciously
demonstrated and enhanced the relative autonomy of the law by
their efforts to define the leading concepts of legal discourse and to
specify the manner in which they should be articulated one with
another. Hence, the unpredictability as regards judicial review cases
of that most consistent of nineteenth-century American judges,
Justice Field (McCurdy, 1975, p. 250).

Horwitz is therefore mistaken when he argues that the reason for
the transition from the antebellum legal instrumentalism to the
later 'legal formalism' was the completion of the law's problem-
solving activities on behalf of the bourgeoisie and the emergence of
a consequent need to 'freeze' the legal advantages they had gained
(Horwitz, 1977, Chapter 8). So far from freezing what were
undoubtedly the bourgeoisie's considerable advantages at law, the
effect of increasing formalism was, at least potentially, to enhance
the law's ability to recognise the rights of non-capitalist groups. In
sum, there is no inherent contradiction between the law's commitment to consistency and the unpredictability of its outcomes from
the point of view of particular litigants. Indeed, the commitment to
consistency is what allowed a certain unpredictability to democratic
capitalist law even before the law's fundamental premises were
qualified, as has been suggested in detail elsewhere (Woodiwiss,
1990a, Chapter 2) with respect to trades unionists.

Conclusion: Consistency and the Possibility of a Modern Absolutism

The general point that this text seeks to make against those such as Horwitz, who work with a notion that the law is only or simply an instrument of capitalist domination, is that such a conception vastly oversimplifies matters by failing to specify precisely what this so-called 'instrument' in fact is. In the present text, it has been argued that the law is a particular set of discourses defined by its strain towards consistency, which has gained the position of being the prime transpositioning mechanism in democratic capitalist societies, which further rests on certain specific conditions of existence and effectivity, and which finally derives its substantive content from the transpositioning demands that are made of it. Moreover, it is also argued that it is only when the nature of law is specified in this way that it becomes possible to understand in full both the manner in which it contributes to capitalist domination (that is, by the sheer fact of the centrality of the concepts 'property', 'contract', and 'the contract of employment' etc, etc) and the less common occasions when it allows the claims of non-capitalist groups. And here it is possible, against the formalists, to agree with the position once enunciated by Holmes but apparently later forgotten by him, and which Gilmore (1977, p. 53) quotes as follows:

> What has been said will explain the failure of all theories which consider the law only from its formal side, whether they attempt to deduce the *corpus* from *a priori* postulates, or fall into the humbler error of supposing the science of the law to reside in the *elegantia juris*, or logical cohesion of part with part. The truth is, that the law is always approaching, and never reaching, consistency. It is forever adopting new principles from life at one end, and it always retains old ones from history at the other, which have not yet been absorbed or sloughed off. It will become entirely consistent only when it ceases to grow.

The formalists thought that, once discovered and specified, legal principles were eternally established; that they thereby gave substance to the rule of law; and that they were therefore almost automatically capable of bringing the rule of law to each new aspect of society brought to the courts. In fact, as Holmes recognised, the process of broadening the rule of law was far from automatic and, indeed, often far from just in its results. As the history of labour law and its effects on the discourses of production makes clear, the expansion of the rule of law into industrial relations was very much a case in point. Not only were the identities of the controlling concepts and principles in doubt and established only in a very *ad hoc* manner (for example the contract of employment itself, Woodiwiss, 1987b, pp. 505–9), but also it took a complex set of changes in the conditions of existence of legal discourse (for example those that produced the *Trades Disputes Act* 1906, in Britain and the *Wagner Act* 1935, in the United States) to obtain even a semblance of system let alone equality before the law in the area of industrial relations.

Ironically, the achievement of such semblances in labour law (Atleson, 1984; Woodiwiss, 1990a), as in other areas (for example contract, see Collins, 1986b), occurred only at the cost of undermining the very substantive consistency that the law had so recently approached. The achievement was the consequence of the legislative articulation, albeit in very different ways, of alternative principles to that of 'liberty', as Dicey (1914) recognised. However, despite the increasing unpredictability that accompanies the pursuit of doctrinal consistency, even under 'normal circumstances', Dworkin's (1986, pp. 239ff) Hercules is condemned to fail in the effort to maintain the fiction of his own and the law's absolute autonomy, let alone 'integrity'. For all their substantive inconsistencies, the discourses he enunciates remain those that are constitutive of capital's hegemony (see Woodiwiss, 1990a, Chapter 8). And this for reasons additional to the fact that the embodiments of capital are the law's most frequent supplicants. Because of the changed circumstances under which they exist, such juridical discourses have come to base themselves on more inclusive but still decidedly inegalitarian notions of corporate or group rather than individual liberty. Because this has proved to be the extent of the 'collectivism' that Dicey so disliked, one may share his concern as to whether or not the continued maintenance of law's autonomy has anything necessarily to do with the maintenance of individual autonomy or freedom, since the former is no longer premissed on the latter. (For a discussion of a legal system wherein the existence of any such connection has always been questionable – that is, Japan – see Woodiwiss, 1988a.) Moreover, one may share Dicey's concern even as one regrets the state's increasing preference for enabling legislation which strikes at the roots of group freedoms too. Such freedoms are decidedly better than none at all – than a return to absolutism, in other words. However, the problem may be even more profound than is currently imagined.

It may be that one reason why those who have sought to defend group freedoms whether they be those of trade unionists or even lawyers, have encountered such an apathetic response is because the sets of social positionings that create the constituencies for such groups no longer organise the majority of the population. The developments summarised by such terms as 'Fordism' and 'post-Fordism' have so transformed the occupational structures of advanced capitalist societies that many individuals, as well as those who would organise them, find it very difficult to imagine a corporate identity separate from that of the entity which employs them (again a comparison with Japan is instructive, see Woodiwiss 1990b). If this is the case, and I think that it is, then the stress on individual rights in the British Charter 88 and in the legislative proposals presently being formulated by British trades unions would seem to be very well advised, as a minimalist response to the threat represented by a modern absolutism, irrespective of the political complexion of the government in power.

This is all that can be said directly about these matters here. However, I hope that enough has been said to indicate that the current threat to freedom under the law has roots that extend far beyond political programmes and even beyond programmes of ideological transformation such as that exemplified by Thatcherism. These roots reach into and are sustained by those structures and processes that are the central and still very opaque objects of sociological enquiry. Thus although the final chapters of the present text might otherwise appear to have little connection with legal matters, in fact this concern continues: the problem to be addressed is that posed by what many, including the postmodernists, now believe to be the illusoriness of the social structural groupings that Marxists and many others have typically thought of as undergirding the more immediately visible groupings, namely social classes.

PART IV
Rethinking Class

7 Law and Production

This part will begin by drawing out the critical implications of the theoretical and substantive arguments developed earlier for some recent, influential efforts to reform Marxism as a prelude to an attempt to reconstruct the theory of class. The sheer discovery of the existence of the discourses of production, if accepted, is enough to make the 'enrichment' strategy pursued by such as Bowles and Gintis (1981) unnecessary, at least with respect to the critical issue of whether or not the labour theory of value itself should incorporate political and ideological elements. Requiring somewhat more elucidation is the critical significance of the foregoing arguments for the reform effort mounted by those who might be called the 'attenuators' of Marxist economic theory, because of their desire to ditch the labour theory of value (for example Cutler et al., 1977; Elster, 1985; Roemer, 1981; Steedman, 1977).

Although there are important differences between, especially, Cutler et al. and the other 'attenuators' and particularly on the issue of the place of 'humanism' in Marxist discourse, nevertheless all of them depend very heavily upon the orthodox periodisation of legal/economic history. However, despite the pivotal significance of a juridically articulated and enforced concept of property for both the cogency of their alternative theories of exploitation and their claims that these remain Marxist, neither group of writers offers anything but the vaguest indication of what they mean by 'property' as a legal term.

Steedman merely states that one of his underlying assumptions is that 'all produced means of production are *owned* by the capitalists' (1977, p. 16, emphasis added). Roemer is marginally more forthcoming when he states that:

Profits are a genuine social surplus in the precise sense that their distribution is determined by property relations, which are guaranteed ultimately by institutions of power and authority, and not by some objectively necessary economic law (Roemer, 1981, p. 86).

145

Similarly underdeveloped are the comments of Elster, who begins his presentation of 'market exploitation: the canonical case' as follows:

> Imagine a set of individuals all equipped with the same amount of labour-power (of the same skill), but differently endowed with other factors of production. In addition to the individuals we must postulate the presence of a state that guarantees property rights and enforces contracts ... (Elster, 1985, p. 172).

Elster does, however, later recognise the importance of the employment contract and with it the centrality of the possessory relation to capitalist private property in that he develops a point that Roemer (1981, p. 147) also makes in passing but ascribes an opposite significance to:

> ... It is misleading to say that this control [quality control A.W.] is an exercise of power, if by that we mean something different from the economic power wielded by the capitalist by virtue of his possession of the means of production. The exercise of power occurs when the [employment A.W.] contract is signed, by the capitalist taking advantage of the lack of property of the worker. The enforcement of the contract is not then a further exercise of power. 'What brings the seller into a relationship of dependency is *solely* the fact that the buyer is the owner of the conditions of labour.' Normally, the contract is enforced by the worker's knowledge that he will be fired if he violates it (Elster, 1985, p. 200).

Despite this recognition, and neglecting the problems created by his fusion of 'possession' and 'control', Elster fails to appreciate and register its significance for what is required of a specifically capitalist concept of private property.

In Cutler et al. (1977, Volume 1) a similar progression commences with the straightforward assertion of the necessity of an unspecified, juridical concept of property as a condition of the existence of capitalist relations of production (ibid., pp. 46, 49). It continues with an appreciation of the specificity required in order to acknowledge the particular relations – axed around possession – between owners and labourers that distinguish capitalism from other economic systems. And it ends with a failure to acknowledge the significance of this for what is required of a legal concept of capitalist private property. As is apparent in the following two quotations, and as with Elster, a similar absorption of the powers given by 'contract' into those given by 'property' is what prevents Cutler et al. from recognising the need for the specificity of capitalist relations of production to be acknowledged legally if one wishes to talk of this being a necessary condition of their existence:

> To say that production takes place under capitalist forms of possession is to say that it presupposes, *inter alia*, legal recognition of the forms of wage-labour contract.
>
> ... the wage-labour contract must always be *determinate*, that is, it must specify definite conditions and obligations on the parties to that contract. There must always be some legal specifications of the forms of contract that are possible and of those that are legally precluded and, within those limits, each wage-labour contract presupposes some further determination of the particular conditions specified in the contracts (ibid., p. 240).
>
> In all cases ... effective possession involves a capacity to control the functioning of means of production in the process of production and to exclude others from their use ... Effective possession is not to be identified with the legal concept of ownership or with the performance of certain functions of direction ... Thus for each mode of possession in separation we have a class of possessors and a class of separated non-possessors. For example, in the case of capitalist relations of production, the capitalist possesses various instruments and raw material in the form of commodities, and workers may engage in production only on condition that they sell their own commodity, labour-power, to the capitalist. Here the capitalist controls and organises the production process in which he brings together certain commodities at the beginning of the process so as to obtain other commodities at the end. The capitalist sells, or tries to sell, his products to other capitalists or to workers. Thus capitalist possession of the means of production involves a definite form of the organisation of the production process in which labour-power is purchased, under definite contractual conditions, from the worker by the capitalist and enters production as his property, as one commodity among others (ibid., pp. 249–50).

The axiomatic dependence of 'contract' on 'property' with respect to the employment relation that both Elster and Cutler et al. assert, occurs, it will be suggested here, because they also share a socially and therefore discursively transcendent concept of property similar to Macfarlane's. This is the concept that Durkheim too regarded as the 'essence' of property: 'the right of a given individual to exclude other individual and collective entities from the usage of a given thing' (Lukes and Scull, 1983, p. 164).

Cutler et al.'s commitment to this definition is suggested, despite their denial of any identity between 'effective possession' and the 'legal concept of ownership' in the first sentence of the second extract taken from them above. Elster's commitment to it may be inferred from his general preference for game-theoretic 'withdrawal statements' as the means to define powers and which would provide exactly such a definition if it were applied to the problem of defining the powers of property holders.

However, the assumption that the employment contract is but an outgrowth of 'property' runs counter to what we know about legal history. 'Property' and 'contract' emerged as the core signs of distinguishable discourses, as the discourses constructed around feudal 'dominium' and petty commodity patriarchy retreated. Capitalist property owners did not gain rights over those that laboured for them on the basis of 'contract' until late in this process of emergence/retreat – until then they depended upon the legal powers of the state or, more often, upon no legal powers at all (for England see Abrahams, 1968; Dobson, 1980; Malcolmson, 1981; Thompson, 1975). Moreover, contractually based and enforced rights over labour, when they eventually emerged, were very restricted and served, at first, to empower labour as well as the capitalist owners (see also Atleson, 1983, p. 13). Thus the discursive subordination of 'contract' to 'property' that is intrinsic to the employment contract was not only a very late development as compared to the existence of capitalist production relations, but also the development that was critical to the completion of the construction of a specifically democratic capitalist legal system.

The critical question that recognition of this neglected history raises for the 'attenuators' is: How can capitalist property rights be understood as the sole or even the most important condition of existence for a distinctively capitalist mode of exploitation if for so long no such rights existed? Amongst the ways in which non-capitalist property rights were initially 'good enough' to allow the reproduction of capitalist relations of production was by their enforcement (for example on the basis of what is sometimes called 'the Tudor industrial code' and the master–servant laws that grew out of it) of capitalist possessory power. However, in order to pre-empt a possible line of defence, it is important to note that in other ways (for example because of notions such as that of 'a just price') such rights imposed limits on capital's freedom and additionally that they were challenged by the rise of combinations. Hence the rise and fall of conspiracy doctrine and the creation of the contract of employment.

The conclusion that these considerations point to is that neither capitalist private property rights nor some surrogate for them can therefore be understood as the sole or even the most important source of a distinctively capitalist mode of exploitation. If the *capitalist* nature of a particular set of production relations can no longer be defensibly defined by reference to 'the conditions of production' prior to the commencement of the actual production process, as all the 'attenuators' suggest, then attention must turn back to the production process itself, the relations that define it and the claims made by the labour theory of value. Put in general terms, the concept 'mode of production', this time in its 'restricted' form (see above, p. 60), may be restored to the position of theoretical and analytical centrality from which Cutler et al. have sought to remove it. And the labour theory of value may be reduced and made more sustainable. Put more specifically, the only claim that need now be made for the labour theory of value is that, in the context of the private monopolisation of possession of property in the means of production, it explains the existence of capitalist exploitation as a function of the 'peculiar property' of labour power as a commodity, that is of its 'use value ... being a source of value, whose actual consumption ... is itself an embodiment of labour, and consequently, a creation of value' (Marx, 1965, p. 167).

All the other claims traditionally made by or on behalf of the theory, most importantly the claim that it also provides a 'measure' of value that ultimately explains the prices of labour power and other commodities, may be referred to the concept of the discourses of production and the re-conceptualisations of the political and other economic dimensions of production and exchange to be found in the works of such as Burawoy and 'the regulation school' (for example Aglietta, 1976; Lipietz, 1985). The specific contribution expected of the concept of the 'discourses of production' here is that it *promises* a means of explaining not just the legal grounds upon which a wage may be demanded and/or paid, but also a means of explaining why particular wages may be demanded or paid: since the latter particularities are constructed in the discourses, including the gendering and racialising ones, that define skills, apportion responsibilities, justify hierarchies, etc. Together with political and other economic determinations, these discourses explain the existence and the structure of internal labour markets and by extension contribute to the understanding of external labour markets also. The point is that, taken together, these determinations provide a means of explaining the prices paid for labour-power, which does not depend upon establishing any quantitative relationship between value and price, or upon making any assumptions about the illusory or epiphenomenal nature of price as compared to value. Exchange relations and their social dimensions may thus be granted their due reality and degree of autonomy.

In this way, then, Cutler et al.'s (1977, Volume 1, pp. 12ff) major objection may be accepted, a means provided for bypassing the related obstacles represented by the problems of 'joint production' and 'heterogeneous labour', so emphasised by Steedman (1977) and the 'rational choicers', *and* the labour theory of value retained as an *explanation* of the fact of exploitation as it exists under the capitalist mode of production. Finally the fate met by the 'attentuators" efforts at reform as a consequence of the results of a little historical curiosity provides strong support for the conviction expressed in the introduction that theorisation is best attempted in a context where it may be disciplined by the rigours of empirical study, rather than in one where it is guided simply by well-established representations of the empirical world.

8 Deconstructing 'Class'

In her bracing polemic against contemporary Marxist attempts to develop more adequate means for understanding the phenomena to which the concept 'class' refers in capitalist societies, Ellen Wood (1986) characterises and indeed claims to explain the occurrence of these attempts as part of a process of theoretical and political 'retreat'. Ironically, given the sources many of her victims draw upon, her text draws much of its power from its rhetorical style rather than from any alternative conceptualisation that might inform it. Wood herself would insist, no doubt, that her text is informed by the conceptualisation to be found in Marx's own work. The problem is, however, that such a response would beg all the questions raised by the work she criticises and which may be reduced to 'What is the Marxist concept of class?' Moreover, as Rattansi (1985) has made clear in his recent paper, Marx's own concept of class remained frustratingly underdeveloped and unclear. Thus what is required is the deconstruction/reconstruction of the Marxist theory of class not its restoration.

Metatheory and the Concept of Class
If one does not share Wood's intolerance of those who would dare to criticise let alone claim to have improved upon the works of the master, the difficulties with which Marx's legacy confronts contemporary Marxists cannot be shrugged off so easily. In line with the earlier parts of this text, an important dimension of the way in which this challenge will be taken up here, and something that will distinguish it very clearly from Wood's stance, will be its attention to 'metatheoretical' issues. Indeed, contra Przeworski, the pursuit of humanism back to its last redoubt in the self-evidently representationalist, one might even say 'Eisensteinian', figure of 'struggle', and the uncovering of the theoretical conditions that sustain it, as they have already been shown to have sustained the figure of fetishism, will structure the narrative of this chapter.[1] It will also create a basis

151

for the later construction of a non-humanist, non-representationalist and non-economistic concept of class in capitalist societies, designed to acknowledge the complexity of classes and especially the particular complexities that follow from the fact that those subjects which embody classes are often gendered (Crompton, Mann, 1986, Davidoff, Hall, 1987) and often racialised (Miles, 1982). In sum, 'the force' that is 'class' will be specified.

Marxists since Althusser have become relatively well aware of the powerful theoretical and analytical effects of metatheoretical assumptions, at least by comparison with non-Marxists. Nevertheless, with the partial exception of those who have taken their lead from Hindess and Hirst (for example Cottrell, 1984; Johnston, 1986), they have proved to be excessively timid in the use they have made of the opportunities and creative possibilities that recognition of this power opens up. That this should be so is doubly surprising in the area of class theory, since the taken-for-grantedness that attaches to representationalist claims was shattered some time ago as a result of the signifier 'class' having been made to refer to very different extra-discursive phenomena by the effects of metatheoretical differences on the construction of particular signifieds. Additionally so, because the best-known and most elaborately confused instance of contemporary class theory owes its confusedness precisely to its failure to observe rigorously the need for metatheoretical consistency. The latter point will be taken up and justified below when the work of Poulantzas is discussed, whilst the former will be illustrated immediately in order that the power being claimed for metatheoretical assumptions in this area of theory may be understood clearly from the beginning. The illustration will be brief since the contrast that I have in mind involves two of the best-known exemplars of contemporary Marxist class theory, Thompson and Poulantzas. Thompson is ontologically a humanist and epistemologically an empiricist and thus the classes that he regards as the product of the capitalist mode of production are composed of and indeed constructed by directly observable, 'struggling' individuals: 'I do not see class as a "structure" ... but as something which in fact happens ... in human relationships' (Thompson, 1964, p. 9).

By contrast, Poulantzas is ontologically a non-humanist and epistemologically a realist and thus for him the classes associated with the capitalist mode of production are the products of a set of 'social relations' that have human 'supports' or 'bearers' but are in themselves the 'effects' of a set of 'structures':

... everything happens as if social classes were the result of an ensemble of structures and of their relations, firstly at the economic level, secondly at the political level and thirdly at the ideological level. A social class can be identified either at the economic level, at the political level, or at the ideological level, and can thus be located with regard to a particular instance. Yet to define a class as such and to grasp it in its concept, we must refer to the ensemble of levels of which it is the effect (Poulantzas, 1973 pp. 63–4).

For Poulantzas, classes cannot be directly observed as groups of struggling individuals. Moreover, the struggles of individuals can be taken as providing indirect evidence of the existence of classes, only if their struggles can be shown to be effects of the pertinent ensemble of structures. In sum, for Thompson classes are groups of people, whilst for Poulantzas they are presumably non-human, structural entities that have determinative effects on individuals.

Non-humanism and the Subject Re-revisited

Before the implications of the sceptical qualifier 'presumably' in the previous sentence are spelt out, one aspect of the metatheoretical stance taken here requires somewhat more development than it has hitherto received (see above, pp. 25–7; 72–3). The reason is that a plethora of empirical data relating to the past, the present and many different societies indicates that individuals do not always or even very often act in ways that one might expect given what is generally termed their 'class position'.

Here a proposition will be advanced that leads to any suggestion that individuals 'have' class positions, being treated with great scepticism. Indeed the inverse proposition will be preferred. Putting this general issue to one side for now, the particular prefatory point that should be made immediately is that a fundamental difference between the stance taken here and that taken in other ostensibly non-humanist texts is that it does not share their apparent belief in the social and therefore sociological irrelevance of the actions of individual or collective human subjects. Positioned as they are (economically, politically and ideologically) subjects are literally the embodiments of such positionings. They are therefore an important part of what gives them their materiality. However, if one agrees with Freud/Lacan, as is the case here, then human subjects, for example, are not *simply* the embodiments of such positionings. Subjects are the understandable but inherently unpredictable mate-

rialisations of positionings and so are capable not only of repro-
ducing said positionings but also of disrupting them. The present
text nevertheless insists that the effectivity of individual or collective actors and of their undeniable struggles is constrained or,
better, shaped by their congruence with what, for want of a better
term, have to be called 'structural forces': if they are congruent with
one or other of what are often opposed 'forces' they will have an
effectivity, whilst if they are not they will be, most often, a sociological irrelevance. However, the requirement of congruence is not a
very strict one in that typically it may be satisfied in different ways,
which therefore must be regarded as representing sets of strategic
choices (cp Jessop, 1986, Chapter 12), regardless of whether what is
at issue is an instance of economic, political, ideological or
synthetic calculation.

Returning to the first of the points just made, what the present
stance most emphatically does not involve, therefore, is a belief that
the sociology it enunciates can explain *on its own* why any individual or group makes particular choices. Such choices may, on the
contrary, only be explained fully with the additional knowledge
generated by metatheoretically compatible social scientific
discourses whose 'rules of formation' were/are such that the individual subject is their object of investigation, that is, by
psychological discourses. If one takes Foucault seriously, the difference between, and the mutual irreducibility of, psychological and
non-humanist sociological discourses are not only social facts but
also conditions of our having any knowledge whatsoever of the realities to which they refer. There exists therefore a discursive gulf
between the two sets of discourses, one that has to be acknowledged
if one wishes to make psychological or sociological sense, let alone
both.[2] Moreover, although classes may only have effects on one
another and in the wider social formation through the actions of
particular human and non-human subjects, there is no reason
either to expect that such subjects should be coherent, consistent or
even conscious class subjects, or to think that the fate of a particular
class depends upon the existence of such subjects. What matters
sociologically, if not politically, is only *that* the effects occur, not
through whom or what they occur, nor how aware the subjects are
of them.

To elaborate somewhat, classes have their effects through the
subjects that they position: sometimes these are individuals, sometimes families, and sometimes communities, corporations or even
nations. Thus, for example, the issue as to whether individuals or

families are the proper units of class analysis, which has recently occupied so much time (for example Crompton, Mann, 1986) is from the present point of view a non-issue, since it is both a product and a demonstration of the irresolvable analytical conundrums forced upon those whose discourses are premissed upon humanism. Additionally, classes have their effects regardless of whether the subjects that embody them are aware of their positionings, or are positioned divergently in the political, economic and ideological spheres. For example, sometimes subjects may be aware of their economic, sometimes of their political, and sometimes of their ideological positionings, but seldom will they be aware of all or any of them consistently. Thus, regardless of whether or not an individual, economically proletarian subject is aware of his or her positioning or indeed is also positioned in high political office and as a shareholder in the same or another enterprise, s/he will still economically embody the working class and as such her or his actions will have certain definite social effects inside and outside of production. This said, should such a subject be critically aware of their positioning, still the occupant of high political office and enamoured of an altogether different conception of title, the continued reproduction of these effects might be rendered problematic.

Humanism and Class

So much, then, for where this attempt at rethinking starts from. It is now time to discuss the concept of class that this stance makes possible. The failure of Marxism to produce a fully non-humanist concept of class has its roots deep in the Marxist canon and particularly in the strong preference for political rather than social scientific readings of the key texts. This widespread preference has had especially unfortunate consequences for the conceptualisation of class because Marx seldom directly addressed the topic in his later and less politically engaged work and so failed to comment on any divergences between the conceptualisations produced by the different kinds of reading. When he did so comment (Rattansi, 1985), a rather different concept is suggested to that found in his earlier work. However, so implicit is this different concept that it is not at all surprising that the original one, which had become established very quickly as productive of the key sign – 'class struggle' – in Marxist/socialist political discourse, was not even challenged, let alone displaced. And this despite the fact that in the earlier work the signifier 'class' was combined with no very definite signified, apart from the inherited one of a human collectivity of an economic kind (Lichtheim, 1961, p. 41).

Even in Marx's pre-Manifesto theoretical works, which were anyway largely unpublished and therefore presumably not influential, one can find little indication of what class may have originally signified for him beyond groups located at the level of 'the division of labour', which are necessarily in conflict with one another as a result of a recurrently developing contradiction between what are referred to as 'productive forces' and 'modes of internal intercourse' (for example private property, see *The German Ideology*). In *The Poverty of Philosophy* and *The Communist Manifesto* these groups were identified as 'classes' and the conflicts between them as 'class struggles', thus establishing these terms as the key signs in Marxist discourse. But, and this point cannot be emphasised too strongly, this was long before the concept of 'labour power' had been distinguished from that of 'labour', and so long before the mode of the appropriation of the surplus had been discovered as the precise relational nexus in which classes are formed and reproduced. Although Marx himself realised the significance of this discovery for the analysis of class relations (Rattansi, 1985, pp. 651–2), neither he nor many, if any, of his subsequent readers realised its potential negative significance for the already established humanistic political rhetoric of class.

The *locus classicus* of the self-conscious reassertion of the originary power of the human subject in response to the causal straitjacket imposed by Marxism's equally well-established commitment to economic reductionism, and therefore of an instance of their unacknowledged interdependence, is Lukacs' reflection on the failures of the Second International, *History and Class Consciousness*. In theoretical terms the critical essay on class consciousness exhibits a marked irony in that it uses a notion central to *Capital*, but neglected by the theorists of the Second International – 'fetishism' – in a discursive setting informed by a neo-Kantian metatheory, to revivify the humanistic class-in-itself/class-for-itself couple that *Capital* otherwise provides a means of superseding. The famous result of this move is that it leads Lukacs to posit a reified realm of appearances that is both produced by and masks an inherently oppressive capitalist economic reality. Since this realm of appearances is also the source of the psychological consciousness shared by individual proletarian subjects the latter must be falsely conscious and may be rescued only by their participation in a 'praxis' decided upon by an enlightened, socialist party leadership which acts in pursuit of the class' true interests.

For these reasons all who embrace the term 'praxis' and apply it to their actions or those of others enthrone an enriched version of the profoundly humanistic notion of 'struggle' at the centre of their thinking about class. In using the term 'praxis' they no doubt imagine that their commitment to an originary subject is their means of escape from economic reductionism, but in fact it is what makes their escape impossible. And this is because it means that the deeper metatheoretical as well as theoretical sources of economic reductionism are still obscured from them. The chief amongst these is humanism itself, since it undergirds the representationalism which causes the premature theoretical closure exemplified by reductionism.

Non-humanism and Class: Incomplete Re-Readings of Marx

In addition to the outright humanists, there are also those like Althusser, who, whilst they have sought to make use of several of the social scientific advances made possible by Saussurian theory, have nevertheless failed to recognise the unwanted humanism and representationalism brought into their discourse by their continued dependence, by now deeply repressed, on the figure of fetishism. The representationalism implicit in the figure of fetishism is one of the principal problems caused by the presence of humanistic tropes in otherwise purportedly non-humanist discourses. It, rather than humanism itself as in assertively humanist texts, is what makes the escape from reductionism so difficult even in ostensibly non-humanist Marxist texts. This is because it informs the discursively prior conception of the mode of appropriation of the surplus shared by even the so-called 'structuralists'; that is, because it explains why it is so casually assumed that the exploiters and the exploited, themselves terms with strongly humanistic connotations, are individual human subjects. Perhaps the single, most influential contemporary instance of this assumption is Balibar's specification of the 'invariant' elements in any mode of production, which begins as follows and in a way that makes clear that Marx too shared it:

> We find a first extremely clear text in *Capital* Volume Two:
> Whatever the social form of production, labourers and means of production always remain *factors* (*Faktoren*) of it. But in a state of separation from each other either of these factors can be such only potentially (*der Möglichkeit nach*). For production to go on at

all they must *combine* (*Verbindung*). The specific manner in which this combination is accomplished distinguishes the different epochs of the structure of society one from another (*Capital*, Vol. II, p. 43 – modified).

Two of the elements we are seeking are indicated here:

(1)   *The labourer* (labour power);
(2)   *The means of production.*

The text goes on:

In the present case, the separation of the free worker from his means of production is the starting-point given, and we have seen how and under what conditions these two elements are united in the hands of the capitalist, namely, as the productive mode of existence of his capital.

Here we find straightaway a third element which, like the other two, also deserves to be called a 'factor':

(3)   *The non-worker, appropriating surplus-labour.*

Elsewhere, Marx describes him as the representative of the 'class of large proprietors' (*Grossbesitzerklasse – Capital*, T.II, p. 185; Vol. I, p. 511). This is the capitalist. Besides this, we find here an element of a different kind which we could call a *connexion* (*relation*) between the preceding elements: it can take two exclusive values: separation (*Trennung*)/property (Althusser, Balibar, 1970, p. 212).

These human subjects may only be of interest to Marx and Balibar in so far as they are the 'personifications', 'representatives' or 'bearers' of certain social relations (for example 'money bags'), or again, the occupants of certain structural positions, 'locations' (Wright, 1978) or whatever. But the theorists' shared failure further to define the entities that are being personified leads to their non-humanism being too readily compromised and to them slipping unawares or even willingly into a conception of these entities as groups of people. Rattansi (1985, p. 662) exemplifies both how this slippage occurs and its contemporary currency when he says in discussing these same invariant elements:

In the *Grundrisse, Capital* and other later works 'relations of production' indexes in actuality *two* sets of *relations between agents and means of production,* i.e., a relation of ownership (and non-ownership) of the means of production and a relation of 'real' appropriation or control over the instruments of production [emphasis added].

That the occurrence of this slippage may owe much to the humanism inherent in a political rhetoric dominated by the notion of 'struggle' will now be suggested by a discussion of Poulantzas' two major texts on class (for the determinant role played by 'politics' throughout Poulantzas' discourse, see Jessop, 1986, passim).

Referring back to the definition of class quoted from Poulantzas above (p. 153), it should be noted that it was necessary to qualify somewhat my claim to be accurately representing it when I described it as referring to 'non-human structural entities' by including the term 'presumably'. This was necessary not only because Poulantzas himself begins the extract with a sentence that includes the qualificatory phrase 'as if', but also because even in his most determinedly non-humanist phase, during which the extract under discussion was written, and with the sole exception of the extract itself, he is seldom so clearly committed to the view that classes are non-human structural entities. Indeed most often and, for example, immediately after the extract he can be found insisting that classes exist at the level of the 'social relations of production'. This insistence culminates in the following passage:

> More exactly, social class is a concept which shows the effects of the ensemble of structures, of the matrix of a mode of production or of a social formation *on the agents which constitute its supports: this concept reveals the effects of the global structure in the field of social relations.* In this sense, if class is indeed a concept, it does not designate a reality which can be placed in the structures: it designates the effect of an ensemble of given structures, an ensemble which determines social relations as class relations (Poulantzas, 1973 p. 68).

But even if Poulantzas cannot grant classes the status of 'structures' he is nevertheless determined that they are not groups of people:

> What concrete results can be inferred from these remarks with respect to the constitution of social classes? Firstly, the constitution of classes is not related to the economic level alone, but consists of an effect of the ensemble of the levels of a mode of production or of a social formation. The organization of instances in economic, political and ideological levels is reflected, in social relations, in economic, political and ideological class practice and in 'struggle' between the practices of the various classes (ibid., p. 69).

There is a striking awkwardness, not to say a failure of sense in the way in which the passage ends – in what sense may 'practices' be said to 'struggle'? This awkwardness suggests that Poulantzas' own struggle with humanism was being lost, since the only way in which it could have been avoided was by him dropping 'struggle between' and 'the practices of', since both of them are implicitly humanist. As it turned out, Poulantzas' equivocation as to the onto-logical identity of classes was to be a major cause of his later confusion, as was his accompanying equivocation on the issue of reductionism. His reason for thinking that 'class' cannot signify a structure is that 'an effect of the structures (namely the class) cannot itself constitute a structure'. Given a more rigorously non-humanist metatheoretical stance, it is difficult to see why the opposite conclusion should not be preferred, unless, that is, another intellectual commitment, another link in the pertinent signifying chain is pulling the other way. One such commitment would be to a base/superstructure model of the social formation, which requires some phenomena to be considered as more important than others, as the producers of others. One source of Poulantzas' continued commitment to just such a model is, of course, his explicit mainte-nance of Althusser's 'determination in the last instance' formulation of the social significance of the economy. Another equally powerful but unacknowledged source is the repetition of the figure of fetishism in his formulation of the structure/conjuncture relation, as will become apparent below when Poulantzas' later work on classes is considered. In sum, then, even in what many, perhaps including Poulantzas himself, came to regard as a text too far in the battle for a non-humanist Marxism and from which they and he sought a route back to the comforts of humanism (for example Clarke, 1980), humanism was still a potent if subordinate presence, which was later to wreak its wholly predictable havoc in his *Classes in Contemporary Capitalism*.

Classes begins very badly from the present point of view when Poulantzas answers the question 'What are social classes in Marxist theory?' as follows:

They are groupings of social agents, defined principally but not exclusively by their place in the production process, that is, in the economic sphere (Poulantzas, 1978, p. 14).

This appears to be a pretty straightforward repetition of the regret-table classical combination of humanism and economic determinism. Things get even worse when in his second proposition Poulantzas tries to extricate himself from the close to nonsensical position he was earlier (p. 160 above) found to be in with respect to his effort to free the notion of struggle from its humanist associations:

> For Marxism, social classes involve in one and the same process both class contradictions and class struggle; social classes do not firstly exist as such, and only then enter into a class struggle. Social classes coincide with class practices, i.e., the class struggle, and are only defined in their mutual opposition (ibid., p. 14).

No longer do 'practices' 'struggle', but rather 'social classes', 'practices' and 'class struggle' 'coincide' with one another! What this seems to mean is that a necessary aspect of the existence of classes is the struggle between them; that is, class struggle is both necessary for classes to exist and a consequence of their existence. The result of this circularity, which I accept is part of an effort, a rather desperate one, to avoid humanism, is a self-defeating, almost existentialist fixation on practice (for Poulantzas' earlier and explicit existentialism as well as a much more positive assessment of his later work see Jessop, 1986). However, this circularity only occurs because Poulantzas regards classes as 'groupings of social agents', or because of, in other words, his own residual humanism. Classes cannot 'firstly exist as such' because if they did, for Poulantzas, this would be the same as saying that agents exist before structures, which would be humanism. So instead of an overt humanism we have a covert one, which, as Poulantzas might have said, 'we may know through its effects'.

These effects are immediately apparent in Poulantzas' third and fourth propositions, which also complete the outline of his basic position. The third begins:

> The class determination, while it coincides with the practices (struggle) of classes and includes political and ideological relations, designates certain objective places occupied by the social agents in the social division of labour: places which are independent of the will of these agents (ibid., p. 14).

Having so defined class 'place' and reasserted his claim to be putting forward a non-humanist analysis, Poulantzas moves on to define what he calls class 'position' and in so doing undermine precisely the same claim. Thus his fourth proposition begins:

> This structural determination of classes, which thus exists only as
> the class struggle, must however, be distinguished from class
> position in each specific conjuncture – the focal point of the
> always unique historic individuality of a social formation, in
> other words the concrete situation of the class struggle. In
> stressing the importance of political and ideological relations in
> determining social classes, and the fact that social classes only
> exist in the form of class struggle and practices, class determina-
> tion must not be reduced, in a voluntarist fashion, to class
> position. The importance of this lies in those cases in which a
> distance arises between the structural determination of classes
> and the class positions in the conjuncture (ibid., pp. 14–15).

Mindful of the historical record, Poulantzas is stressing here that
class struggles and practices do not always take the form or possess
the content that their structural origins might lead one to expect.
Additionally, he is concerned to differentiate his position from a
'voluntarist' (that is, overtly humanist) one, which would involve
reducing 'place' to 'position'. The problem is, however, that apart
from this negative statement about the relationship between what
are very hard to describe as other than two levels, Poulantzas has
very little to say about it. Moreover, what he does say is what causes
one to doubt that his position is in fact that much different from a
humanist one. Proposition five opens by asserting the primacy of
'place' relative to 'position', and proposition six by asserting that 'in
the determination of social classes, the principal role is played by
place in the economic relations.' For all his dismissal of Lukacs
(ibid., p. 16), it seems that not only has Poulantzas not entirely rid
himself of dependence on the base/superstructure metaphor, but
also that in so far as he has done so then it is by deploying the
reality/appearance couple basic to the notion of fetishism as developed by Lukacs. This he uses to provide what seems to me to be
both the undeclared but most likely rationale for the 'place'/
'position' distinction and the formers' primacy, and also, more originally, to provide a new way of thinking the relations between the
economic, political and ideological dimensions of the production
process:

This dominant role of the relations of production over the

productive forces and the labour process is what gives rise to the constitutive role of political and ideological relations in the structural determination of social classes. The relations of production and the relationships which comprise them (economic ownership/possession) are expressed in the form of powers which derive from them, in other words class powers; these powers are constitutively tied to the political and ideological relations which sanction and legitimize them. These relations are not simply added on to relations of production that are 'already there', but are themselves present, in the form specific to each mode of production, in the constitution of the relations of production. The process of production and exploitation is at the same time a process of reproduction of the relations of political and ideological domination and subordination (Poulantzas, 1978, p. 21).

As I read this passage, the first sentence seems to be saying that the nature of the economy in general is such that it requires that production should have political and ideological dimensions, whilst the second seems to be saying that what makes the presence of these dimensions necessary is the need for 'economic' powers to be sanctioned and legitimised. Taken together they therefore seem to be saying that economic reality produces not a separate realm of political and ideological appearances, which was Marx and Lukacs' position, but the necessary form of its own appearance. Thus, albeit in a novel way, Poulantzas' argument takes the same form as the figure of fetishism, a similarity which is also suggested at a further deconstructive remove by the way in which the term 'powers' is used. For Poulantzas fetishism explains the intrinsically multidimensional nature of production relations rather than their relation to the necessarily external but nevertheless dependent political and economic realms as is the case for Marx and Lukacs.

Thus far my argument that Poulantzas' covert humanism may be known by its effects has been confined to pointing to the spectral presence of the figure of fetishism in his work, which figure depends for its existence on a humanist ontology (p. 45 above). In other words, it has been an argument by implication. However, Poulantzas' humanism is not simply an implicit presence, since what lies behind his unconscious deployment of the figure of fetishism and therefore explains the primacy that he continues to grant to the economy is his commitment to a variant of Balibar's concept of mode of production which he introduces as follows:

In a society divided into classes, the relations of production

consist of a double relationship which encompasses men's relations to nature in material production. The two relationships are,
first, the relationship between agents of production and the
object and means of labour (the productive forces); second, and
through this, relations between men and other men, class relations (ibid., p. 18).

The casual and unselfconscious humanism of this passage is every
bit as frank and disruptive as that found in Balibar and Marx. And it
has the same source in a failure to define the nature of the class
entities that 'men' 'personify' or whatever. Finally, it allows the
same slippage in the referent of 'class' from something non-human
to something very human, as is clear from Poulantzas' succeeding
and illustrative accounts of the feudal and capitalist modes of
production (ibid., p. 19). The difference is that in Poulantzas'
discourse the overdetermining role of the centrality of the notion of
'struggle' is much more explicit; necessarily so, because at some
level Poulantzas knew that non-humanism threatened its traditional place in Marxist discourse. As he was to say in his last book,
with more passion than *theoretical* justification: '... struggles [are,
A.W.] lodged in the very heart of the relations of production and
exploitation' (Poulantzas, 1980, p. 15).[3]

Non-humanism and Class: Missing the Point

Like Poulantzas but unlike Wright (1985) and Elster (1985), Cutler
et al. (1977) recognise the pertinence of ontological issues to the
conceptualisation of class. The disappointing thing about their
work is that, although it poses the issue of humanism/non-
humanism quite sharply, it misses the most important point and
concludes by simply adding non-human agents, such as joint-stock
companies, to human agents as the possible occupants of 'loci of
decision' in a very narrowly defined (that is, wholly economic) class
relation. The very phrase 'loci of decision', like Poulantzas' terms
'place' and 'position', implies that classes require agents not just as a
condition of their existence, which is unexceptionable, but if they
are to possess any social effectivity. The humanist implications of
this denial of the independent existence of classes are not altered
one jot by the insistence that some of the necessary agents may be
non-human. How this missing of the point is achieved will be
explained, but briefly and only in enough detail to facilitate the
start of the presentation of a reconceptualisation of class.

That Hindess and Hirst should be party to an argument that fails to get to grips with the problems posed by humanism is rather surprising, given their earlier enthusiasm for precisely the non-humanist dimension of Althusser's writings. It is an occurrence, however, that may be explained relatively straightforwardly as the consequence of the conclusions they latterly drew from their reading of Foucault and which served to distance them from their Althusserian past (Hindess, Hirst, 1977). Fatefully, these conclusions were epistemological, or, better, anti-epistemological rather than ontological. They led to what may best be termed 'an accidently postmodernist' denial of any claim, at least any claim imaginable by Hindess and Hirst, to scientificity for Marxism and indeed social science in general, on the grounds that extra-discursively verifiable knowledge of any phenomena – discursive or extra-discursive – is impossible.

The adoption of a realist epistemology enables one to sidestep Hindess and Hirst's point, since the former does not regard scientificity as being tied to verificationism. In addition it is possible to read Foucault, and indeed much else in the 'structuralist' tradition in another way, the critical implications of which for Marxism are different and constructive rather than simply negative (see the introduction and Chapter 3 above). In terms of such a reading Foucault provides both a largely implicit critique of Marxism's failure to accept the reality and autonomy of the ideological realm and a means of correcting it. By extension he also provides therefore a means for more adequately theorising *any* of the objects of study of concern to Marxists, such as those referred to by the terms 'production', 'law' and 'class'. This point will be put to one side for the time being, since what is of more immediate interest is the fact that Hindess and Hirst's conclusions led them, like Laclau and Mouffe, to view issues of epistemology rather than ontology as at the root of Marxism's analytical problems, and worse, again like Laclau and Mouffe, to view the imperatives of the struggle for socialism, in an almost Sorelian way, as the sole touchstone of Marxism's analytical adequacy.

Hindess and Hirst are preoccupied with producing 'theory relevant to the *struggle* for socialism' (Cutler et al., 1977, p. 5, emphasis added) and thus in danger of elaborating a discourse that, consciously or not, is likely to be permeated with humanism and representationalism – theory is very unlikely ever to be as immediately relevant to struggle as they suggest, unless, of course one thinks of a class as a group of people waiting to be instructed. It is, then, hardly surprising that their diagnosis of the ills afflicting

Marxism as primarily epistemological should so strongly mark both the lead-up to and their actual discussion of class in the attempt to reconstitute Marxist theory which they and others co-authored (Cutler et al., 1977). The lead-up includes a rigorous critique of the classical version of the labour theory of value, on the grounds that it rests upon an idealist concept of measurement derived from Hegel, and with which critique I have already stated my partial agreement. However, because they think their critique invalidates all the claims that might be made on the theory's behalf, the lead-up also includes an attempt to replace 'exploitation' as the central category in the Marxist explanation of what happens in the capitalist economy with an alternative, which I find neither theoretically justifiable nor empirically supportable (see above pp. 146–50). Again, this point may be put to one side for now.

What is more important on this occasion is that Cutler et al.'s epistemological diagnosis leads them to regard economic reductionism as the ultimate metatheoretical cause of the problems they find with Marxist class theory in general, one of which is the assumption that only humans may be regarded as class agents. In other words their conception of the relationship between reductionism and humanism as the twin obstacles to a more adequate concept of class is the reverse, in terms of discursive causation, of what is being argued here. Their rejection of epistemology appears to have led to a reversal of what is normally considered to be the proper discursive ordering wherein premisses precede theory. Whether or not this reversal is intended, indeed whether or not it is valid, and in a certain Foucauldian sense it may be, Cutler et al. do not register, let alone justify, its occurrence, which leads one to suspect that it might have produced some unanticipated effects within their discourse such as the unconscious return of humanism and representationalism of concern here. (For signs of a similarly unconscious return, see the resort to Heidigger in Laclau and Mouffe, 1987.) Whatever may be the hidden effects of this reversal, its visible effects are clear and extraordinary.

Misdirected by the reading of Foucault that they share with Hindess and Hirst, encouraged by their resulting, entirely negative epistemological critique of the labour theory of value, and with their way back cut off by their inversion of the premiss/theory relation, Cutler et al. can only solve the problem of economic reductionism by *fiat*, or 'dogmatically' as they might say. Their notorious principle of 'necessary non-correspondence' represents in the end a simple declaration of the autonomy each sphere must have, whether it be the political, the economic or the ideological. Its extraordinary consequence for the concept of class is what one sympathetic critic (Johnston, 1986) has termed approvingly its 'disaggregation':

> If classes are conceived as categories of economic agent then they cannot also be conceived as political and cultural agencies. It follows that political institutions and practices, ideologies and other cultural forms cannot be conceived as classes (Cutler et al., 1977, p. 231).

However, in the absence of their dogmatic autonomisation of the various realms, resort to the same reformulation of the relationship between the realms as that suggested by Cutler et al. (that is, conditions of existence rather than levels) allows one to discover the path to the very middle way of 'relative autonomy' that they insist cannot exist. In its turn, discovery of this middle way additionally allows the formulation of precisely the non-humanist, non-essentialist and multi-dimensional concept of class that they also say is impossible.

Notes

1. Przeworski summarises his position thus:

   > I believe that the challenge of methodological individualism must be accepted. The only alternative would be to agree with G.A. Cohen that '... Marxism is fundamentally concerned not with behaviour, but with the forces and relations constraining and directing it...' This seems to me more like a screenplay for Star Wars than for social theory. Somehow I would think that for historical materialism the motor of history is class struggle, not The Force (Przeworski, 1986).

2. Since most sociologies, whether they are Interactionist, Functionalist, Weberian or indeed Marxist, have not acknowledged the unsurpassability of this discursive gulf, one is left with the question as to what sort of sense, if any, they make if it is not grounded in what I am suggesting are properly psychological or sociological discourses? While I do not intend to offer anything like a full answer to this question, I would say in passing that they do, of course, make a certain sense (for

example as 'unchained melodies' in the case of the prolife-
rating class schema?). However, because of the incoherences
and aporia that are the consequences of the absence of any
such grounding, the opportunity is created for ethical notions
to insinuate themselves into such discourses in order to fill or,
more often, obscure such gaps. In other words they tend to
project how individual/collective subjects *ought* to behave if
certain representations/assumptions were true; for example if a
certain form of action were typical of given groups (Weber), if
there were shared values (Parsons) or if, as members of classes,
they acted in accordance with their interests (Marx). The
suggestion that there is an ethical dimension to these notions
is reinforced by the ease with which the person/group, society,
or class that fails to behave in the projected fashion is
condemned or is diagnosed as suffering from some form of
pathology (for example 'false consciousness'). Similar reinforcement may be derived from the less common occasions
when a redemptionist note is struck, as when it is declared
that a particular class schema allows one to say something to
the effect that 'the manual working class which is after all the
real working class has remained true to its interests' (see
Heath, 1987).

3. If Poulantzas has sought to rescue the Marxist concept of class
    from the twin threats of humanism and economic reduc-
    tionism by fetishising 'the class struggle', at least it can be said
    that he is aware of the problems posed by these two threats.
    Unfortunately, the same cannot be said of Erik Wright (1978,
    1985). Until recently (1987), although he elaborates a concep-
    tion of 'class structure' which owes something to Althusser,
    Wright has betrayed no concern whatsoever as regards the
    issues raised by the problematisation of humanism. Indeed he
    has criticised Poulantzas for his half-hearted challenge to the
    primacy of the economic and so has remained firmly wedded
    to what Rattansi has called 'Manifesto Marxism', albeit of
    highly sophisticated, self-produced kind: 'Marxism ... is not
    primarily a theory of class structure; it is above all a theory of
    class struggle' (Wright, 1978, p. 98).

    It is not at all surprising, therefore, that latterly Wright
    should have been overwhelmed when he heard the sirens of
    'rational choice Marxism', especially as it has been developed
    by John Roemer (1982), since for them Marxism's humanism
    and economic reductionism are its greatest strengths and
    provide the bases upon which it may be developed by being

articulated with ideas produced by any number of non-Marxist and humanist schools of thought. It is therefore also not at all surprising that neo-Weberians such as Rose et al. (1987) should have greeted the publication of Wright's most recent book as the occasion for considerable rejoicing, especially since the book followed the 'rational choicers' in remaining more orthodox as regards humanism than reductionism.

9 Reconstructing 'Class'

The site has been cleared and the tools laid out. The reconstruction of 'class' may now begin. In other words the effort must now be made to realise the conceptual possibility that too quickly passed through Poulantzas' mind when he said, 'everything happens as if social classes were the result of an ensemble of structures and their relations' (see p. 153 above). The reasons why a non-humanist concept of class failed to emerge in Poulantzas' discourse, have already been set out and so need not be repeated here. What does need to be repeated, however, is that what pre-empts the possibility of a non-humanist and multi-dimensional concept of class in Poulantzas' discourse, as in Cutler et al.'s, is a dogmatism, which indicates the occurrence of a moment of great articulatory strain in the pertinent signifying chains. The strain is caused by the fact that to follow up on the possibility that is being denied would challenge the place of too many other cherished signs, such as 'determination in the last instance', 'fetishism' and, most cherished of all, 'struggle'. What is denied is often hidden away, and we have seen already how diligently Poulantzas covered his tracks. So well did he cover them that he was able to hide from himself the fact that he had something to hide (that is, it allowed him to continue to denounce the humanism of others to the end). Such a theory is thus unlikely to prove a very dependable guide for others, no matter how formidable their tracking skills, and they are likely to be sent off along false trails.

The dogmatism that pre-empts the realisation of the selfsame possibility within Cutler et al.'s discourse is much less deeply buried within it, in the sense that it protects the place of far fewer signs and I doubt that many, if any, are particularly cherished. Indeed theirs is an almost casual dogmatism, arising from what looks like a simple error concerning the necessary ordering of theoretical discourses, an eccentric reading of Foucault, and involving a simple denial that classes can have political and ideological dimensions.

However, their simple error may be easily corrected, their eccentric reading readily replaced with another, and their many other gains retained as a result. In what follows an alternative to Cutler et al.'s attempt to re-theorise class will be presented, on the grounds that this promises to be the most economical way of providing a fully non-humanist, non-reductionist and multi-dimensional concept of class, which neither protects nor depends upon any, even vestigally representationalist notions.

Cutler et al. are forced to deny the possibility of a multi-dimensional concept of class because they believe that otherwise there is no way of properly acknowledging the autonomy of the political or ideological realms. They believe this because they think that economic reductionism is the cause of Marxism's pervasive humanism. And the reason, in turn, that they think *this* is their belief that the ultimate source of economic reductionism is the epistemological idealism that they find in the heart of the labour theory of value. Finally, they so privilege epistemological concerns because of the anti-epistemological conclusion they draw from their reading of Foucault. For them, the recognition of the impossibility of epistemology opens up the royal road to the assertion of the truth about 'class'! It should be noted, however, that even this would appear to have involved too big a claim for Hindess (1987, pp. 110, 123–4), who now argues that classes do not exist. In explaining this conclusion, he makes explicit what was implicit in his earlier collaborative texts, namely their unconsciously but profoundly humanist refusal, which instructively they share with those by such as Przeworski, to allow the existence of any forms of being that are not 'actors' (that is, not themselves capable of decision-making). The refusal is justified on the inevitably representationalist, if negative, grounds that it is not classes who actually struggle. (For a similarly surprising and ultimately representational justification for refusing a place to the category of 'class' in socialist theoretical discourse, see Laclau, Mouffe, 1985, p. 166.)

By retracing the steps that led to this truly nihilistic conclusion – there is nothing to picture – and by picking up the constructive points already made in the discussion of Cutler et al., a more plebian road may be opened up to another destination – a multi-dimensional concept of class. One difference will be that progress along this road will be governed both by the requirement for theoretical creativity that stems from the need to maintain a rigorous non-humanism and by the epistemological protocols of realism, which require that it should be temporarily closed any time there is a need to gain the consent of the 'facts'. Progress along this road will be based upon a reading of Foucault, which finds in his texts a critique of Marxism's failure to accept the reality and autonomy of the ideological sphere and a means of correcting this. More specifically and more pertinently, such a reading leads to a different sort of criticism being made of the labour theory of value, a substantive one which sees the undeniable presence of idealism in the discourse that produced it as responsible for the over-extension of the theory's explanatory power rather than for any intrinsic economic reductionism. If all that is wrong with the labour theory of value is its explanatory over-extension, and if this may be avoided by acknowledging the presence of ideological and indeed political dimensions within production, then not only need the labour theory of value not be junked, but also and at last a non-humanist and non-reductionist concept of class may be formulated that may be made to refer to structural entities which neither act nor struggle.

The first move, then, must be to refuse a suggestion that has hitherto proved to be irresistible. Namely, that the specification of the mode of surplus appropriation specific to the capitalist mode of production instantly and fully defines the positions of classes of capitalist and proletarian *agents*. This refusal apart, the specification of the mode of production provided by Balibar (see above p. 157) is acceptable here with only one further proviso, which is that it be read as signifying what Wolpe (1980) has termed its 'restricted' (that is, simply economic) form. As a consequence, here the discernment of the capitalist mode of production at the level of capital in general in relation to any set of production relations is deemed sufficient only to define the set of economic positions which are differentiated by what Cutler et al. have termed usefully 'the relations of possession and separation' and that are partially constitutive of the world of production.

Forgetting the labour theory of value for a moment, stripped of its humanist and reductionist props, this is as much as classical Marxism can contribute. However, it is a most important contribution since (pace Cutler et al.) what it provides is the vital but hitherto elusive means of escaping the metaphorical conception of classes as either groups of agents or agents in their own right engaged in struggle; that is, it provides the means whereby such conceptions may be displaced by a concept of classes as distinguishable ensembles of more than economic positions that are – and this is the critical point – nevertheless still part of a single structure. What makes this so critical is the fact that, once classes are conceptualised as part of a single structure, the processes that divide and therefore the boundary that divides them may be conceptualised as a shared one. In other words, one need no longer think representationally, as the metaphor directs, in terms of two armies confronting one another in an 'arena' or with a field ('terrain') in between, where the changing compositions and relative strengths of the two can only be related to what is imagined to be a pertinent underlying structure with the greatest of difficulty, if at all. Rather, one may think of any set of classes as a structural unity which is divided into two as a necessary consequence of the relations that constitute it as a whole. The line of division will gain or lose definition as a direct and equally necessary consequence of any changes in its constitutive relations. Thus, classes need no longer be thought of as armies confronting and attacking one another but rather as the products of tectonic forces that over time divide sets of economic, political and ideological positions more or less completely from one another. Nor, at a more abstract level, need their relationships to one another be understood in terms of what Althusser (1970) has termed 'linear causality', which must remain the case if one maintains, no matter how unconsciously, an empiricist/humanist metatheoretical stance. Rather their relationships may be understood in terms of what are called 'causal mechanisms' as is appropriate if one adopts a realist/non-humanist stance (Sayer, 1984).

Thus, whilst it is agreed here with the early Wright (1978), as against Poulantzas (1978), that the capitalist mode of production can only give rise to two and not three possible classes, it is important at the structural level to understand that the theory currently being expounded has no room for Wright's 'contradictory class locations', although this has proved to be a highly suggestive notion to the present author. The reason for this is, first, because, like Poulantzas' class 'places' and Cutler et al.'s 'loci', such 'locations' require agents to occupy them as a necessary condition of a class' effectivity, with the result that the premature theoretical closure that is currently being rectified occurs. And second, because any particular set of positions is on one side of the dividing line or the other, or on neither. In the last case it is an instance of a breach in the boundary between the classes. However, since the location of the boundary may change over time, it is also possible that particular human embodiments may sometimes be positioned by one class and sometimes by the other (that is, they may be 'embourgeoisified' or 'proletarianised'). The consequences that this train of thought has for how the problem posed by the existence of the so-called 'new middle class' may best be approached, and for how the insight contained in Wright's notion of 'contradictory class locations' may be taken advantage of, will be indicated below.

For now the more important task and a necessary prerequisite for any such discussion is the continuance of the present theoretical effort. What must be provided, if the position being elaborated is to be empirically plausible as well as useful, is some specification of how the concrete complexity of classes and their social effects may be grasped. To do this one has first to define the political and ideological dimensions of class so that the specification of the basic structures of the class entities may be completed. Again the pertinent level of analysis is the most abstract one (that is, that which pertains to any set of capitalist ideological and political relations), the interest being in the discovery or otherwise of the existence of divisions in these structures, such as may be suggested by the existence of competing party ideologies and differential party access to state power. However, it is important to emphasise here, for example, that the concrete existence of any such ideologies and differential access only *suggests* the possible existence of class entities but by no means proves it. In order to prove the existence of such entities it is necessary to show that any putative ideological and political class divisions are in fact related to the economic divisions already specified and so are constitutive of classes. In other words a way has to be found of discovering whether or not any aspects of the economic, ideological and political structures in social formations are not only imbricated with, but also interpenetrate one another and so have reciprocally structuring effects.

In the most general terms, the making of this discovery requires that a means be found of moving on from the theorisation of the workplace (see pp. 73–6 above) that may be gained from synthesising the insights and concepts which Marx, Burawoy and Laclau and Mouffe have already provided as regards the economic, the political and the ideological respectively. As a corollary, this discovery also requires that because of the osmotic relationships between classes and their conditions of existence, it is not possible that class entities, formed in the workplace, as in part they undoubtedly are, should be creatures that inhabit only that institutional setting. On the contrary their inherent dependence upon the structures that define the wider social formation necessarily means that they must possess a capacity to produce effects beyond the

workplace, and therefore that they are truly entities of critical significance in society and for sociology.

However, and here I consciously echo Weber's discussion of
'class, status and party', the osmotic transfers necessary for the existence of classes neither exhaust the content of the spheres,
including the economic, that comprise their conditions of existence, nor even monopolise those aspects of them on which they
draw. It must therefore be emphasised that classes are neither the
only nor always (contra Lockwood, 1986) the most important social
entities. This said, classes are nevertheless often the most socially
significant of such entities. Unlike the entities constituted primarily
on the basis of, for example, gendering and racialising discourses,
they are necessarily multi-dimensional and therefore have the
complex, self-constitutive, internal structure that guarantees them a
wide social pertinence. (On this point, putting aside our marked
metatheoretical differences, I agree with Lockwood.) By contrast,
the other entities are not necessarily so elaborately structured. What
is more, since the human subjects that embody classes are always
gendered and often racialised, it is most likely that classes will
provide the medium through which gendering and racialising
discourses and the other entities they support are either sustained or
transformed.

With his distinction between particular capitals and capital in
general and with his provision of the means to think the interrelation between these spheres of capital's existence, Marx allowed the
acknowledgement and understanding of the pertinent osmotic
processes within the economic sphere. In our distinctions between
the political in general and 'the politics of production' and between
the ideological in general and 'the discourses of production', along
with our provision of the means to think the interrelation between
them, Burawoy (1985, Chapter 3) and I have begun to do the same
for the political and ideological realms. When one considers the
three osmotic processes and the structures that support them as
they operate, subsist and have interactive effects within individual
workplaces and social formations, one may discern, without
recourse to the subjects that embody them, an outline of the main
lineaments of the classes that so significantly structure capitalist
societies at the micro and macro levels.

Capital, Labour and the Relations between Them
Economically, the capitalist class comprises that set of positions
defined by the capitalist relations of possession and separation

which possesses means of production, in the sense that in these positions inheres the capacity to set them in motion. Politically, the capitalist class comprises that set of positions defined by the relations of 'discipline against resistance' in which inheres the power to control the process of production so as to ensure that a surplus is produced. Finally, ideologically, the capitalist class comprises that set of positions defined by the relations of signification in which inheres the entitlements, most often but not necessarily the legal rights, required for the maintenance of the other two sets of positions, and therefore to ensuring that the position of possession is also the position to which any surplus accrues.

Following the same reasoning, the working class may be defined as that set of positions in which *inheres* no possession of means of production, no power to challenge the production of a surplus, and no significatory basis upon which to challenge either of these disadvantageous positions. (Whether or not the human or non-human subjects which are positioned by and so partly embody such a set of positions share these lacks is a separate and empirical question.) When all these conditions are met, and only then, may one talk in a non-humanist way of the existence of a capitalist or a working class. As a corollary, if any one or other of them is not met one can speak only of certain necessary elements, but not the classes themselves, being in existence. The reason for this insistence on all the conditions being met before one can speak of the existence of a class is because only then will the necessary, reciprocally constraining and therefore self-constitutive processes be possible, which are now what must be specified for each class.

How, then, do economic, political and ideological divisions at the levels of the social formation and the unit of production become those structural ensembles that are here termed 'classes'? What are the reciprocally interpenetrative processes that produce classes under capitalism? This is the point at which the retained and stripped-down version of the labour theory of value plays an essential role. Since, under capitalism, these processes are those that allow the capitalist class to appropriate surplus-value. Surplus-value is the difference between necessary and surplus labour. Thus it cannot exist unless there also exists an entity that can ensure that such a difference is produced at the level of the unit of capital and at that of capital in general. For such an entity to exist it must comprise an ensemble of economic, political and ideological positions which can, *qua* ensemble, produce such a difference and enforce its own retention of it. No such surplus may exist, let alone be retained, unless an entity exists: first, that monopolises possession of the means of production, as Marx insisted in the famous section of *Capital* Volume I entitled 'The So-Called Primitive Accumulation'; second, that exercises a 'dictatorship' in production, as Marx (1968, pp. 549–50) put it rather exaggeratedly; and third, that enjoys what is most often a legal right of title to its possessions.

Thus the processes that constitute the capitalist class as an entity that is irreducible to human beings are those reciprocal constraints that make monopoly possession, 'dictatorship' over production and a right of title the mutually entailed positions that they have to be if a capitalist class is to exist. None of these positions would hold if the others didn't, and only the requirements that surplus-value should be produced and appropriated ensures their co-presence. In the absence of any of them not only would the ensemble cease to exist, but so too would its positioning effects on subjects, since there would be nothing to constrain them, to fix them; for example whether one has in mind the ensembles of positions themselves or the groups formed by their positioning effects, no monopoly of possession would long survive the absence of a 'dictatorship' over production and/or the absence of a legal or some other right of title. In sum, then, it is the production and, in this case, the appropriation of surplus-value that causes the economic, political and ideological divisions at the levels of the workplace and the social formation to become the structural ensemble of positions that is the capitalist class.

As regards the working class, the reciprocally interpenetrative positions that comprise it are necessarily the mirror image of those that produce the capitalist class. They are therefore those that explain its incapacity, *qua* structural ensemble, to prevent either the existence of a difference between necessary and surplus labour or the capitalist class's appropriation of it. Thus the processes that constitute the working class are those reciprocal constraints that make lack of possession of the means of production, subservience to capital's 'dictatorship' over production and exclusion from any right to title a mutually entailed ensemble of positions. As with the capitalist class, none of these positions would hold if the others didn't and only the requirements that the working class should interfere neither with the production of a difference between necessary and surplus labour nor its appropriation by the capitalist class ensures their co-presence. Again, it is the production and in this case the expropriation of surplus-value that causes the economic, political and ideological divisions at the levels of the workplace and the social formation to become the structural ensemble of positions that is the working class.

These, then, are the rudiments of the structural ensembles that are the two great classes of capitalist society. As such these are the minimum conditions that need to be satisfied before one can talk of either class existing. Needless to say, specification of these positions does not exhaustively describe even the abstractly conceivable structures of these classes. However, before an indication of the nature of their complex internal structures may be provided one must note that classes also have continuing and additional, reciprocally structuring effects upon one another as a result of their sharing of a common boundary within a single structure. What follows cannot do more than indicate the significance of this point, since once one moves beyond the specification of the abstract, minimum conditions for a class's existence it is hard not to talk concretely and thereby run the risk of a return to representationalism. (The structural tensions and therefore the nature of the continuing, reciprocally structuring effects as between the two classes will vary from social formation to social formation, because, of course, the general structures upon which classes osmotically depend are different also.)

Nevertheless, it is possible to say, in substantive if not theoretical agreement with Edwards (1979), Gordon et al. (1982), Crompton and Jones (1984) and many others, that the internal structures of the two classes and their social effects will reflect not simply the nature and variety of the means of production deployed, the type of 'dictatorship' exercised over production, the forms of title in existence, but also the nature and variety of the other osmotic processes that may come to structure concrete production relations (for an exemplification of the latter process as regards politics and ideology see Stedman-Jones' (1983) discussion of Chartism). The former set of variations may lead to varying forms and degrees of segmentation within classes and fractionalisation amongst their embodiments. Similarly, the latter set may lead to classes as a whole or particular segments being imbricated with and hence additionally structured by economic, political or ideological positions that have no necessary pertinence to the production of surplus-value, but which nevertheless will almost always affect indirectly if not directly the structure of classes themselves and therefore their social effects by the additional constraints they impose upon the nature of the subjects that can embody particular sets or sub-sets of class positionings (for example a requirement that skilled labour power, or indeed capital, should be white, male, protestant, Ulster Unionist and capable of 'O' level Maths).[1] Thus concrete classes and their effects are likely to be marked and affected by such factors as levels of technological development, international and domestic market conditions and a whole range of political and ideological conditions. For example: the first and second may speed or slow changes to the mix of means of production deployed; the third may alter the forms taken by the 'dictatorship' over production; and the fourth, as has just been suggested, may add a plurality of legal and extra-legal requirements both to those subjects in which title to the means of production may be embodied and to those who may embody the particular positionings or combinations thereof that constitute the two classes.[2]

In sum, concrete classes are likely to possess highly complex and variable structures, and to have even more complex social effects. This complexity of structure and especially of superincumbent requirements may have negative effects upon the internal coherence of classes *qua* structural ensembles (that is, they may atrophy), as well as on the groupings of subjects that variously and in part embody them (that is, they may fragment). And it may therefore reduce a class' capacity to survive any further destructuring pressures that may arise from time to time in response to the exigencies that flow either from problems in the ongoing production of surplus-value or from changes resulting from the tectonic forces and osmotic processes that link them and any superincumbent positionings with their conditions of existence. Thus classes as such do not struggle but rather, because of their nature as antagonistic components of a single structure, restructure and destructure one another and therefore the groupings of subjects that embody them. [3]

Destructuring, Restructuring and the 'New Middle Class'

This chapter will now approach its end with a very brief discussion of the significance of the so-called 'new middle class' in contemporary advanced capitalist societies. What will be proposed is a new conception of social mobility in that the phenomena to which the phrase 'new middle class' refers should be re-conceptualised: (a) as a shifting, even permeable boundary zone between the two great classes; (b) as, therefore, the most critical site of the structuring/destructuring tension that is necessarily produced between them by their shared, constitutive dependence on the production of surplus-value; and, finally (c) as a crucial indicator of the balance of class forces obtaining in any particular society.[4]

Once classes are conceptualised as non-human entities there is no structural problem of the middle class, since even when the boundary between the two classes is disintegrating no new set of positions is formed within the existing ensemble. What is a problem, however, and this is what hitherto has been thought of confusedly as a problem of 'class' rather than 'class-related' analysis, is the effect on subjects of their being the embodiments of the diverse sets of positionings produced by the multiform nature of capitalist production, especially where the process of disintegration is underway. And this is the case even when one ignores the super-incumbent positionings mentioned above. For example, where one has what are variously known as 'entrepreneurial' or 'competitive' production relations and such a social formation as existed in mid-Victorian Britain, the constraints imposed by being positioned as either an embodiment of capital or labour are very likely to be clear, mutually reinforcing and consistent in their effects, whether one is considering economic, political or ideological positionings. Where such production relations are dominant, and in the absence of other sources of division, one may expect, without forgetting their intrinsic unpredictability, the behaviour of subjects to correspond quite closely to what may be imagined, not as the promptings of the classes and their supposed 'interests' but as the actions necessary either to escape from the constraints inherent in proletarian positionings or to sustain those advantages inherent in capitalist positionings.

By contrast, where one has what are known as 'corporate' or 'monopoly' production relations and such a social formation as exists in the contemporary United States, the constraints imposed by being positioned as an embodiment of either capital or labour are very unlikely to be clear, mutually reinforcing or consistent in their effects. Not least because if one occupies a position that is somewhere in the nowadays very extensive middle of the hierarchies created to administer the production and circulation processes, one is likely to be positioned as an embodiment of capital *and* labour. Thus, for example, a manager is positioned always as the possessor of some part of the power necessary to set the means of production in motion and to attempt to ensure that surplus-value accrues to capital. But managers are also positioned most often as lacking title in that same capital. Similarly, a filing clerk is seldom positioned as a possessor of either power but may be nevertheless a title holder, albeit of a very subordinate kind. Thus one may talk of subjects – human and non-human – being positioned by 'contradictory class positionings', even if one may not talk with Wright of a class made up of the occupants of 'contradictory class-locations' – a small change in terminology signifying a big difference in conceptualisation.

What the contrast between the relative clarity of the positionings of subjects by classes under entrepreneurial capitalist relations and their opacity under corporate capitalist relations suggests are two points. First, that differences in production relations lead to considerable variation in the location of the boundary between the subjects that embody class relations from production unit to production unit. Second, that changes to such relations, and in particular the predominance of the corporate set, leads to the blurring of the boundary itself as one or both groups of subjects is or are destructured, that is, cease to share the same set of positionings.

Historically, it has been subjects embodying proletarian positionings that have been most affected by such destructuring as the tasks inherent in the appropriation of surplus-value have exceeded the physical and even monetary capabilities of title holders. Consequently, segments of those without title have been separated-off, usually by invoking one or more superincumbent positionings, and given 'the opportunity' to exercise one or more of the possessory, disciplinary or title-holding powers of capital, whether as accountants, managers, foremen, shareholders or whatever, and thereby escape some part of the constraints otherwise imposed upon them by their otherwise proletarian positionings.

The corollary of the destructuring of the relations between the embodiments of the working class has been the destructuring, albeit to a lesser degree, of the relations between those embodying capitalist positionings. The latter have had to share the rights and powers of title with employee pension funds and the rights and powers of possession and even sometimes control with unions and/ or other employee representatives. In most contemporary advanced capitalist societies capital retains its hegemony, in the pre-Gramscian sense, thanks to the persistence of certain conditions (for example, a certain level of corporate profitability, political competition for the middle-class vote and the presence of an appropriate hegemonic or at least dominant ideology). In their absence the aforementioned beneficiaries of contradictory positionings may either lose the powers that separate them from the remainder of those without title, or their exercise of such powers may lose its worth for capital with consequent negative effects on their incomes, other perquisites and loyalty. Thus, although the expansion of 'the new middle class' always indicates the occurrence of a certain underlying destructuring, whether this is likely to be to the benefit of the embodiments of capitalist or working class positionings depends upon other and contingent conditions whose nature has to be established separately for each society.[5]

Class Destructuring and the Possibility of Socialism

If either class destructures and thereby dissolves the other, and this is only one possible and unlikely scenario, neither capitalism nor the remaining class would continue to exist. What they were replaced by would depend upon which was the destructured class, which, if any, were the remaining superincumbent positionings and how auspicious were their conditions of existence. If the proletariat were destructured, the superincumbent positionings were benign and their conditions of existence auspicious, socialism would be what replaced capitalism. If one were not so lucky and either the capitalist class (as in the USSR in 1917), or the proletariat were destructured and the superincumbent positionings were malign and/or the conditions of existence inauspicious, there is as yet no agreement as to what sign to use in referring to such a social formation. However, 'barbarism' would seem to me to be an appropriate working designation, as indeed it seemed to Marx and to those leading postmodernists who once saw the choice before humanity as one between 'Socialism or Barbarism'. Barbarism is made no less appalling by the realisation that the 'theme park' rather than the 'iron cage' or 'the gulag' may more accurately prefigure it.

Without doubt one of the most ironic and tragic consequences of Marxism's long-term commitment to a humanist ontology has been the commitment of some parts of the socialist and communist left to the preservation of a proletariat of 'good people', untainted by any share in property ownership. Where carried through to a successful and supposedly revolutionary conclusion, the unintended social-structural consequence of this has been and would be again the preservation of a set of positions and positionings, albeit no longer proletarian, characterised by lack of title, possession and control, and hence highly susceptible to resubordination to those positioned by another set of positions in which title, possession and control were claimed to inhere. And this could be on the basis of privileging one or other of any number of superincumbent positionings such as 'race', religion, gender, sexual preference or party affiliation.

Thus what the present non-humanist stance makes even clearer than before is that, for the sake of all 'good people', the victory of the working class would be its own dissolution; that is, the rights and powers inherent in capital would by then be shared out amongst the whole population and not simply amongst those separated off into 'the new middle class'. The challenge to the Left is to find ways of ensuring not only that this occurs but also that this multiply-held wealth is used in a socially responsible and democratically accountable manner.

Notes

1. The existence of such superincumbent positionings is likely to be an important part of any explanation for the common incoherence of class subjects that was mentioned earlier, since they may also be positioned by other, possibly opposed, non-class ensembles of positionings.
2. On this point see also the very suggestive paper by Wolpe (1986), which for all its parallels with the present one remains separated from it by precisely the casual, residual humanism inherited from Marx and Althusser that was criticised above, p. 157.
3. Apart from suggesting how a defensible sociological sense may be made of the results obtained by Weberian and 'Manifesto Marxist' accounts of 'class struggle', this formulation additionally appears to suggest a way in which the dispute currently raging between Crewe (1986) and Heath et al. (1987) may be resolved; that is, it allows both that classes continue to be politically significant in contemporary Britain as Heath et al. insist, but without opportunistically redefining their identities as they do, and that individuals act inconsistently as Crewe suggests. However, the non-representationalism that allows this formulation is, of course, what makes it an unacceptable basis for resolving the differences between the two parties, since both are profoundly representationalist in their metatheoretical assumptions. For this reason they appear to be condemned to continue arguing about their respective methodological competences, oblivious to the fact that such a focus of argument suggests a naive empiricism that both parties would otherwise wish to reject.

4. In what follows only one section of 'the new middle class' is discussed, which is that section produced by private capital in any sphere of economic life. Although this section represents the archetype of the new middle class, it is important to bear in mind that its relative importance varies greatly as between advanced capitalist societies and as a consequence of the varying size of the section produced by the state. Many ingenious attempts (for example, Carchedi, 1977) have been made to identify the latter group in class terms. I find them all to be unsatisfactory. The approach to the conceptualisation of classes put forward here should cause one to doubt that any such attempt could be successful. In other words, my view is that Cutler et al. (1977, p. 289) are very likely to be correct when they suggest that there is no reason to suppose that economic class-relations must encompass all members of the social formation. This said, work remains to be done not only on the nature of the state as a sociological entity and on its articulation with classes, but also more pertinently on the effects of the positions and positionings thus generated on the subjects that embody the state. In sum, not only is the coherence of the notion of 'the new middle class' very problematic, but so too is its coherence as a group of subjects.

5. In two works in progress (Woodiwiss, 1988a; 1988b) I endeavour to assess the significance of the postwar growth of 'the new middle class' in Japan and the United States.

Conclusion: Towards a Sociology without Metaphors

The law may or may not be a particularly effective way of changing society, but the effort to improve our understanding of it may again prove, as it did for the founders, a highly effective way of changing sociology. Likewise, a better sociology of the facts that come before the courts and lawmakers, in both senses of the term, is required, if we are to produce a better understanding of the law, let alone better laws. The most general contention advanced here has been the somewhat ironic one that postmodernism has an important role to play in the pursuit of these improvements, provided that its limits are appreciated. For this reason, 'Post-representationalism' rather than 'postmodernism' better signifies what has been sought here.

The reasons for accepting and valuing the distinguishing characteristics of Marxist economic theory remain persuasive (for example Wolfe, Callari, Roberts, 1984), as do the reasons for believing that Marxism provides the best basis upon which to develop a political science worthy of the name (for example Jessop, 1982, 1986, passim). The argument here has been that the reasons for the failure to utilise effectively the conceptual basics thus provided in the construction of a properly synthetic sociology are threefold: a lack of awareness of the significance for theorising of Saussure's revolution in the understanding of language; a more general neglect of the language-borne discursive dimension of social life; and a resulting inability to produce the techniques necessary to discover these problems, understand their causes and correct them. Once this set of failures has been overcome, it is possible to rediscover the constructive dimension of the activity termed 'critique', and to do so in such a way as to increase the theoretical gain from research. I have tried to make clear how this may be done in the course of my efforts to rethink production, law and class. It is also now possible to restore to its rightful place at the centre of theoretical concern the issue as to how the interpenetration of the various spheres of social life is to be understood. Too often in the past these spheres

185

have been analysed as if they are really as isolated from one another as the necessity of their separate conceptualisation might appear to suggest. In this text the terms whose presence most clearly signals the occurrence of such a restoration are: 'transudation', 'transpositioning', 'osmosis', 'techtonic' and 'superincumbent' – all terms that, in one way or another, directly address the problems of linkage and interpenetration.

Finally and in sum, it is possible to confront the source of contemporary theory's anxiety and as a result escape from the repetition of the hopeless task to which humanism has hitherto condemned it; that is, that of trying to aggregate individual human beings into groups and thence into societies. It is possible instead to begin to construct a *base* that is truly a sociology and not an impossible social psychology, whether of 'action', 'interaction', 'struggle' or, most recently, 'strategy' (see Crow, 1989). Thus, what is required is not just a positive scepticism that empowers the sociological imagination so that it can suggest what else might exist apart from human and non-human subjects, but also a stoicism that allows sociology to appreciate its limits. The most important limit is, in the end, the disciplinarily imposed one that no sociology may be built by *generalising* about either human or non-human subjects. Individual human subjects *qua* subjects may only be understood by psychology and even it, given the metatheoretical stance adopted here, cannot base itself upon such generalising. Nevertheless, provided the psychology deployed is metatheoretically compatible, the knowledge it produces may be combined with that produced by the sort of sociology envisioned in this text. As a result, subjects' relations to and effects on their social-structural environments may be illuminated, as may the nature of any collective subjects so formed, whether human or non-human. However, it should never be forgotten that any additional knowledge so gained is exactly that, *additional* knowledge, which, while it may be used to illuminate the topics traditionally of interest to social psychologists, historians and humanist sociologists, cannot be used to produce theory *de novo*. In sum, on account of both their intrinsic unpredictability and the fact that they are in no sense exhaustive of what subsists within the realm of the social, subjects cannot serve as the objects of study for sociology.

As has been indicated on many occasions in this text, the most common indicator of the inadequacy of unreconstructed Marxist theoretical discourse is its recurrent resort, especially when addressing issues of linkage, to metaphorical devices, principally those of 'base/superstructure', 'fetishism' and 'struggle'.[1] The condition that connects these symptoms of theoretical underdevelopment with the representationalist and humanist modes of theorising that produce them is the failure to recognise the significance of the fact that, as Foucault (1974) has demonstrated and as has just been assumed in the discussion of the relations between psychology and sociology, theoretical discourses are made possible by discursive formations, whose 'rules of formation' constrain their pertinence within certain discursive and non-discursive limits; that is, Marxist theory does not simply name the primary substantive object of its interest as 'the economy' but, given the 'rules of formation', which account for its conditions of possibility/existence, the real objects of its referential concern could not be other than those generally understood by this term.

The corollary of this is that the real objects of concern in the ideological and political realms must similarly only be fully and properly illuminable by recourse to those discourses whose associated discursive formations and 'rules of formation' are specific to them and therefore different from those that produced and now sustain 'economics'. Hence the use here of the terms 'signification' and 'discipline against resistance' to signify the core relations in the ideological and political realms respectively. Hence also the use of the terms 'the ideological' and 'the political' to signify the complexes of institutions in which they predominate and to which they are generally taken to refer. In sum, with Foucault's help, it is possible to acknowledge theoretically a sense of the real and irreducible differences between what we currently understand to be the fundamental dimensions of sociality. The significance of these differences is variously obscured, minimised or denied whenever the old Marxist metaphors are present. Clearly, the challenge that remains is to formulate a conception of sociality that can both maintain the acknowledgement of these differences and facilitate the understanding of their concrete imbrication and interpenetration.

In sum, the present text points towards a conception of societies or social formations that has nothing in common with those signified so reassuringly but in the end so elusively by, for example, architectural or spatial metaphors. On the contrary, it conceives of them as a particular kind of aggregate of theoretically identifiable entities and their interactive effects. Each of these has some of their effects through subjects but never only because of them. Additionally and critically, the conception of the social formation advanced here privileges none of these entities, arguing instead that they only come to comprise bounded entities as a consequence of their reciprocally structuring effects. Such entities, in turn, produce what are usually, but not necessarily, national social formations.

Societies, therefore, are not to be understood as in any sense free-standing edifices but rather as ensembles of ensembles of positions, which are themselves produced by inexhaustible and unmonopolisable processes, and which for a longer or shorter time impose constraints upon one another. Workplaces, markets, legal systems and classes, for example, are thus but particular instances, albeit often especially important ones, of the possible concrete entities that are produced in the course of the operation of such reciprocal constraints and which in turn recursively help to reproduce the underlying structures and relations. There is simply no way in which a concrete instance of the interactive effects of even so artificially limited a set of such recursive relations may be visualised in a single representation. This is because any such instance (for example, a strike) is at least four other observable 'things' at the same time (for example, a workplace relation, a market relation, a legal relation and a class relation). This is the point whose negative significance for representationalist approaches to social theory is regularly obscured by theorists' insufficiently radical and rigorous rejection of the equivalences that are popularly thought to obtain between the terms 'society', 'social formation' and 'nation state'. Given such a rejection, 'society' may only be realised as an imaginary and abstract model which while it may owe something or even a great deal to the results of efforts made to make it refer to the extra-theoretical world, is never, with any degree of certainty, the same as the latter.

The final claim, then, to be made on behalf of the approach exemplified here, is that it promises to provide something which has often been promised in the past but never yet delivered, namely, the means whereby social theorists may finally free themselves from the thrall of the nation state. The need for such a move arises because, whether theorists have been aware of it or not, the nation state has too often been the ultimate pre-given. It is the picturable 'home' (sometimes happy, sometimes not) whose structure all varieties of sociology have typically sought to understand by representing it in terms of their architectural and other metaphors. However, the nation state is not a legitimate first or even second object of theoretical speculation, since it, unlike production, law, and class, is only a concrete entity and thus may only be understood as an instance of the concrete interactive effects of such structural entities. These processes and entities themselves are the proper objects of sociological speculation and, ultimately, they are 'homeless'. This is a point whose significance humanist sociologies have found very difficult to acknowledge (for a notable, if extreme, exception, see Mann, 1986, pp. 14–17). Generally, they have no satisfactory means of sustaining an insight that has been generated within many of them, especially Marxism, that the boundaries between states are as likely to be dissolved as they are to be created by processes that are otherwise supposed to be 'internal' to them. Now, more than ever, this is an insight that must be sustained and developed if sociology is to understand what is increasingly obviously a 'trans-national' world, within which new and non-unitary structures of sociality are becoming daily more apparent.

Notes

1. It must, of course, be confessed that many of the terms I use are drawn from other than social scientific discourses and thus that there is a sense in which their use represents a metaphorical mode of reasoning. However, my defence is that their presence in this text causes no problems, since their appearance herein rests upon explicit and determinate theoretical conditions whereby they are combined with signifieds which are different to those with which they were combined in the discourses from whence they were borrowed. Nevertheless, given the metatheoretical stance taken here, these terms recommend themselves as prime candidates for deconstructive criticism. Whatever may be their ultimate status, they will have served their purpose if their use and/or criticism contributes to the reorientation of social scientific thought sought here.

Bibliography

Abercrombie, N., Hill, S., Turner, B. (1982) *The Dominant Ideology Thesis*, Allen and Unwin, London.

Abercrombie, N. et al. (1986) *Sovereign Individuals of Capitalism*, Allen and Unwin, London.

Abercrombie, N. et al. (1990) *Discourses of Dominance*, Unwin Hyman, London.

Abrahams, G. (1968) *Trade unions and the Law*, Cassel, London.

Abrahamson, B., Brostrom, A. (1980) *The Rights of Labour*, Sage, Beverley Hills.

Abrams, P. (1982) *Historical Sociology*, Cornell University Press, Ithaca.

Ackerman, B.A. (1980) *Social Justice and the Liberal State*, Yale University Press, New Haven.

Ackerman, B.A. (1983) *Reconstructing American Law*, Harvard University Press, Cambridge, Mass.

Adams, P., Minson, J. (1978) 'The Subject of Feminism', *M/F*, 2.

Aglietta, M. (1976) *The Theory of Capitalist Regulation*, Verso, London.

Alexander, J. (1982) *Theoretical Logic in Sociology*, 4 vols, Routledge and Kegan Paul, London.

Alexander, J., Giesen, B., Munch, R., Smelser, N. (eds)(1987) *The Macro-Micro Link*, University of California Press, Berkeley.

Althusser, L. (1969) *For Marx*, Allen Lane, London.

Althusser, L. (1971) *Lenin and Philosophy*, New Left Books, London.

Althusser, L., Balibar, R. (1970) *Reading Capital*, New Left Books, London.

Anderson, P. (1983) *In The Tracks of Historical Materialism*, Verso, London.

Annette, J. (1970) 'Bentham's Fear of Hobgoblins...', in Fine, B. (1979).

Archard, D. (1984) *Consciousness and the Unconscious*, Hutchinson, London.

Armstrong, P.S., Goodman, J., Hyman, J. (1981) *Ideology and Shop-floor Industrial Relations*, Croom Helm, London.

Atiyah, P.S. (1979) *The Rise and Fall of Freedom of Contract*, Oxford University Press, Oxford.

Atleson, J. (1984) *Values and Assumptions in American Labour Law*, University of Massachusetts Press, Amhurst.

Austin, J. (1913) *Lectures on Jurisprudence*, MacCray, London.

Baker, J.H. (1979) *An Introduction to English Legal History*, Butterworth, London.

Balkin, J. (1987) 'Deconstructive Practice and Legal Theory' *Yale Law Journal*, 96, p. 743.

Barthes, R. (1972) *Mythologies*, Cape, London.

Barthes, R. (1975) *S/Z*, Cape, London.

Beirne, P., Quinny, R. (eds) *Marxism and Law*, Wiley, New York.

Bennett, T. (1979) *Formalism and Marxism*, Methuen, London.

Bentham, J. (1970) *An Introduction to the Principles of Morals and Justice*, Athlone, London.

Benton, E. (1977) *Philosophical Foundations of the Three Sociologies*, Routledge, London.

Benton, E. (1984) *The Rise and Fall of Structural Marxism*, Macmillan, London.

Benton, E. (1984) 'Biological Ideas and their Cultural Uses' in Brown, s.c. (1984).

Benton, E. (1988) 'Humanism = Speciesism: Marx on Humans and Animals', *Radical Philosophy*, 50.

Benveniste, E. (1971) *Problems in General Linguistics*, Miami University Press, Miami.

Berman, H.J. (1983) *Law and Revolution*, Harvard University Press, Cambridge, Mass.

Bhaskar, R. (1978) *A Realist Theory of Science*, Harvester, Brighton.

Bhaskar, R. (1985) *Scientific Realism and Human Emancipation*, Verso, London.

Bhaskar, R. (1989) *Reclaiming Reality*, Verso, London.

Boudin, L. (1968) *Government by Judiciary*, 2 vols, Russell and Russell, New York.

Bowles, R. (1982) *Law and Economy*, Martin Robertson, Oxford.

Bowles, S., Gintis, H. (1981) 'Structure and Practice in the Labour Theory of Value', *Review of Radical Political Economies*, 12, 4.

Braverman, H. (1974) *Labour and Monopoly Capitalism*, Monthly Review Press, London.

Bridwell, R., Whitten, R. (1977) *The Constitution and the Common Law*, D.C. Heath, Lexington.

Brown, B., Cousins, M. (1980) 'The Linguistic Fault: the Case of Foucault's Archaeolgy', *Economy and Society*, 9. 3.

Brown, S.C. (1984) *Objectives and Cultural Divergence*, Royal Institute of Philosophy, Cambridge.

Buchanan, A.E. (1982) *Marx and Justice...*, Methuen, London.

Buci-Glucksmann, C. (1980) *Gramsci and the State*, Lawrence and Wishart, London.

Burawoy, M. (1979) *Manufacturing Consent: Changes in the Labour Process and Monopoly Capitalism*, University of Chicago Press, Chicago.

Burawoy, M. (1985) *The Politics of Production*, Verso, London.

Burton, F., Carlen, P. (1979) *Official Discourse*, Routledge, London.

Cain, M., Hunt, A. (1979) *Marx and Engels on Law*, Academic Press, London.

Carchedi, G. (1977) *On the Economic Identification of Social Classes*, Routledge, London.

Castoriadis, C. (1987) *The Imaginary Institution of Society*, Polity, Cambridge.

Chase, W. (1982) *The American Law School and the Rise of Administrative Government*, University of Wisconsin Press, Madison.

Christie, G. (1969) 'Objectivity in Law', *Yale Law Journal*, 78, p. 1311.

Christie, G. (1982) *Laws, Norms and Authority*, Duckworth, London.

Clarke, S. et al. (1980) *One-dimensional Marxism*, Motive, London.

Cohen, G.A. (1978) *Marx's Theory of History*, Verso, London.

Collins, H. (1986) *The Law of Contract*, Weidenfeld and Nicolson, London.

Collins, H. (1982a) 'Capitalist Discipline and Corporatist Law', pts 1 & 2, *The Industrial Law Journal*, ll, pp. 78–93; 170–7.

Collins, H. (1982b) *Marxism and Law*, Clarendon Press, Oxford.

Cottrell, A. (1984) *Social Classes in Marxist Theory*, Routledge, London.

Cousins, M., Hussain, A. (1984) *Michel Foucault*, Macmillan, London.

Coward, R., Ellis, J. (1977) *Language and Materialism*, Routledge, London.

Crewe, I. (1986) 'On the Death and Resurrection of Class Voting', *Political Studies*, xxxiv, 4.

Crompton, R.R., Jones, G. (1984) *White-collar Proletariat: Deskilling and Gender in Clerical Work*, Macmillan, London.

Crompton, R., Mann, M. (eds) (1986) *Gender and Stratification*, Polity, Cambridge.

Crow, G. (1989) 'The Use of the Concept of "Strategy" in Recent Sociological Literature', *Sociology*, 23, 1.

Cutler, T., Hindess, B., Hirst ,P., Hussain, A. (1977) *Marx's Capital and Capitalism Today*, 2 vols, Routledge and Kegan Paul, London.

Dalton, C. (1985) 'An Essay on the Deconstruction of Contract Doctrines', *Yale Law Journal*, 98, p. 997.

Daniels, N. (ed.) (1975) *Reading Rawls*, Basil Blackwell, Oxford.

Davidoff, L., Hall, C. (1987) *Family Fortunes: Men and Women of the English Middle-class 1780–1850*, Hutchinson, London.

de Vaus, D. (1986) *Surveys in Social Research*, Allen and Unwin.

Derrida, J. (1977) *Of Grammatology*, Johns Hopkins, Baltimore.

Derrida, J. (1978) *Writing and Difference*, Routledge, London.

Dews, P. (1988) *Logics of Disintegration*, Verso, London.

Dicey, A.V. (1914) *Law and Opinion in 19th Century England*, Macmillan, London.

Dobson, C.R. (1980) *Masters and Journeymen*, Croom Helm, London.

Dreyfus, H., Rabinow, P. (1982) *Michel Foucault: Beyond Structuralism and Hermeneutics*, Harvester, London.

Durkheim, E. (1964a) *The Rules of Sociological Method*, Macmillan, London.

Durkheim, E. (1964b) *The Elementary Forms of Religious Life*, Allen and Unwin, London.

Dworkin, R. (1977) *Taking Rights Seriously*, Duckworth, London.

Dworkin, R. (1986) *Law's Empire*, Fontana, London.

Eagleton, T. (1976) *Criticism and Ideology*, New Left Books, London.

Easthope, A. (1983) *Poetry as Discourse*, Methuen, London.

Easthope, A. (1988) *British Post-Structuralism*, Routledge, London.

Edelman, B. (1979) *Ownership of the Image*, Routledge, London.

Edwards, R. (1979) *Contested Terrain: the Transformation of the Workplace in the 20th Century*, Oxford University Press, New York.

Elster, J. (1985) *Making Sense of Marx*, Cambridge University Press, Cambridge.

Feinman, J. (1976) 'The Development of the Employment at Will Rule', *The American Journal of Legal History*, xx, p. 1.

Fine, B. et al. (eds) (1979) *Capitalism and the Rule of Law*, Hutchinson, London.

Fine, B. (1984) *Democracy and the Rule of Law*, Pluto, London.

Flanders, A., Clegg, H. (eds) (1954) *The System of Industrial Relations in Great Britain*, Basil Blackwell, Oxford.

Foucault, M. (1967) *Madness and Civilisation*, Tavistock, London.

Foucault, M. (1970) *The Order of Things*, Tavistock, London.

Foucault, M. (1974) *The Archeology of Knowledge*, Tavistock, London.

Foucault, M. (1979) *The History of Sexuality*, vol. 1, Penguin, Harmondsworth.

Fox, A. (1966) 'Industrial Sociology and Industrial Relations', *Royal Commission Research Paper*, 3.

Fox, A. (1974) *Beyond Contract*, Faber and Faber, London.

Fryer, B. et al. (1981) *Law, State and Society*, Croom Helm, London.

Gabel, P., Feinman, J. (1982) 'Contract Law as Ideology' in Kairys (1982).

Gane, M. (1988) *On Durkheim's Rules of Sociological Method*, Routledge, London.

Geras, N. (1971) 'Essence and Appearance, Aspects of Fetishism in Marx's Capital', *New Left Review*, 65.

Geras, N. (1987) 'Post-Marxism?', *New Left Review*, 163.

Giddens, A. (1971) 'Durkheim's Political Sociology', *Sociological Review*, 19, pp. 447–519.

Giddens, A. (1985) *The Constitution of Society*, Polity, Cambridge.

Gilmore, G. (1974) *The Death of Contract*, Ohio State University Press, Columbus.

Gilmore, G. (1977) *The Ages of American Law*, Yale University Press, New Haven.

Goodrich, P. (1984) 'Law and Language', *Journal of Law and Society*, 11, 1.

Goodrich, P. (1986) *Reading the Law*, Basil Blackwell, Oxford.

Gordon, D., Edwards, R., Reich, M. (1982) *Segmented Work, Divided Workers*, Cambridge University Press, Cambridge.

Graham, K. (ed.) (1982) *Contemporary Political Philosophy: Radical Studies*, Cambridge University Press, Cambridge.

Grau, L.W. (1982) 'Whatever Happened to Politics?', in Beirne, P., Quinney, R. (1982).

Haines, B.W. (1980) 'English Labour Law and the Separation from Contract', *Journal of Legal History*, 1,3.

Halevy, E. (1972) *The Growth of Philosophic Radicalism*, Faber, London.

Harre, R. (1970) *Causal Powers*, Blackwell, Oxford.

Harris, R. (1988) *Language, Saussure and Wittgenstein*, Routledge, London.

Harris, Z. (1963) *Discourse Analysis Reprints*, Mouton, The Hague.

Hart, H.L.A. (1961) *The Concept of Law*, Oxford University Press, Oxford.

Hart, H.L.A. (1983) *Essays in Jurisprudence and Philosophy*, Oxford University Press, Oxford.

Harvey, D. (1989) *The Condition of Post-Modernity*, Blackwell, Oxford.

Hay, D, et al. (1975) *Albion's Fatal Tree*, Allen Lane, London.

Hayek, F.A. (1973) *Law, Legislation and Liberty*, Routledge, London.

Hayek, F.A. (1980) *1980s Unemployment and the Unions*, Institute of Economic Affairs, London.

Heath, A. (1987) 'Trendless Fluctuation: a Reply to Crewe', *Political Studies*, xxxv, 2.

Held, D. (1980) *An Introduction to Critical Theory*, Hutchinson, London.

Henry, S. (1983) *Private Justice: Towards Integrated Theorising in the Sociology of Law*, Routledge, London.

Hindess, B. (1987) *Politics and Class Analysis*, Blackwell, London.

Hindess, B.(1988) *Choice, Rationality and Social Theory*, Unwin Hyman, London.

Hindess, B., Hirst, P. (1975) *Pre-Capitalist Modes of Production*, Routledge, London.

Hindess, B., Hirst, P. (1977) *Mode of Production and Social Formation*, Macmillan, London.

Hirst, P. (1975) *Durkheim, Bernard and Epistemology*, Routledge, London.

Hirst, P. (1979) *On Law and Ideology*, Macmillan, London.

Holloway, J., Picciotto, S. (eds) (1978) *State and Capital*, Arnold, London.

Horwitz, M. (1977) *The Transformation of American Law*, Harvard University Press, Cambridge, Mass.

Hunt, A. (1977) *The Sociological Movement in Law*, Macmillan, London.

Hyman, R., Brough, I. (1975) *Social Values and Industrial Relations*, Basil Blackwell, Oxford.

Institute for Economic Affairs (1987) *Trade Unions: Public Goods or Public Bads*, Readings, London.

Jackson, B. (1985) *Semiotics and Legal Theory*, Routledge, London.

Jacobson, R. (1960) 'Concluding Statement: Linguistics and Poetics', in T.A. Sebeok (ed.) (1960).

Jameson, F. (1984) 'Post-Modernism, or the Cultural Logic of Late Capitalism', *New Left Review*, 146.

Jameson, F. (1987) *The Political Unconscious*, Methuen, London.

Jessop, R. (l980) 'On Recent Marxist Theories of Law, the State and Juridical Political Ideology', *International Journal of the Sociology of Law*, 8, 4.

Jessop, B. (1982) *The Capitalist State*, Martin Robertson, Oxford.

Jessop, B. (1986) *Nicos Poulantzas: Marxist Theory and Political Strategy*, Macmillan, London.

Jessop, B. (1987) 'Conservative Regimes and the Transition to Post-Fordism: the Cases of Great Britain and West Germany', mimeo, Department of Government, University of Essex.

Johnston, L. (1986) *Marxism, Class Analysis and Socialist Pluralism*, Allen and Unwin, London.

Jones, K. (1982) *Law and Economy*, Academic Press, Canada.

Kahn-Freund, O. (1954) 'Legal Framework' in Flanders, A., Clegg, H. (1954).

Kahn-Freund, O. (1977) *Labour and the Law*, Stevens, London.

Kahn-Freund, O. (1980) *Labour Law and Politics in Weimar Germany*, Basil Blackwell, Oxford.

Kairys, D. (1982) *The Politics of Law*, Pantheon, New York.

Kavanagh, T. M. (ed.) (1989) *The Limits of Theory*, Stanford University Press, Stanford.

Kay, G., Mott, J. (1982) *Political Order and the Law of Labour*, Macmillan, London.

Keat, R., Urry, J. (1975) *Social Theory as Science*, Routledge, London.

Kellner, D. (1989) *Post-Modernism/Jameson/Critique*, Maisonneuve Press, Washington.

Kennedy, D. (1979) 'The Structure of Blackstone's Commentaries', *Buffalo Law Review*, 28, p. 205.

Klare, K. (1978) 'Judicial Deradicalisation of the Wagner Act and the Origins of Modern Legal Consciousness, 1937–1941', *Minnesota Law Review*, 62, 3.

Klare, K. (1981) 'Labour Law as Ideology', *Industrial Relations Law Journal*, 4.

Klare, K. (1982) 'Critical Theory and Labour Relations Law', in Kairys, D. (ed.) (1982).

Knorr-Cetina, K., Cicourel, A. (1981) *Advances in Social Theory and Methodology*, Routledge, London.

Kronman, A.T. (1983) *Max Weber*, Arnold, London.

Lacan, J. (1977) *Ecrits*, Tavistock, London.

Laclau, E. (1977) *Politics and Ideology in Marxist Theory*, Verso, London.

Laclau, E., Mouffe, C. (1985) *Hegemony and Socialist Strategy*, Verso, London.

Laclau, E., Mouffe, C. (1987) 'Post-Marxism without Apologies', *New Left Review*, 166.

Larrain, J. (1983) *Marxism and Ideology*, Macmillan, London.

Lawson, H., Appignanesi, L. (eds) (1989) *Dismantling Truth: Reality in the Post-Modern World*, Weidenfeld and Nicolson, London.

Lee, D. (1980) 'Skill, Craft and Class: a Theoretical Critique and a Critical Case', *Sociology*, 15, 1.

Lewis, R. (1976) 'The Historical Development of Labour Law', *British Journal of Industrial Relations*, 14, p. 1.

Lewis, R. (1979) 'Kahn-Freund and Labour Law: an Outline Critique', *Industrial Law Journal*, 8, pp. 202–21.

Lewis, R., Simpson, B. (1981) *Striking a Balance?*, Martin Robertson, Oxford.

Lichtheim, G. (1961) *Marxism*, Routledge, London.

Lipietz, A. (1985) *The Enchanted World*, Verso, London.

Littler, C. (1982) *The Development of the Labour Process: A Comparative Analysis*, Heinemann, London.

Lockwood, D. (1981) 'The Weakest Link in the Chain? Some Comments on the Marxist Theory of Action,' in Simpson and Simpson (1981).

Lockwood, D. (1986) 'Class, Status and Gender' in Crompton and Mann (1986).

Lukes, S., Scull, A. (1983) *Durkheim and the Law*, Martin Robertson, Oxford.

Lyotard, J.F. (1985) , *The Post-Modern Condition*, Manchester University Press, Manchester.

Lyotard, J.F. (1987) *Just Gaming*, Manchester University Press, Manchester.

Macdonell, D. (1986) *Theories of Discourse*, Blackwell, Oxford.

Macfarlane, A. (1979) *The Origins of English Individualism*, Cambridge University Press, Cambridge.

Macpherson, C.B. (1977) *The Life and Times of Liberal Democracy*, Oxford University Press, New York.

Malcolm, J. (1982) *Psychoanalysis: The Impossible Profession*, Picador, London.

Malcolmson, R. (1981) *Life and Labour in England 1700-1780*, Hutchinson, London.

Mann, M. (1986) *The Sources of Social Power*, Cambridge University Press, Cambridge.

Marsh, C. (1988) *Exploring Data: An Introduction to Data Analysis for Social Scientists*, Polity Press, Cambridge.

Marx, K. (1964) *Economic and Philosophical Manuscripts*, International Publishers, New York.

Marx, K. (1965) *Capital*, vol. 1, Lawrence and Wishart, London.

Marx, K. (1970) *The German Ideology*, Lawrence and Wishart, London.

Marx, K. et al. (1972) *On Historical Materialism*, Progress Publishers, Moscow.

McCurdy, C.W. (1975) 'Justice Field and the Jurisprudence of Government-Business Relations' in Friedman, L.M., Scheiber, H.N. (eds) (1975).

Merritt, A. (1982) 'The Historical Role of Law in the Regulation of Employment', *Australian Journal of Law and Society*, 1, 1.

Miles, R. (1982) *Racism and Migrant Labour*, Routledge, London.

Miller, J.A. (1977–8) 'Suture: Elements of the Logic of the Signifier', *Screen*, 18, 4.

Mills, C.W. (1963) *The Marxists*, Penguin, Harmondsworth.

Milsom, S. (1981) *Historical Foundations of the Common Law*, Butterworth, London.

Minson, J. (1980) 'Strategies for Socialists? Foucault's Conception of Power', *Economy and Society*, 9.1.

Nelson, W. (1982) *The Roots of American Bureaucracy, 1830–1900*, Harvard University Press, Cambridge.

Norman, R. (1982) 'Does Equality Destroy Liberty?', in K. Graham (ed.) (1982).

Norris, C. (1982) *On Deconstruction...*, Methuen, London.

Norris, C. (1988) 'Law, Deconstruction, and the Resistance to Theory', *Journal of Law and Society*, 15, 2.

Palmer, J., Pearce, F. (1984) 'Legal Discourse and State Power: Foucault and the Juridical Relation', *International Journal of the Sociology of Law*, 11, 4.

Parker, I. (1989) *The Crisis in Modern Social Psychology – and How to End it*, Routledge, London.

Parsons, T. (1949) *The Structure of Social Action*, Free Press, Glencoe.

Pashukanis, E.B. (1978) *Law and Marxism*, Ink Links, London.

Pearce, F. (1989) *The Radical Durkheim*, Unwin Hyman, London.

Pearce, F. (1988) 'The Struggle for Foucault', *International Journal of the Sociology of Law*, 16, 2.

Pecheux, M. (1982) *Language, Semantics and Ideology*, Macmillan, London.

Perelman, C. (1963) *The Idea of Justice and the Problem of Argument*, Routledge, London.

Perelman, C. (1980) *Justice, Law and Argument*, Reidel, Dordrecht.

Pollock, F., Maitland, F. (1968) *History of English Law*, Cambridge University Press, Cambridge.

Polyani, K. (1957) *The Great Transformation*, Beacon Press, Boston.

Posner, R. (1981) *The Economics of Justice*, Harvard University Press, Cambridge, Mass.

Poulantzas, N. (1973) *Political Power and Social Class*, New Left Books, London.

Poulantzas, N. (1974) *Fascism and Dictatorship*, Verso, London.

Poulantzas, N. (1975) *Classes in Contemporary Capitalism*, New Left Books, London.

Poulantzas, N. (1980) *State, Power, Socialism*, Verso, London.

Pritt, D.N. (1970) *Law, Class and Society*, 2 vols, Lawrence and Wishart, London.

Przeworski, A. (1985) 'Marxism and Rational Choice', *Politics and Society*, 14, 4.

Rattansi, A. (1985) 'End of an Orthodoxy? The Critique of Sociology's View of Marx and Class', *Sociological Review*, 33, 4.

Rawls, J. (1971) *A Theory of Justice*, Clarendon Press, Oxford.

Renner, K. (1949) *The Institutions of Private Law and their Social Functions*, Routledge, London.

Rex, J., Mason, D. (1986) *Themes in Race and Ethnic Relations*, Cambridge University Press, Cambridge.

Robbins, L. (1981) 'Economists and Trade Unions' in Institute of Economic Affairs, *Readings*, 17.

Roemer, J. (1981) *Analytical Foundations of Marxian Economic Theory*, Cambridge University Press, Cambridge.

Rorty, R. (1979) *Philosophy and the Mirror of Nature*, Princeton University Press, Princeton.

Rorty, R. (1982) *Consequences of Pragmatism*, Harvester Press, Brighton.

Rose, D. et al. (1986) 'Constructing the (W)right Classes', *Sociology*, 20, p. 440.

Rose, G. (1984) *Dialectic of Nihilism*, Basil Blackwell, Oxford.

Rose, N. (1977) 'Fetishism and Ideology', *Ideology and Consciousness*, 2.

Rossi, I. (1983) *From a Sociology of Symbols to a Sociology of Signs*, Columbia University Press, New York.

Rubin, G.R. Sugarman, D. (1984) *Law, Economy and Society, 1750–1914*, Professional Books, Abingdon.

Saussure, F. de (1974) *Course in General Linguistics*, Fontana, London.

Sayer, A. (1984) *Method in Social Science*, Hutchinson, London.

Sebeok, T.A. (1960) *Style in Language*, MIT Press, Cambridge, Mass.

Selznick, P. (1980) *Law, Society and Industrial Justice*, Transaction Books, New York.

Simpson, A.W. (1976) *A History of the Common Law of Contracts*, Oxford University Press, Oxford.

Simpson, A.W. (1979) 'The Horwitz Thesis and the History of Contracts', *University of Chicago Law Review*, 46, p. 533.

Simpson, R., Simpson, I. (eds)(1981) *Research in the Sociology of Work*, JAI Press, Greenwich.

Skillen, A. (1977) *Ruling Illusions*, Harvester, Hassocks.

Stedman-Jones, G. (1983) *Languages of Class*, Cambridge University Press, Cambridge.

Steedman, I. (1977) *Marx after Sraffa*, Verso, London.

Stevens, R. (1983) *Law School: Legal Education in America from the 1850s to the 1980s*, University of North Carolina Press, Chapel Hill.

Stone, K. (1981) 'The Post-war Paradigm in American Labour Law', *The Yale Law Journal*, 90, p. 1509.

Strinati, D. (1982) *Capitalism, the State and Industrial Relations*, Croom Helm, London.

Sturrock, J. (1986) *Structuralism*, Fontana, London.

Sugarman, D. (1980) 'A Review of the Transformation of American Law', *British Journal of Law and Society*, 7, p. 297.

Sugarman, D. (ed.) (1983) *Legality, Ideology and the State*, Academic Press, London.

Sugarman, D. (1984) 'Law, Economy and the State in England, 1750–1914: Some Major Issues', in Rubin, G., Sugarman, D. (eds) (1984).

Sugarman, D. (1986) 'Legal Theory, the Common Law Mind and the Making of the Textbook Tradition', in Twining (1986).

Sutherland, A. (1967) *The Law at Harvard*, Harvard University Press, Cambridge, Mass.

Therborn, G. (1984) 'New Questions of Subjectivity', *New Left Review*, 143.

Thompson, E.P. (1964) *The Making of the English Working Class*, Gollancz, London.

Thompson, E.P. (1975) *Whigs and Hunters*, Penguin, Harmondsworth.

Thompson, E.P. (1978) *The Poverty of Theory*, Merlin, London.

Tigar, M., Levy, M. (1977) *Law and the Rise of Capitalism*, Monthly Review Press, New York.

Tomlins, C.L. (1985) *The State and the Unions*, Cambridge University Press, New York.

Trigg, R. (1981) *Reality at Risk*, Harvester, Brighton.

Tully, J. (ed.) (1988) *Meaning and Context: Quentin Skinner and his Critics*, Princeton University Press, Princeton.

Tushnet, M. (1977) 'Perspectives on the Development of American Law', *Wisconsin Law Review*, 44, p. 81.

Twining, W. (1973) *Karl Llewellyn and the Realist Movement*, Weidenfeld and Nicolson, London.

Twining, W. (ed.) (1986) *Legal Theory and the Common Law*, Blackwell, Oxford.

Unger, R. (1976) *Law in Modern Society*, Free Press, New York.

Unger, R. (1986) *Politics: a Work in Constructive Social Theory*, Cambridge University Press, Cambridge.

Weber, M. (1978) *Economy and Society*, 2 vols, University of California, Berkeley.

Weber, M. (1980) *The General Economic History*, Transaction Books, New York.

Willer, D., Willer, J. (1973) *Systematic Empiricism*, Prentice-Hall, Englewood Cliffs.

Williamson, C. (1960) *American Suffrage: From Property to Democracy, 1760–1860*, Princeton University Press, Princeton.

Winch, P. (1958) *The Idea of a Social Science*, Routledge, London.

Wittgenstein, L. (1958) *Philosophical Investigations*, Blackwell, Oxford.

Wolff, R., Callari, A. Roberts, B. (1984) 'A Marxian Alternative to the Traditional Transformation Problem', *Review of Radical Political Economics*, 16, 1.

Wolff, R.P. (ed.) (1977) *Understanding Rawls*, Princeton University Press, Princeton.

Wolpe, H. (ed.) (1980) *The Articulation of Modes of Production*, Routledge, London.

Wolpe, H. (1986) 'Class Concepts, Class Struggle and Racism', in Rex, J., Mason, D. (1986).

Wood, E. (1986) *The New True Socialism*, Verso, London.

Wood, H.G. (1886) *A Treatise on the Law of Master and Servant*, J. Parsons, Albany, New York.

Woodiwiss, A. (1978) 'Critical Theory and the Capitalist State', *Economy and Society*, 7, 2.

Woodiwiss, A. (1985) 'A Theoretical Prologue to a Socialist Historiography of Labour Law: Law, Discourse and Transpositioning', *International Journal of the Sociology of Law*, 13, 1.

Woodiwiss, A. (1987a) 'The Discourses of Production (pt. I): Law, Industrial Relations and Ideology', *Economy and Society*, 17, 3.

Woodiwiss, A. (1987b) 'The Discourses of Production (pt. II): The Contract of Employment and the Emergence of Democratic Capitalist Law in Britain and the United States', *Economy and Society*, 17, 4.

Woodiwiss, A. (1988a) 'Law, Unions and the State in Japan', mimeo, work in progress.

Woodiwiss, A. (1988b) 'Class, Crisis and Recovery in the Postwar United States', mimeo, work in progress.

Woodiwiss, A. (1990a) *Rights v. Conspiracy: A Sociological Essay on the History of American Labour Law*, Berg, Oxford, New York, Hamburg.

Woodiwiss, A. (1990b) 'Rereading Japan: Possession, Law and the Necessity of Hegemony', in Abercrombie et al. (1990) (eds).

Wright, E.O. (1978) *Class, Crisis and the State*, New Left Books, London.

Wright, E.O. (1985) *Classes*, Verso, London.

Wright, E.O. et al. (1987) 'Marxism and Methodological Individualism', *New Left Review*, 162.

Index

Abrahamson, B. and Brostrom, A., 99–100
absolutism, 140, 141
Althusser, L., 48–50
Armstrong, P.S. (et al.), 40–2
articulation, theory of, 64–71, 77

Barthes, R., 62
base/superstructure, 29, 187
Braverman, H., *Labour and Monopoly Capitalism*, 48, 50
British Charter 88, 141
Burawoy, M., 50–6

capital and labour relations, 175–9
capitalist class, definition, 175–6, 177
capitalist law, origins of, 132–4
capitalist mode of production, 60–1, 172, 173
capitalist private property, 146–9
capitalist relations of production, 128–9, 133, 146–7, 158–9
   corporate, 181
   entrepreneurial, 181
certainty, 6–8, 20
Christie, G., 108–10
class,
   concept of, 151–3
   effect of, 154–5
   in Marx, 13, 151, 155–6, 161
   as non-human entities, 159
class position, 153, 154–5, 161–2, 173–4, 181–2
   capitalist, 175–7, 182
   working, 176, 177–9, 182

class powers, and production, 163
class struggle, 155, 157, 160–2, 164, 168, 187
Collins, Hugh, 114–15
commodity production, 101–2
common law, 137
conceptual v. empirical, 7–8
consciousness (false), 3
consistency,
   in law, 108–12, 117–18, 135–6, 139–40
   in legal discourse, 121–3
contract,
   in legal discourse, 134
   and property, 128, 131, 147–8
contract of employment, 74–6, 92–3, 94–5, 128–9, 148–9
   inequality of, 98
critical legal theory, 15, 18, 122
customary law, 90
Cutler, T., et al., 145, 146–8, 150, 167, 170–2

deconstruction,
   and the law, 34–5
   in social science, 33–4
democratic capitalism, 120, 124
democratic capitalist law, 135–6
Derrida, J., *différance*, 29, 31, 32
destructuring of class positionings, 179, 181–3
dictatorship in production, 177, 179
discourse, 4, 35, 63–4, 108, 111
   law as, 118–20
   and Marxism, 19–20

political, 3, 4
and reality, 28–30
and social science, 27–8
theory of, 2, 61–2, 68
discourses of production, 73–6,
149–50
and classical Marxism, 43–6,
117
and contemporary Marxism,
46–50
discursive change, 112–14
discursive formation, 26, 33,
63–4, 66–7
rules of, 35, 73, 75, 187
Durkheim, Emile, 57, 127
*Professional Ethics and Civic
Morals*, 128
Dworkin, R., 83–5

economic reductionism, 160,
168–9, 171
Marxist, 5, 9, 10, 19, 45
Edelman, B., 98–9, 110
Elster, J., 146, 147–8
empiricism, 7–8, 10
in jurisprudence, 136–8
Employment Act (1980) (UK), 17,
92–3
epistemology, 31
in Marx, 165–6
equal and unequal rights, 89–90
equality, in law, 81, 82–5
exchange of equal values (Marx),
89–90

factors of production, 157–8
fetishism, 47–8, 156, 157, 162–3,
187
of commodities, 44–7, 104–6
feudal law, and property, 132–3
Foucault, Michel, 32, 35, 62,
63–4, 111–12
freedom under the law, 140, 141

Hayek, F.A., and law, 82–3
Hindess, B. and Hirst, P., 164–6

humanism, 2, 5, 6–7, 10, 41–2
in class, 152–3, 155–7, 160–1,
162–4, 170–1
in liberal jurisprudence, 121
Hyman, R. and Brough, I., 47–8

idealism/realism, 8, 68–70
ideology,
and class, 115
and state, 106–7
ideology in industrial relations,
47–8, 51–2, 54
incommensurability, 39–43, 76
individual rights, 141
industrial relations, 39, 40–1
and discourse of production,
73–5
ideology in, 47–8, 51
see also labour law
Industrial Relations Act (1971), 94
interpellation, 49–50, 113, 115, 119

Japan, 140, 141
Jones, K., 130–1
jurisprudence,
liberal, 82–8, 92–7
and reconstruction, 14–15
socialist, 88–92, 97–100
see also law

Kahn-Freund, O., 74, 93–5, 113
knowledge, in metatheory, 7

labour law, 139–41
and liberal jurisprudence, 92–7
and socialist jurisprudence, 97–
100
see also industrial relations
labour movement, and law, 16–18
labour process theory, 48
labour relations, 133–4
see also capitalist relations of
production
labour theory of value, 18–19, 89,
100, 145, 149, 150, 166, 172,
176–7

labour v. capital, 180
Laclau, E. and Mouffe, C., 64–6, 67–9, 70–1, 74, 171
language, 3, 12, 57–9, 67, 185
langue, 31, 32, 58, 59, 61–2
law,
  autonomy of, 135–6, 140
  centrality of, 13–14
  and consistency, 108–12, 117–18
  and deconstruction, 34–5
  as discourse, 115–17, 118–20
  and economics, 18–19
  nature of, 139
  need for consistency, 117–18
  and state, 115–16
  theory in United States, 15–17
  see also jurisprudence; labour law
legal formalism, 138, 139
legal history, periodisation, 125–9
legal realism, 15, 21, 34
liberal jurisprudence,
  and equality, 82–4
  and labour law, 92–7
liberty, and rule of law, 81, 83–4, 85–8
linguistic reference, 31–2

macro–micro problem, 39–40, 41
Marx, Karl,
  Capital, 18–19, 44, 89, 177
  Critique of the Gotha Programme, 89–90
  The German Ideology, 43–4, 45, 89
Marxism, 10, 12
  and class, 13, 151, 155–6
  classical, 43–6
  contemporary, 46–50
  and jurisprudence, 88–9
  labour theory of value, 18–19
  and postmodernism, 19–20
  see also economic reductionism
master-servant laws, 74, 133

metaphor, 186–7
  sociology without, 185–9
  of workplace, 42, 52–4
metatheory, 6, 65
  and concept of class, 151–3
middle class, new, 174, 179–83, 184
Minnesota Rate Case, 1890, 128
mode of production, 149, 157, 172
  restricted concept of, 60–1, 149

nation state, 188–9
nodal points, 66, 70, 74
non-human entities, 3–5, 159
  see also non-humanism
non-humanism, 20, 72–3, 153–5
  and class, 152–3, 157, 164–7
  in legal discourse, 120–3
  and realism, 25–6
non-representationalist approach to theory, 8–13

osmosis in class structure, 174, 175, 179
ownership, 18, 130–2
  see also property

parliament, supremacy of, 16, 17
parole, 31, 32, 58, 61–2
Pashukanis, E.B. *Law and Marxism*, 103–6
periodisation of legal history, 125–9
positive scepticism, 6, 9
post-Fordism, 14, 21, 141
post-structuralism, 5
postmodernism, 2, 5–6, 11–13, 185
  limits of, 28–30, 31
  and Marxism, 19–20
Poulantzas, N., 111, 119, 153, 159–64
praxis, 157
production, 55
  capitalist relations of, 146–7, 149

and class powers, 163
in Marx, 43–4
means of, 177
mode of, 60–1, 149
relations of, 51, 53, 178, 180
proletariat, danger of preserving,
  182–3
property,
  definition, 148
  history of, 127–9
  law of, 13, 102–3
  as legal term, 145

Rawls, John, on equality, 84–5
realism, 6, 11–13, 21, 28–9
realism/idealism, 68–70
reconstructing class, 170–5
reconstructing legal theory, 15–17
reductionism *see* economic
  reductionism
reference, 9, 30–2, 58
Renner, K. *Institutions of Private
  Law...*, 101–3, 105–6
representationalism, 2, 4, 20,
  48–50, 157, 185
  rejection of, 6, 7
rule of law, and liberty, 81, 83–4,
  85–8
rules of formation *see* discursive
  formation

Saussure, F. de, 2, 31–2, 57–9, 63,
  67
scientific jurisprudence, 136–7
scientific realism, 5–6, 7, 10–12,
  21, 32
Selznick, P., 96–7
signification, 3, 29–30, 57–9, 67,
  187
social formation, 187–8
social mobility, 179–80
socialism, as a result of
  destructuring, 182–4
socialist jurisprudence, and labour
  law, 97–100
society, nature of, 188

sociology,
  limits of, 186
  and psychology, 25–7
  task of, 26–7
state,
  and ideology, 106–7
  and law, 82–3, 111–12
  power of, 112
Statutes of Labourers, 132
structural entities, 4
structural unity of class, 172–3
structure of class, 178–9
Sugarman, D., 16, 114–15
surplus value, and capitalism,
  176–8
Sweden, labour law, 99–100

Taft Hartley Act (1947) (US), 92–3
textbooks, legal, 126–7, 137–8
theoreticism, 10
theory, non-representationalist
  approach, 8–13
totality, 65–6, 70
transpositioning, 113–14, 116–17,
  118
  in legal discourse, 121–2, 134–8
  modes of, 117
Trigg, R., 69

Unger, R., 85–8, 120
United Kingdom, and US legal
  theory, 15–16
United States,
  capitalist production relations,
    133–4
  and labour law, 98
  legal theory in, 15–17, 137–8
  production relations, 180

Wagner Act (1935) (US), 96
Wolpe, Harold, 60, 61
Wood, Ellen, 151
working class, definition, 176,
  177
workplace, 73–6, 174
  metaphor of, 42, 52–4